THE CORPORATE WARRIOR

Successful Strategies from Military Leaders to Win Your Business Battles

BY JAMES P. FARWELL

Print – ISBN: 978-1-944480-74-5
EPUB – 978-1-944480-75-2
WEB PDF – 978-1-1-944480-76-9

ROTHSTEIN PUBLISHING
A Division of Rothstein Associates Inc.

www.rothsteinpublishing.com

THE CORPORATE WARRIOR

Successful Strategies from Military Leaders

to Win Your Business Battles

BY JAMES P. FARWELL

COPYRIGHT ©2022, James P. Farwell

All Rights Reserved. No part of this publication may be reproduced, stored in a retrieval system, or transmitted in any form by any means, electronic, mechanical, photocopying, recording, or otherwise, without the express prior permission of the Publisher.

The Publisher or Authors assume no responsibility for any injury or damage to persons or property as a matter of product liability, negligence or otherwise, or from any use or operation of any methods, products, instructions, or ideas contained in the material herein. Local laws, standards, and regulations should always be consulted first, as well as your legal counsel before considering any advice offered in this book.

Print – ISBN: 978-1-944480-74-5
EPUB – 978-1-944480-75-2
WEB PDF – 978-1-1-944480-76-9
Library of Congress Control Number: 2021950822

ROTHSTEIN PUBLISHING
A Division of Rothstein Associates Inc.

4 Arapaho Road
Brookfield, Connecticut 06804 USA
203.740.7400
info@rothstein.com
www.rothsteinpublishing.com

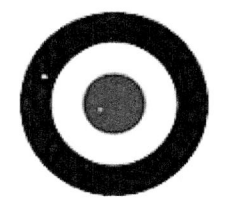

WHAT YOUR COLLEAGUES ARE SAYING ABOUT THE CORPORATE WARRIOR

"This fascinating book takes us behind the scenes to see what corporate heads and business owners have done right, done wrong, and shows how today's leaders can use the advice to successfully course-correct. I recommend this book as well to former military men like myself. When our initial careers wind down, many of us will serve on corporate boards, or work directly inside corporations, as I now do. For us, these examples serve as vivid reminders of what we, too, can take away from each other's military tactics and strategies."

Admiral James ("Jim") George Stavridis (Ret), Supreme Allied Commander – Europe (SACEUR), retired four-star United States Navy admiral, and bestselling author, is currently an operating executive with the Carlyle Group and chair of the board of counselors at McLarty Associates.

"Every business leader should put **The Corporate Warrior** at the top of their reading list. It is an incredibly insightful and thought-provoking work. Especially as we think about marketing and managing for the future."

John P. Kotts, CEO, Kotts Capital

"Informative, entertaining, a must-read for every executive at all levels."

Boysie Bollinger, Chairman and CEO, Bollinger Enterprises, Bollinger Shipyards, Inc.

"A top expert in strategic communication, James Farwell's excellent book informs and entertains through colorful examples and cogent analysis. Highly recommended."

General (Ret) Joseph L. Votel, fmr. Commander, US SPECIAL OPERATIONS COMMAND and US CENTRAL COMMAND

"This is a very sensible business book which will remind you through its dozens and dozens of examples of the available options to resolve crucial situations powerfully or poorly, sensibly, or stupidly. Is this a book about leaders and leadership? Certainly! Is this a book about strategy? Definitely! This book is really focused on you and on helping you advance your career in significant ways."

James E. Lukaszewski, ABC, Fellow IABC, APR, Fellow PRSA, BEPS Emeritus Chairman, The Lukaszewski Group

---

"Grab this book and learn from it. James Farwell has captured the essence of the New Wave in business that has propelled so many companies to amazing success, from Amazon and Nike to Harry's razor blade company, among many others. He applies lessons from military strategy to show how entrepreneurs can achieve the same type of incredible success in their arenas."

Amb./Lt. Gen. Dell Dailey, former Director for the Center of Special Operations, US SPECIAL OPERATIONS COMMAND, and former U.S. State Department Coordinator for Counter-Terrorism

"The insights and ideas James Farwell offers in **The Corporate Warrior** are invaluable for management and wise leadership."

Frank Stewart, CEO. of Stewart Capital and former CEO of Stewart Enterprises, the global leader in the funerals and cemetery business

---

"A lively, entertaining read, THE CORPORATE WARRIOR offers key insights into how business executives can maximize the impact of their marketing. I loved it."
Bill Goldring, Chairman, Sazerac Company, America's largest distiller. www.Sazerac.com. www.BuffaloTrace.com

---

"James Farwell ranks among the world's most influential experts on strategic communications. His latest contribution offers fascinating illustrations from both the military and corporate worlds. Farwell shows how you can apply precepts from the military to build an image profile, sell a product, and handle crisis communications."

Dr. Neville Bolt, Director, King's Centre for Strategic Communication, King's College; Editor-in-Chief, NATO's s peer-reviewed journal, Defense Strategic Communications.

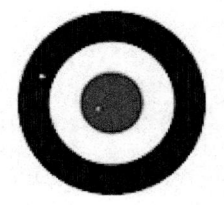

DEDICATION

For Ronald A. Faucheux

All statements of fact, opinion, or analysis expressed are my own and do not, on national security issues, reflect the official positions or views of the U.S. government. Nothing in the contents should be construed as asserting or implying U.S. government authentication of information or endorsement of the views expressed.

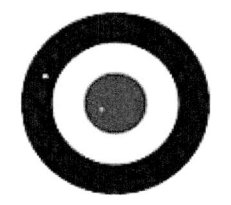

FOREWORD

By Admiral James ("Jim") George Stavridis

Like James Farwell, I have always held that leaders in the military and the business world have much in common. Both must clash with or compete against adversaries and emerge victoriously. Like war and the world of global politics, business is an ongoing, tough-minded competition.

As a retired Admiral who had the honor of serving as Supreme Allied Commander – Europe and today an executive with The Carlyle Group, I know from personal experience and observation that executives and entrepreneurs can learn a great deal from each other.

Were he with us today, the great Sun Tzu would almost certainly agree. Among the sage advice he gives military commanders in his iconic The Art of War is this: *strategy without tactics is the slowest route to victory. Tactics without strategy are the noise before defeat.*

This book lays out insightful strategies and tactics that apply to the military and industry.

James has interviewed dozens of military leaders – generals, admirals, colonels, flag officers – and CEOS of various businesses, public and private. In relaying their advice from the frontlines of military strategies and practices, he provides vital information on how executives can overtake and beat competitors in challenging marketplaces.

This fascinating book takes us behind the scenes to see what corporate heads and business owners have done right, done wrong, and shows how today's leaders can use the advice to successfully course-correct. Case studies range from footwear endorsed by prominent athletes to a brand-new type of razor for men and everything in between. It's informative, and the lively writing makes a great read.

I recommend this book as well to former military men like myself. When our initial careers wind down, many of us will serve on corporate boards, or work directly inside corporations, as I now do. For us, these examples serve as vivid reminders of what we, too, can take away from each other's military tactics and strategies.

Sun Tzu also wrote: *If you know the enemy and know yourself, you need not fear the result of a hundred battles. If you know yourself but not the enemy, for every victory gained, you will also suffer a defeat. If you know neither the enemy nor yourself, you will succumb in every battle."*

Exchange the word "enemy" for "competition," follow James' logic and examples, and you will see Sun Tzu's timeless advice in modern dress. Know your competition and know who you are and how what you offer differs, and you have a solid foundation for growth and success. Recognize that strategy is an art as much as a science. Provide strong moral leadership, and root your company in strong, positive values including integrity, loyalty, excellence, hard work, and above all, a commitment to improving the lives of others.

If you concentrate only on what you offer and not the competition's pluses and minuses, you may survive for a while, but you will not grow. If you're blind to who and what your brand and your company really are, who your competition is, and what your audiences genuinely want, the battle is already lost – kind of like those dinosaurs of old who kept running even after a tiger gnawed on one of their legs. By the time they tried to shake the aggressor off, it was too late. They went down with a thud.

James shows you companies that mirror all three of these aspects: they knew, they grew. But, they had a blind spot for the competition; they stagnated. They didn't do their due diligence and were somewhat delusional about their strengths – they died a slow death.

If you heed the advice here, you might avoid the fate of the dinosaurs and evolve into the most successful version of yourself. Now hop to it!

Admiral James ("Jim") George Stavridis (Ret), Supreme Allied Commander – Europe (SACEUR), a retired four-star United States Navy admiral, and bestselling author, is currently an operating executive with the Carlyle Group and chair of the board of counselors at McLarty Associates. His novel, "2034: A Novel of the Next World War," was published in March 2021.
https://admiralstav.com/

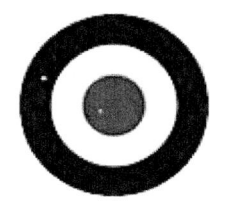

Jim Lukaszewski, America's Crisis Guru® on *The Corporate Warrior*

I believe you will find this unusual, in that it's customary to ask the author to identify the target audiences of the book in which you are about to be a guest author; James Farwell's answer was powerfully refreshing. When I suggested that maybe it's a leadership book, he responded quickly and decisively that this is a book for those who may already be guiding leaders or managers and who, themselves, expect to be leaders of tomorrow.

If this is you, you are at the right place, and you are holding in your hands a career-building resource that covers many of the most urgent issues that you, as a future senior manager/leader, will encounter on your journey. Farwell wisely observed that today's leaders have more than likely already decided how to handle various critical organizational situations. Changing their minds and altering their opinions is harder and harder for them as they reach the highest levels of management and leadership.

Here's the proof: First, there are an extraordinary number of examples of successful and missed opportunities, of surprise successes and of some real boneheaded mistakes. This book provides up-and-coming leaders and managers with a variety of useful and thoughtful examples that enlighten and enhance the importance of whatever advice is suggested or recommended.

This is also a very sensible business book which will remind you through its dozens and dozens of examples of the available options to resolve crucial situations powerfully or poorly, sensibly, or stupidly. The wisdom of this approach is to empower effective advice by providing options for decision-making from which a leader may consider changing a strategy that can powerfully alter outcomes. And, of course, as an influencer, you stand ready to absorb the blame if shifted in your direction or be a silent hero as the leader takes responsibility for success.

My 40+ year career has largely been devoted to helping leaders and their organizations prepare for, respond to, and recover from crises. I typically arrive on the scene after-the-fact. One of the larger lessons, perhaps the largest I have learned, is the propensity for leaders and senior managers to intentionally make, even repeat, bad choices.

Some of the examples chosen in this book present poor decisions made intentionally that go unchallenged, sometimes as a result of the increasing speed required to make effective competitive decisions. Too often, decisions get made simply because a senior manager or leader has the power to make them. This book advances your experience through understanding the tension, stress and urgency that causes errors and misjudgments of critical situations.

Is this a book about leaders and leadership, *certainly*!

Is this a book about strategy, *definitely*!

This book is really focused on you, and on helping you advance your career in significant ways. The main advice Farwell offers is that you will advance more significantly and rapidly throughout your career if you focus first on being an increasingly *trusted strategic advisor*. Be a trust builder and others will trust you more rapidly in return.

James E. Lukaszewski

ABC, Fellow IABC, APR, Fellow PRSA,
BEPS Emeritus
Chairman
The Lukaszewski Group
Minneapolis, Minnesota
https://www.e911.com/

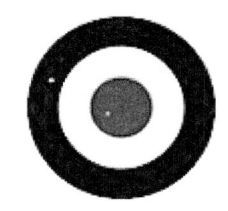

PREFACE

If you're a middle or upper-middle-level executive, or a business school student, *The Corporate Warrior* is for you. It's about leadership and lays out specifically how to think through and execute strategic plans for marketing and sales, crisis communication, as well as dealing with social media and the cyberworld.

Success in strategic planning – whether corporate or military – starts with leadership that understands the competitive playing field, defines success, and forges winning strategies, plans, operations, and tactics. But the top leadership is only as strong as people like yourself, who provide ideas, plans, and critical analysis, and then execute strategic thinking.

Modern business faces challenges that parallel the battles waged by the military. The military's precepts translate to industry. I've advised C-suite CEOs, CFOs, and COOs, from major multi-national companies such as RJR Nabisco, Philip Morris, Freeport-McMoran, Monsanto, Entergy Corporation, Microsoft, Boeing, and Monsanto, among others.

The Corporate Warrior draws upon interviews with dozens of retired generals, admirals, and senior officers,[1] along with Pentagon and intelligence officials who moved to the business world and applied their military expertise to industry.

I've worked closely with senior officers in the US and United Kingdom for twenty years. People often ask me my assessment of them. I can summarize them collectively in two words: *awe-inspiring.* They're intelligent, dynamic,

---

[1] Senior officers include Colonels. Many people mistakenly believe that flag officers are the driving force in the military. Some are very hands-on, but others set policy. Colonels drive operations, based on guidance from commanders.

disciplined, focused, and result-oriented. They exude an aura of leadership. They respond to imaginative, innovative thinking from the people who rank below them on the ladder of authority.

This book draws on my own experience of two decades as a strategic advisor to the US Department of Defense, the US Special Operations Command, the US Strategic Command, major corporations, candidates for public office, and a cybersecurity attorney.

The Corporate Warrior uses some examples drawn from *Information Warfare* (Quantico: Marine Corps University Press, 2020) – which I wrote for commanders and operators (ordinary soldiers) – to provide comparisons to industry approaches. This book is my fifth as an author or co-author analyzing strategic communication and information warfare.

Chapter One: Understand the Global Competitive Marketplace describes how the military and national security leaders see the world as a marketplace for the global *competition of ideas*. It's the world in which you must compete. In today's world, you must use every channel of communication, from social media to personal engagement to traditional media, as you compete to influence target audiences and shape behavior. The world is changing rapidly. Approaches to strategy and communication need to stay ahead of the curve. But understanding the arena in which competition occurs is vital if you're going to prevail.

Chapter Two: Define Success explains the notion of *winning*. In both the military and industry, successful strategic communication starts with defining success. What constitutes winning? How do you measure that? The military thinks about achieving particular conditions that define an "end-state," the situation on the ground once operations conclude. The failure to specify that clearly in Iraq until 2007 and for nearly twenty years in Afghanistan produced headaches in Iraq and defeat in Afghanistan. Victories achieved in the 1991 Gulf War or taking down Panama President Manuel Antonio Noriega stemmed from clarity of vision. The key for you, whether starting your own business or joining a larger enterprise, is to understand what success requires.

Chapter Three: Identify Obstacles requires that you understand the society, culture, history, leadership, and values of any target audience. The military contends with hostile adversaries, unfamiliar cultures, target populations focused on local agendas. Our actions may or may not interest them. Different societies embrace different values. Remember the word *values;* it's become a cliché in US politics. But value-driven companies and governments focused on improving lives are more likely to succeed. In this chapter, corporate examples illustrate the precept. For example, after drowning in red tape, IBM reincarnated its identity. Apple urged customers to think differently. Nike built success around a narrative that you can improve your life through sports. Starbucks understood the power of connections in a culture in which many people feel isolated.

Chapter Four: Understand Your Target Audience examines how you *target audiences*. The military faces a more complex challenge: you can change consumer tastes, but you can rarely change the fixed political beliefs or convictions of military target audiences. You need to understand your target audience. What do they think about what interests you? What do keywords mean to different people? What language do you use to communicate ideas?

Chapter Five: Elements of Strategy analyzes *strategy and tactics*. Strategy has been notoriously difficult to define. The military and industry face similar challenges, although they may surmount them differently. The US military operates at three confluent levels: *strategic, operational, tactical*. Strategy in the West exists at a grand and a tactical level. Other nations employ different terms. Russia doesn't embrace the language "grand strategy[2]" – it employs a notion of "national strategy" that has distinct nuances. Industry has seen its share of grand strategic successes. In this chapter, we'll look at Nike, IBM, Apple, and Starbucks. Their marketing epitomizes strategic excellence.

Chapter Six: Critical Elements of a Strategic Communications Plan looks at how *story and narrative* play in strategy. People make sense of events through the roles that people play in shaping events and outcomes. The story sets forth *what* people do. The narrative explains *why* actors take their actions. Anything you do – sell a service, market a product, run for office, defeat a military adversary, win over target audiences – involves a story. You get nowhere unless you understand who you want to talk to and what you want from them. Target audiences make sense of all this, of what people do, why, and how, through stories. Actors, action, events – we watch or listen to these to understand.

---

[2] The term "grand strategy" seems to have originated with military historian Liddell Hart. The word "strategy" was first seen in the book *Strategy*, written by Sima Biao in the Jin Dynasty at the end of the third century, although it comes from the Greek word *strategos*, meaning army leader. See: China's Science of Military Strategy, *China Aerospace Studies Institute* (2013): https://www.airuniversity.af.edu/Portals/10/CASI/documents/Translations/2021-02-08%20Chinese%20Military%20Thoughts-%20In%20their%20own%20words%20Science%20of%20Military%20Strategy%202013.pdf?ver=NxAWg4BPw_NylEjxaha8Aw%3d%3d.

Chapter Seven: Developing Your Story and Narrative explains how you apply strategy and tactics, story, and narrative to *get results*. There is no formula. You tailor actions to each situation. Achieving objectives entails complicated, nuanced steps. You distinguish among the indispensable, influential, and inessential players. You divide responsibilities, secure buy-in from stakeholders, instill accountability and responsibility, and pose the right questions to the right stakeholders at the right time.

Chapter Eight: Overcoming Obstacles to Your Success analyzes how *obstacles* are part of life. We can't wish them away. In warfare and the commercial world, you must identify them and be smart and practical in devising communication and other strategies to overcome them. And I assert: Americans are geniuses at believing that bad people are stupid and do the wrong thing. Looked at in terms of their goals, they are often smart and do the right thing. Never underestimate an obstacle. The seemingly small ones may be what kills you. That's why Mike Bloomberg's insight that you "win the tough battles by inches" is so powerful.

Chapter Nine: How Strategic Communication is Vital to Crisis Management dissects *crisis communication*. Iraq offers an excellent example of how the military dealt with the Abu Ghraib scandal. You can learn a lot from Johnson & Johnson's handling of the Tylenol scare, Union Carbide's troubled response to the Bhopal disaster, Boeing's fiasco over its Supermax 737 jets, and how Starbucks addressed ethnic sensitivities.

Chapter Ten: Cybersecurity Resilience describes how cybersecurity and cyber issues affect reputation, business interruption, shareholder value, and liability. You cannot eliminate cyber threats. You can manage them. Cybersecurity is a pressing issue. People think it's just about technology. Wrong! Your Chief Information Security Officer (CISO) is too often put in the IT box. He or she must be part of *management*, not IT operation. Cyber is a very difficult, complex field. Strategic communication is vital, and how you employ it may determine whether you keep your reputation, your business operations functioning, your stock prices high, and yourself insulated from legal liability. Once lost, these assets are hard to recover.

Strategic planning and communication embrace science. But as much as anything, it's art. Whether you are military or industry, you can learn from one another. You can increase profits and market share by drawing lessons on how successful leaders forge and execute strategies, operations, plans, and tactics.

A lifelong passion for campaigns and understanding strategic communication inspired me to write this book. Information binds us and our communities in a world characterized by connectivity and networks. It is a principal way that we define our identity, describe our ideas, and connect with one another. The ends, ways, and means that govern strategies for making such connections have long fascinated me. I hope this book sheds light on that dynamic, informing as well as entertaining you.

James P. Farwell
New Orleans, Louisiana
February 2022

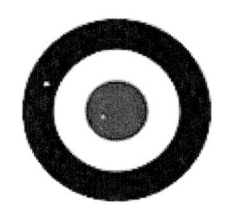

CONTENTS

WHAT YOUR COLLEAGUES ARE SAYING ABOUT THE CORPORATE WARRIOR iii

DEDICATION vi

FOREWORD By Admiral James ("Jim") George Stavridis vii

Jim Lukaszewski, America's Crisis Guru® on *The Corporate Warrior* xi

PREFACE xiii

CONTENTS xix

CHAPTER ONE   UNDERSTAND THE GLOBAL COMPETITIVE MARKETPLACE 1

   The Theory of Special Operations Teaches Lessons 2

   How Do These Precepts Affect Target Audiences? 10

   Apple Surges Us Into a New World 13

   Nike Summons the Hero Within Us 14

   Saks Strikes Back at the Evil Empire 15

   Starbucks Offers a World Apart We Can Enjoy at Home 17

   Discussion Questions 19

CHAPTER TWO   DEFINE SUCCESS 21

   Acquiring the Knowledge 23

   Lessons from Iraq and Afghanistan 26

The Drug Wars and Centers of Gravity 28

Mexico's Challenge 29

Lessons for Executives 31

The Hope Diamond of Razor Blades 31

Gillette Pays for Its Hubris 33

Innocent and the Three College Guys 33

The Diaper Wars 35

Values and Centers of Gravity 35

Discussion Questions 37

CHAPTER THREE   WHAT OBSTACLES MUST YOU OVERCOME? 39

Malaysia 58

A Commercial Parallel 59

Discussion Questions 64

CHAPTER FOUR   UNDERSTAND YOUR TARGET AUDIENCE 65

Nike Gets It 66

Daisy's Explosive Impact 69

Corporate Home Runs 70

Vital Precepts 71

Discussion Questions 75

CHAPTER FIVE   ELEMENTS OF STRATEGY 77

Grand Strategy 78

An Israeli View 82

Strategy and Industry 82

Strategic Positioning 86

Nothing Good Comes Easy 87

A Presidential Comparison 87

Reason Persuades, Emotion Motivates 88

What About Humor? 91

Quirky Works 93

1984: Go with Your Gut Instinct 95

Perceptions of Status Motivate 96

Levis are Hip 97

Tailor Your Strategy to the Culture 99

Discussion Questions 101

CHAPTER SIX   CRITICAL ELEMENTS OF A STRATEGIC COMMUNICATION PLAN 103

Discussion Questions 126

CHAPTER SEVEN   DEVELOPING YOUR STORY AND NARRATIVE 127

Emotional Intelligence 129

Seizing the Moral High Ground 131

Deeds Matter as Much as Words 132

Whose Narratives and Stories Are Emotionally Resonant? 133

Dove's Self-Esteem Project 137

Discussion Questions 143

CHAPTER EIGHT   OVERCOMING OBSTACLES TO YOUR SUCCESS **145**

Coca-Cola 153

The Pepsi Challenge 156

EAGLE CLAW 157

The Challenger Disaster 159

It Happens to Companies Too 160

Social Media 168

Discussion Questions 177

CHAPTER NINE   HOW VITAL IS STRATEGIC COMMUNICATION TO CRISIS MANAGEMENT? 179

A Military Example: Abu Ghraib 179

Tylenol 185

Union Carbide 187

Boeing 191

 Starbucks 194
 Exxon Valdez 196
 Key Lessons About Crisis Management 197
 Discussion Questions 216

CHAPTER TEN CYBERSECURITY RESILIENCE 217
 Defending Against Attacks 220
 Looking at Industry 223
 The Broader Implications 226
 Strategic Communication to Protect Companies 228
 Infectious Disease Pandemics 234
 Discussion Questions 239

CONCLUSION 241
INDEX 249
ACKNOWLEDGMENTS 267
CREDITS 276
ABOUT THE AUTHOR 277
ABOUT ROTHSTEIN PUBLISHING 280

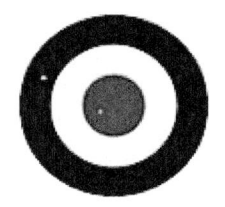

Business strategy is the battleplan for

A better future.

— Patrick Dixon

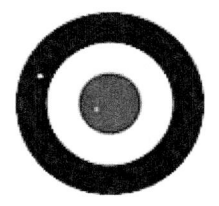

CHAPTER ONE
UNDERSTAND THE GLOBAL COMPETITIVE MARKETPLACE

This book is about what you can learn from military and national security leaders and apply their lessons to leadership and marketing in industry. The 21st-century operating environment forces you and your companies to be as adaptable, agile, and flexible as the military. Changes in technology don't change the essence of warfare or its "frictions," as Count Carl von Clausewitz described that notion in his classic book, <u>On War.</u> But new technology changes – and will keep changing – the way we think and operate. The military employs a notion called Operational Art to describe how it forges and executes strategy, operations, and tactics. You can apply lessons from it to strengthen leadership and strategic communication for a small or large enterprise.

Let's start with the overview on winning on a competitive playing field widely employed by military commanders. United Kingdom General Sir Richard Shirreff served as the Deputy Commander of NATO and was one of the few four-star Generals in the British army. Today he runs a large and successful strategic consulting company with a global footprint. He talks from a commander's perspective, but his insights apply up and down the line to any business.

Sir Richard observes that "The military applies force to achieve a political aim, while CEOs conduct business operations to generate revenue. So two fundamentally different outcomes are required. But I would argue that in the same way that 21st-century commanders need to understand the minds of target audiences in their operating environments, CEOs have to do the same for their customers. Both need a strategy. Both need plans. Both need to define desired outcomes, and many of the steps in that process are parallel."[3]

He adds: "Business executives today must understand the environment in which they operate. They have to replay many of the same criteria as military commanders. It's about more than customers, shareholders, and suppliers. It involves many other stakeholders, including local communities, regulators, governments, the media, national or regional policies that affect corporate operations. You have to win and maintain consent among communities to operate. That can be a sensitive challenge for many companies, especially those whose actions are subject to regulators."[4]

Four-Star General (Ret) Joseph L. Votel served as the Commander of the US JOINT SPECIAL OPERATIONS COMMAND – the operational arm of Special Operations and the US SPECIAL OPERATIONS COMMAND, and the US CENTRAL COMMAND. His commands included Iraq and Afghanistan. Today he serves as the CEO of Business Executives for National Security (BENS). Votel sees a new, globally competitive environment but feels that commanders have an advantage. "The challenge for CEOs is that they don't have as much help as military leaders. We have national security guidance, ambassadors, State Department and Pentagon regional experts, the intelligence community, and outreach into broad information networks. But the challenges are parallel. They both have to deal with what Count Carl von Clausewitz called the *frictions* of warfare – sudden, unexpected shifts in ground realities."[5]

The Theory of Special Operations Teaches Lessons

Friction also characterizes shifting marketplaces, whether advancing technology, consumer demand, or competition drives these shifts. How should you deal with this challenge? One option is to apply lessons from the "Theory of Special Operations." Special Operations forces conduct tactical operations that create

---

[3] Interview with General (Ret) Sir Richard Shirreff, May 5, 2021.
[4] Id.
[5] Interview with General (Ret) Joseph L. Votel, May 5, 2021.

strategic effects. They seek *relative superiority* in a strategic situation to achieve a narrowly defined objective.

Admiral William H. McRaven served as the Commander of the US SPECIAL OPERATIONS COMMAND and the JOINT SPECIAL OPERATIONS COMMAND. He commanded Usama bin Laden's takedown in Abbottabad, Pakistan. McRaven describes relative superiority as "the condition that exists when a small force gains a decisive advantage over a large or well-defended enemy. It is how special operations forces achieve the decisive advantage that explains their success. In essence, special operations forces gain that advantage when they have a simple plan, carefully concealed, realistically rehearsed and executed with surprise, speed, and purpose."[6] It is achieved at the "pivotal moment in an engagement," and requires "courage, intellect, boldness, and perseverance or what Clausewitz calls the moral factors."[7]

World War II furnished important examples. Some were successes. Some were failures. Each offers lessons in the need to plan carefully. The British modified an old destroyer, *HMS Campbeltown,* into a floating bomb, sailed it across the English Channel, rammed it into the German-held dry dock at Saint Nazaire, France, and blew it up. The goal was to destroy submarine pens and knock out a base to maintain the battleship *Tirpitz,* the *Bismarck's* sister ship. They did knock out the base. But they didn't assess the potential risk properly. The operation cost 169 soldiers killed and 200 taken prisoner. Admiral McRaven concluded that the operation wasn't worth the risk.[8]

On the German side, SS Capt. Otto Skorzeny conducted a daring glider assault on an Italian stronghold on top of Gran Sasso peak in the Apennines Mountains to rescue Benito Mussolini. It was a model of special operations success. So were the 1976 Israeli raid at Entebbe to rescue Israeli hostages and the raid that took out bin Laden.

Former Supreme Allied Commander – Europe, Admiral James G. Stavridis, whose enormous talent made him one of our most widely admired and respected flag officers, sees four key lessons Special Operations can teach executives. A

---

[6] The language quoted comes from Admiral McRaven's Masters Thesis for the Naval Postgraduate School, "The Theory of Special Operations," 1977, p. 2, which he later refined into his classic book, Spec Ops (New York: Ballantine, 1995). He sets out his theory in the first chapter and illustrates it with eight case studies. I had the honor of advising USSOCOM while he was its Commander.

[7] William H. McRaven, Spec Ops, supra, p. 4-5.

[8] Id, Chapters 4 (Saint Nazaire) and 6 (Norway). A later attack off Norway by a midget submarine got the job done and sank the battleship. McRaven praised that operation.

cerebral retired four-star whose home includes a 5,000-volume library, today he is a senior executive with The Carlyle Group, a significant private equity, asset management, and financial services firm. Here is how he describes the lessons:

> "First, innovation. That's being open to new ideas and promoting people who have good new ideas. Don't be afraid to fail as you attempt them. Put resources behind these ideas coherently and thoughtfully. Second, apply resources smartly. Everyone confronts finite resources. Special forces are small elite teams that cut bureaucracy, use resources efficiently, and place individual responsibility within small teams. Business needs to do that as well. Third, leadership. This speaks for itself. Finally, recognize the pivotal role – increasing every day – that technology plays. You see that today in business, where the electric car is disrupting and revolutionizing the automobile industry. Technological change, of course, is nothing new. At Agincourt, English bowmen slaughtered French knights in their heavy armor.[9]"

Agincourt offers a lesson in how technology affects the psychology of warfare. The longbow revolutionized a means of warfare, although not its nature. Convinced it would increase bloodshed, the Pope denounced it, in effect, as an illegal weapon of mass destruction. The airplane and nuclear weapons would later prompt similar complaints.

Innovation plays a central role in military and commercial strategic thinking. Maj. Gen. (Ret) John Davis served with USSOCOM, US CYBER COMMAND, and as the principal military adviser on cyber to the Secretary of Defense. Today he is a senior executive with Palo Alto Networks. Placing a premium on continuous innovation, Davis observes that "in today's digital world, innovative changes are dramatic and happen extremely quickly. Intelligence and information are perishable. You can't easily plan accurately for more than eighteen months because the pace of disruption through changes in technology is so high."[10]

---

[9] Interview with Admiral (Ret) James G. Stavridis, June 2, 2021.
[10] Interview with Maj. Gen. (Ret) John Davis, March 28, 2021.

Central to this dynamic is that digital connections expand our ability to create new links with people, groups, organizations, and movements. Networks form when nodes emerge, whether comprised of people, computers, mobile devices, drones, or any connective object. Digital networking technologies empower new social and organizational networks. These transcend borders. They form a global system. That gives rise to innovative ways of thinking and technology integral to strategic thinking.

This evolution helps define the information environment. Dr. Ofer Fridman is a former Deputy Commander of Israel's Tank Battalion and today serves as Director of Operations in the Centre for Strategic Communication, Department of War Studies at Kings College, University of London. He observes,

> "the information environment is often understood as a sum of its parts – all the messengers, recipients, as well as means of communication (televisions, newspapers, radios, the internet, and social media) – but it is more than objects and infrastructure. The essence of today's information environment comes not from its technological, biological, or cognitive elements, but the *interactions* between them."[11]

The Taliban's sudden defeat of the Government of Afghanistan in 2021 well illustrates the point. Victory followed within weeks of the US withdrawing most of its forces from the country. Few battles erupted. The Taliban's victory was the product of innovative, cutting-edge *information warfare* that capitalized on social media and every other form of communication. US President Joe Biden asserted that his advisers believed the government would stand for a year to eighteen months.

Succumbing to the Taliban message that its victory was inevitable and unwilling to die for a central government that lacked legitimacy, the army and its political allies surrendered or switched sides. The Taliban took Kabul without firing a shot. That would have been unthinkable in prior eras. The victory affirmed what strategic communication experts had long argued: the Taliban may look like unsophisticated ruffians and their political philosophy would arguably have flourished during the Dark Ages. But its long-term use of social media and

---

[11] Interview with Ofer Fridman by Zoom, April 21, 2021.

grassroots communications, from "night letters" to social media, was cutting-edge. It earned strong – if grudging – respect from the U.S. military.

The Taliban's innovative use of information warfare satisfied the principal goal of warfare. Ofer Fridman is an expert on Russian strategy.[12] He observes that this goal is to "achieve desired aims in the shortest time and with the least sacrifices."[13]

Russian commentators add nuanced dimensions to understanding the nature of war. The views of Genrikh Antonovich Leer, a 19th-century founding father of Russian strategic thinking who served as director of the Nicholas General Staff Academy, remain fresh today. Like Stavridis, he stresses the need to use resources wisely. He viewed the human being as "the main instrument of war," and a resource to be deployed prudently. Like Napoleon, he stressed the importance of time. The more rapidly you get things done, the fewer resources you expend and the greater your ability to generate momentum. Napoleon said that "in war and politics, a moment once lost will never return." Both Leer and Napoleon agreed that while "masters of other arts create only when they feel inspired, during a war one has to be inspired at every given moment" in nerve-wracking circumstances.[14]

Stavridis, Fridman, and Leer stress the pivotal role of strong leadership. What traits define such leadership?

First, you need *resourceful* leaders. You want people with "an ability to find solutions in any possible scenario" and "an ability to discern the best way of action according to known conditions." Second, *character* counts. People follow leaders they look up to, not stumble-bums or cheats. Third is the ability to make decisions rapidly. Count Carl von Clausewitz emphasized that "in war, what is important is not to dare to do the best thing, but *to dare to do anything, as far as anything can be energetically executed."* The worst thing one can decide in war is to choose nothing."[15]

---

[12] See, e.g., Ofer Fridman, <u>Strategiya: The Foundations of the Russian Art of Strategy,</u> (London: Hurst & Company, 2021).
[13] Interview with Ofer Fridman, June 7, 2021.
[14] Genrikh Leer, as translated and interpreted by Ofer Fridman, <u>Strategiya</u>, supra, p. 26.
[15] Interview with Ofer Fridman, June 7, 2021. Fridman is citing Jean-Thomas Rocquancourt and Napoleon's Marshal, Michel Ney.

Finally, bear in mind Napoleon's declaration that three-quarters of success depends upon moral leadership.[16] That echoes Admiral Stavridis and Sir Richard Shirreff, who root leadership in strong, positive values. Corporate counselors like Jim Lukaszewski, Virgil Scudder, and Jim Stengel argue these traits are essential to corporate success.

Consider some commercial examples. Steve Jobs's bold leadership in airing a single television ad introducing the McIntosh computer changed that industry. Startups like Warby Parker, Harry's Razors, Ben & Jerry's ice cream, Bonobos tailored clothing, the travel company Away, Paint company Backdrop, cookware company Potluck, Nom Nom Fresh Dog Food, SprezzaBox men's accessories, Stance Socks, and Innocent Drinks applied principles familiar to Special Operations operators to seize market share. In each case, innovative leaders devised strategies to surmount parochial challenges and seize or increase market share. Imagination and initiative paid off.

Had Jobs' gambit failed, Apple might have collapsed. The above start-up companies faced seemingly overwhelming obstacles. They focused on achieving narrow goals in their specific markets. Besting larger competitors in every category was unthinkable. They selected the actions that lay within their resources and imagination and executed them brilliantly.

What character traits matter most? A handful stand out: integrity, fidelity to truth; commitment to excellence; courage; loyalty to an organization; and the broader intent of purposing their organization to improve lives. These values anchor a credible rationale for appeals to emotional intelligence and reason. Communication and marketing have few universal rules, but here's one. Imprint it on your brain: *reason persuades, but emotion motivates*.

Admiral Bobby Inman served with distinction as Director of the National Security Agency and Deputy Director of the Central Intelligence Agency. Admiral Inman offers additional insights into leadership.

---

[16] In a letter to his brother, Napoleon stated: "In war, three-quarters turns personal character and relations; the balance on manpower and materials counts only for the remaining quarter." Correspondance de Napoleon Ier publiee par ordre de L'Empereur Napoleon III, Vol. 17 (Paris, 1868), p. 471-472; citation provided by Ofer Fridman.

> "To lead people and to make plans work, you need to understand the people with whom you are working and engaging. You need to know their concerns, worries, problems, and ambitions. The demonstration of your interest and concern for what worries them is the key to creating empathy. And always, you need to be truthful and transparent."[17]

General David Petraeus earned a reputation for outstanding leadership as the Commander of U.S. and Coalition Forces in Iraq and Afghanistan. Later, he led the Central Intelligence Agency during important achievements in the global war on terror. After leaving government, he joined KKR, a global investment firm, where he established and Chairs its Global Institute, and with which he later was made a Partner. Petraeus has immersed himself in global and corporate perspectives and what makes leadership succeed. His views are worth hearing.

Petraeus' guidance for communication is simple: *Be first with the truth*. In Iraq, he characterized that as "the biggest of the big ideas that guided our information and public affairs strategies."

Petraeus believes that strategic leaders, those at the top of organizations, have to perform four tasks. First, they have to get the big ideas right. Second, they have to communicate the big ideas throughout the breadth and depth of the organization they lead. Third, they have to oversee the execution of the big ideas. And fourth, they have to determine how the big ideas need to be refined so that they can repeat the process repeatedly.

Most commentators on the Surge in Iraq in 2007-2008 identify its successes in Baghdad as pivotal to the overall campaign's success. Petraeus argues that the success there was exemplary of the achievements throughout the country – which were guided by the big ideas that were the foundation of the Iraq Surge. As Petraeus noted, "The surge that mattered most was not the surge of forces, it was the surge of ideas, the changes to the overarching strategy, which were in the most important respects, 180 degrees." The biggest of the big ideas was the need to "live with the people" to secure them. That required U.S. forces to reverse the strategy of the previous years, which had seen American soldiers leaving the neighborhoods, consolidating on big bases, and handing off security tasks to the Iraqi Security Forces.

---

[17] Interview with Admiral Bobby Inman, April 9, 2021.

Another of Petraeus' big ideas was this reality:

> "A military force cannot kill or capture its way out of an industrial-strength insurgency; rather, it has to reconcile with as many of the rank-and-file of the insurgents as is possible, while pursuing the 'irreconcilable' leaders of the insurgent and extremist movements even more relentlessly than before, as they have to be captured or killed."

Petraeus had, in fact, a whole series of ideas captured in the counterinsurgency guidance that he published to the command not long after taking control. It was a series of warnings. And, when it came to dealing with the press, again, the big idea was to "Be first with the truth." As Petraeus explained:

> "We sought to beat our enemies to the headlines with as accurate a report as was possible in each situation, updating what we provided as additional information arrived. We explicitly rejected trying to 'spin' the press or to 'put lipstick on pigs.' Instead, we sought to provide the most accurate information we could get to the media, our Iraqi counterparts, the Iraqi people, our higher headquarters, etc., as quickly as possible.
>
> "We also believed that we had to be accessible to the press – and I set the example in that regard. Beyond that, we thought that the press had obligations, as well: first, to get the facts right and to accurately report them; second, to provide relevant contextual details (as the actions taken need to be judged based on the context); and third, to properly characterize what happened (e.g., not describing an overarching endeavor as challenged just because one element of it was challenged).
>
> "Finally, we also recognized three realities in dealing with the press: you can't win if you don't play; you can't lose if you don't play, but we have to play as if we owe it to America's mothers and

> fathers and to our fellow citizens to explain what we are seeking to do with their sons and daughters in uniform."[18]

Reporting on the surge, Pulitzer-winning journalist Thomas Ricks said that leadership like Petraeus' made a difference in stabilizing the ground.[19] J. David Patterson served as a Special Assistant to Deputy Secretary of Defense Paul Wolfowitz and witnessed Petraeus in action.

> "One lesson that Petraeus' success teaches, is that he embodied the idea that successful commanders have the unquestionable ability to command – and are *visibly seen* to be in command. That builds confidence, increases morale, instills message discipline, and produces a winning battle rhythm. Petraeus excelled at that."[20]

How Do These Precepts Affect Target Audiences?

Military theatres of operation involve engagement and conflict with populations who may be indifferent, or hostile and dangerous. Neutralizing adversaries and converting fence-sitters is challenging. No one in Gaul, Britain, Spain, or North Africa greeted the Romans as liberators. Julius Caesar's war killed over a million people. That's a lot of folks in any era, but in his, the planet's entire population was only 200 million. Yet Romans viewed him as a "great man." He understood the importance of winning over people and neutralizing fence-sitters or opponents.

Conversely, Napoleon may have provided France with a civil code, the Arc de Triomphe and the Invalides, and he reorganized education. But drunk on warfare, he compounded rather than converted enemies. Bloodlust destroyed him.

---

[18] Interview with General David Petraeus, April 14, 2021.
[19] Ricks also credits General Raymond T. Odierno, who commanded the III Corps from May 2006 to May 2008, with helping to devise the American strategy. He later served as Chief of Staff of the Army.
[20] Interview with Dave Patterson, April 20, 2021.

Continuous warfare in Europe killed between 3.2 and 6.5 million people and tore the Continent apart.[21]

Corporations are lucky. People may dislike a computer, detergent, or cologne. But no one is going to express their dissent by chopping off heads. Executives tend to think about communications more narrowly. So how the military feels about winning offers valuable insights into how executives can strengthen or change brand loyalty and manage crises.

The military flubs it sometimes. The 2003 War in Iraq cratered over an early failure to define the mission clearly and, until 2007, a failure of credibility. Iraqis grew cynical about the Coalition's goals. They rejected the narrative that the Coalition wanted to help skeptical Iraqis. Was the goal to eliminate weapons of mass destruction? Was it to topple Saddam, "drain the swamp"[22] in the Middle East, and make way for a new, democratic world order? Was it to build Iraq into a modern state? Or was it, as Al Qaeda in Iraq skillfully argued, to conduct a Christian crusade to repress Islam and Muslims, occupy Muslim land, and pirate Muslim wealth?

As we move beyond the theory of Special Operations, a successful strategy requires understanding the world and looking over the horizon. Futurist Gerd Leonhard predicts "humanity will change more in the next twenty years than in the three hundred years."[23] The advent of virtual reality, artificial intelligence, neurotechnology, 5G, quantum computing, and other new technologies seem to affirm his forecast. Networks and connectivity define the nature of today's era. Understanding how to capitalize on them is pivotal.

You need a holistic approach. Austin Branch served as the Senior Director for Information Operations at the Pentagon and is a leading expert. He points out that "appreciating the information environment requires learning the culture and language of any place you operate. Understand what interests target audiences.

---

[21] In today's world, Napoleon is criticized for tolerating or embracing slavery, a flaw that affects any assessment of him as an individual, but no one denies that he was a compelling figure whose actions affected the flow of history.

[22] See: Tom Engelhardt, "Draining the Swamp," *Huffington Post*, January 5, 2017: https://www.huffpost.com/entry/draining-the-swamp-then-and-now_b_13978450. A lot of excellent books on the 2003 Iraq War have been written. Especially recommended are George Packer, Assassin's Gate, (London: Thorndike, 2006), Thomas Ricks, Fiasco (New York: Penguin Books, 2006), and Andrew J. Bacevich, America's War (New York: Random House, 2016).

[23] Gerd Leonhard, "10 Future Principles and what they mean for EU policy makers," EU FTA 2018:Â https://www.futuristgerd.com/2018/06/my-presentation-at-the-fta-2018-eu-commission-event-inn-brussels-today-9-future-principles-for-policy-makers/

In a conflict zone, is it their security? In a civilian world, is it the quality of life? What hopes and fears drive people? What do they feel they need? How do they perceive communicators and understand what their interests are?"[24]

Branch stresses forging relationships between government and private industry to build on their mutual strengths. He notes that "the relationship is not primarily as a source of understanding and information but identifying where their interests intersect and respecting corporate privacy and independence. In a connected world defined by networks, the best way that executives and government can learn from one another is to establish networks that benefit from the actions and communications of commonly oriented actors. Cultivating trust in network relationships is essential."[25]

The National Defense Strategy – amplified in March 2021 by President Joe Biden's Interim National Security Strategic Guidance[26] – aims to meet the complex security environment in a multi-polar world. Adversaries pose competition in disruptive battle spaces. Great power competition is about leveraging influence for strategic gain. Executives face a comparable challenge. A hundred years ago, executives worried about competitors across state borders; today, south China, Malaysia, Germany, or Mexico furnish much of the competition.

A coherent strategy is essential. The US intervened in Libya citing the rather new doctrine of a Responsibility to Protect innocent civilians. The current chaos dramatizes the failure to think through actions. By contrast, assistance the US provided to southeast Asians when the 2004 tsunami struck fourteen Asian countries, or the 2002 intervention into the West African nation of Liberia to stop a civil war, shows the good one can achieve.

Clear-cut Commander's Briefs defined goals. US forces carried out the planning envisioned. The tsunami relief efforts alleviated vast suffering. The Liberia mission stopped bloodshed and stabilized matters. In each case, wise strategy and knowing ground realities spelled the difference.[27]

---

[24] Interview with Austin Branch, March 26, 2021.
[25] Second interview with Austin Branch, May 25, 2021.
[26] See: President Joseph R Biden, Jr., *Interim National Security Strategic Guidance*, March 2021: https://www.whitehouse.gov/wp-content/uploads/2021/03/NSC-1v2.pdf and U.S. Department of Defense, *Summary of the National Defense Strategy of the United States of America*, 2018: https://dod.defense.gov/Portals/1/Documents/pubs/2018-National-Defense-Strategy-Summary.pdf
[27] I participated in the provision of advice through a defense contractor to the Combined Joint Task Force-Horn of Africa (CJTF-HOA) that examined how the Command could leverage existing

As executives, you can learn from those successes so long as you recognize the limits of strategic communication. You cannot change deeply held beliefs; your goal is to channel emotions and ideas to those beliefs. Marketing guru Herbert Jack Rotfeld years ago told it like it is: "No marketing plan could impel Auburn University men to start wearing skirts to class."[28] Nor could influential operations in Afghanistan motivate Afghans to prefer centralized over localized government. You have to avoid stupidity. Rotfeld recounts the potato chip company in Argentina that ran an ad depicting Adolph Hitler becoming a nicer guy after eating his chips. The ad concluded by morphing the Nazi swastika into the company logo.[29]

 Global brands such as Nike and Coca-Cola tailor strategies to diverse cultures. Your company may currently focus on local or regional markets, but success still requires innovative thinking, rooting the company in the values of integrity, excellence, loyalty, and improving lives. Four examples mark how visionary leadership scores points.

Apple Surges Us Into a New World

During the 1984 Super Bowl, Apple announced its new Macintosh computer with a bang. It hired film director Ridley Scott, who directed the films *Aliens* and *Gladiator*, to do a million-dollar television blockbuster spot that cast PCs as the tools of an authoritarian state. Created by Lee Glow with a sly reference to George Orwell's *1984*,[30] the scale is epic. The story dramatizes the exploit of an athletic heroine who casts a javelin hammer at a TV screen featuring a ranting Big Brother. The imagery symbolized control of technology by the few. The javelin shatters the screen. Shackles that had dehumanized people burst.

Apple proclaimed a new world. This is tuh today as it was 36 years ago. Indeed, a parody that drew millions of YouTube views helped jump-start Barack Obama's 2008 Presidential campaign, resonating with the select, young, and hip market Apple sought to reach. The tone, approach, and visual vocabulary communicated a narrative, theme, and message that struck a powerful emotional

---

programs to carry out its peacekeeping mission. Our examination of the Liberian intervention significantly influenced our recommendations.
[28] Herbert Jack Rotfeld, Misplaced Marketing, (Westport: Quorum, 2001), p. 4.
[29] Id., p. 147.
[30] https://www.youtube.com/watch?v=PsjMmAqmblQ. Glow was the Creative Director of TBWA/Worldwide.

chord. The ad urged independent thinkers to rebel against the conventional establishment and to "think different."[31]

Apple is now legendary. It changed the way we thought about computers. Computer geeks insist to me that the differences between Macintosh computers and PCs don't matter. We ordinary mortals find its ease of use and elegance a godsend. Founder Steve Jobs declared: "Apple is not about making boxes. Its core value is that we believe people with passion can change the world for the better." In his view, "People who are crazy enough to believe they can change the world are the ones who do."[32]

The message is powerful, emotional, and appeals to our idealism. It inspires and motivates us to act. Apple's campaigns even today draw a friendly but clear contrast with PCs and drive the point that Apple is for the imaginative and the independent. I have nothing against PCs. The 17th century produced a lot of fine technology, and for Mac users like me, we know deep in our hearts that's where PC technology belongs. We just look ahead to the future and what new, cutting-edge technology harbors. It's colorful, hip, official ad for 2021 captures that spirit.[33]

Nike Summons the Hero Within Us

Peek inside Nike's brand strategy, and you'll find the classic story of the hero's journey, notably relayed in Joseph Campbell's books.[34] Nike positions us as both heroes and villains. The slogan "Just do it" cuts across nationality, culture, gender, and age. Nike fosters the belief that we all can overcome doubt, hesitation, and fear through dedication, discipline, and hard work. We can endure the suffering of physical training, transcend weakness, and find our inner

---

[31] Apple, "Introducing the MacIntosh:" https://www.youtube.com/watch?v=2zfqw8nhUwA. In 2008, Barack Obama supporters adapted the spot into a mash-up that cost little money to discredit the conventional wisdom that Hillary Clinton had locked up the Democratic nomination. In place of Big Brother. we saw Hillary. The rebel wore an iPod on her waist, emphasizing the modernity of the mash-up. The spot generated cheers and enthusiasm. Tactics like these ignited the grassroots campaign of a charismatic candidate and propelled this political underdog to victory in the nomination contest and the general election. The narrative and theme projected Obama as a charismatic outsider in tune with the times, a sharp contrast to the nearly septuagenarian Clinton, whose campaign had a lock on party machinery.
[32] https://www.youtube.com/watch?v=keCwRdbwNQY
[33] https://www.youtube.com/watch?v=b0IatUaFIc0
[34] Joseph Campbell, The Hero's Journey, (New York: New World Library, 2014)

strength. We can each become a hero.[35] Nike's philosophy is that sports can improve our lives and help us to fulfill ourselves.

Nike, Reebok, Adidas, and their competitors don't connect their communication to a scientific breakdown of what makes their shoes distinctive. Instead, they use language, images, symbols, and action to define *what it means* for you to use their products. They appeal to our deeply held values. They shape our identity, but Nike does it best.

Nike ads touch deep emotional chords in playing to the aspirations of women, younger competitors, and those growing older. Nike urges us to compete against the villain in ourselves – laziness, sloth, doubt, lack of discipline, or hard work – in pushing ourselves to the limit and breaking through the pain to fulfill ourselves. Its strategy does not sell a product. It sells a *vision* of self-improvement. **Just do it.** The shoes, a *swoosh* punctuating the slogan, represent a symbol of commitment.

An online video about Nike founder Bill Bowerman narrated by actor Sam Elliot sums up Nike's theme: *Don't do anything unless you care enough about it to be a winner.*[36] Nike maintains strong message discipline across media channels, nations, and cultures. The message is that those who wear Nike shoes have what it takes to capitalize on sports and to improve your life.

Saks Strikes Back at the Evil Empire

Powerhouses like Amazon have disrupted retailing. Online shopping is eating into traditional store-based sales.[37] A visionary and futurist, Amazon founder Jeff Bezos has re-imagined how technology can propel a revolution. He argues that

---

[35] Graeme Newell, "Nike Brand strategy: emotional branding using the story of heroism:" http://602communications.com/nike-brand-strategy-emotional-branding-using-the-story-of-heroism/

[36] "Running Nike: The Bill Bowerman Story:" https://www.youtube.com/watch?v=aQYBULq1UkA. The video roots Nike's story in Nike founder Bill Bowerman's life story and values. Bowerman summons us to give our best to become a better person, open our minds to new ideas, strengthen teamwork, ignore failure and do what it takes to achieve our goals.

[37] Kate Rooney, "Online shopping overtakes a major part of retail for the first time ever," *CNBC.com*, April 2, 2019: https://www.cnbc.com/2019/04/02/online-shopping-officially-overtakes-brick-and-mortar-retail-for-the-first-time-ever.html

customers are the winners, but his victory leaves many retailers in a ditch. Malls that inspired films like *Mallrats* are closing. By 2022, one in four may vanish.[38]

The military thinks in terms of end-states, not outcomes. The achievement of each objective creates a state of affairs that will give rise to new goals. As former Secretary of State George Shultz famously declared, "In politics, nothing is ever settled." This holds for the military and executives. Starting in 2016, and continuing today, Saks Fifth Avenue has taken the lead in striking back with a fresh vision that caters to high-end shoppers who relish an exciting, personalized shopping experience.

Since its founding in 1867, Saks Fifth Avenue has prized its status as a luxury retailer. It answers the online competition by providing a satisfying real-life experience that makes people feel special. You can't do that online. Saks touts excitement. It appeals to our desire for status, suggesting that only the elite shop there. In-store iPads and in-store delivery of items ordered online show cutting-edge technical sensibility to tastes. Saks' Brookfield location in Lower Manhattan promises to take consumers through "a shopping journey equipped with digital touchpoints." It makes shopping *fun* as well as satisfying.

Chief Merchant Tracy Margolies says that "Every person who comes into Saks wants to feel empowered. They want to stand for fashion."[39] Saks provides personal shoppers a hotline called "Saks Save Me." It allows clients to drop off items for lunchtime alterations or shoe repairs. Saks makeup artists make house calls. Saks connects online shoppers to in-store associates. Saks stores feature high-end restaurants.[40] Saks caters to a high-end audience. The brand understands that delivery of a high-end experience is a classic form of good strategic communication.[41]

---

[38] Abha Bhattarai, "Malls are dying. The thriving ones are spending millions to reinvent themselves," *Washington Post*, November 22, 2019: https://www.washingtonpost.com/business/2019/11/22/malls-are-dying-only-these-ones-have-figured-out-secrets-success-internet-age/. She cites a Credit Suisse report for the 2022 mall closure forecast affecting one in four malls.

[39] Lauren Sherman, "Inside the Reinvention of Saks Fifth Avenue," *businessoffashion.com*, September 6, 2016: https://www.businessoffashion.com/articles/intelligence/saks-fifth-avenue-brookfield-place

[40] Id.

[41] Centric Digital, "Strategy," December 20, 2016: https://centricdigital.com/blog/customer-experience/how-saks-sacks-its-competitors-with-a-better-customer-experience-strategy/ Saks competitor Bergdorf Goodman installed digital mirrors that allow customers to take pictures

In 2021, its CEO, Mark Metrick, declared that Saks was doubling down on what he termed the retailer's "luxury disrupted" strategy. The strategy builds on the high-touch personal approach while aggressively marketing online in social media. The impact of COVID on store attendance mandated that strategy. "We've put lots of technology in the hands of our associates," he says. "Our stylists in our stores have generated nearly $150 million in revenue from technology, from being able to use it on websites to fulfill their customers' needs before the stores were open [after COVID forced their temporary closure] and then even after they were open and folks didn't want to come in."[42]

As a venerable retailer, some might wonder if SAKS might become stodgy. Actually, the brand has chosen innovative leaders who combined technology, personal service, and fashion to thrive. SAKS teaches an important lesson for those who wonder how to keep a long-time brand on the cutting edge. If you're going to go for top-shelf customers, you better behave like you're top-shelf and provide a Top of the Mark experience.

Starbucks Offers a World Apart We Can Enjoy at Home

Starbucks CEO Howard Schultz proved a lackluster candidate for public office. He dropped his 2020 ambition to run for President as an independent. He discovered what political professionals have long known: the principles of political communication transfer well into commercial advertising and corporate communication, but that doesn't usually work in reverse. Yet Schultz was a genius at turning coffee, an everyday commodity, into a high-end work of art.

Schultz glamorized the notion of a *barista,* the person behind the counter who makes a wide range of primary and colorful coffee drinks and delivers exotic coffee beans from around the world. Like Saks' leaders, he understood that creating a story, narrative, theme, and message about the *experience* sells.

---

with garments in the store. Tiffany uses augmented reality that lets customers try on experiences in its remote shopping channel. Id.
[42] George Anderson, "NRF 2021: SAKS doubles down on its 'luxury disrupted' strategy," *Retail Wire*, August 31, 2021: https://www.retailwire.com/discussion/nrf-2021-saks-doubles-down-on-its-luxury-disrupted-strategy/

His coffee drinks bear exotic names: Frappuccino, Blonde Cappuccino, Espresso Con Panna, Blonde Peppermint Mocha, London Fog Tea Latte. Starbucks designs its cafes as destinations: places where people meet, drink coffee, talk, make new friends. One of my former neighbors – she's nuts but committed – is an early bird. Life traumatizes her unless she rises at 4:30 a.m. to go to Starbucks for coffee. That's a bit much for me, but it's a free country. Gold medal to Schultz.

Soon enough, Starbucks was serving 70 million cups a day with a $15 billion market cap. Then it got complacent, and sales sagged, requiring a fresh new start. He closed 800 stores, laid off 400 employees, and brought the workforce to New Orleans to re-train *baristas* to make espresso. Clever marketing, Starbucks Cards, and mobile payments further boosted revenues. Reinvention defines Schultz's leadership, which persists even though in 2017, he turned over the CEO reins to Kevin Johnson.[43]

Starbucks' *strategy* began with a vision: connect peoples' lives. *Operations* have embraced the entire globe. *Tactics* have focused on how Starbucks positioned itself in the marketplace, the physical appearance and operation of each store, and the nature and training of its employees, promotions. Schultz articulated a message of corporate responsibility. He hired 10,000 veterans and military spouses. He believes that the values of public spirit and helping others are right and smart.

Success in a globally competitive economy requires making strategic business judgments that predict megatrends likely to define global culture in the coming decades. Our top military leaders think like that. The leaders of Apple, Nike, and Starbucks offer excellent examples for corporate leaders who likewise strive to look into the future for the direction and growth of their business.

Let's all take a lesson.

---

[43] David A. Kaplan, "Starbucks: The Art of Endless Transformation," *Inc.com*, June 2014: https://www.washingtonpost.com/business/2019/11/22/malls-are-dying-only-these-ones-have-figured-out-secrets-success-internet-age/

Discussion Questions

1. What do you want your leadership and marketing to achieve? Can you draw a parallel between your ambitions and those of pioneers like Jobs, Bowerman, and Shultz?

2. If just anybody could do what you dream of, why do you matter? As you develop goals for strategic communication or marketing, whether large or small, what breaks through the clutter and enables you to stand apart?

3. Is there new technology – or older technology you can repurpose – that moves you forward and helps you to achieve your goals?

4. Admiral McRaven's theory of Special Operations may be especially relevant for startups. His approach seeks to achieve *local superiority*. It's a tactic that achieves strategic effects. Jobs pulled it off with computers, Bowerman with shoes – initially he just bought shoes from Japan and slapped his own label on them – and Shultz with coffee. Think about it: coffee costs almost nothing. In the U.S., his stores get a couple of bucks for Starbucks coffee. In Australia, it's almost *five dollars*. They aimed to achieve specific goals. You don't have to achieve every goal in one swoop. What goals lend themselves to your achieving such local superiority, and that form steppingstones to broader success?

5. Do you agree or disagree with Jim Stengel that the most successful executives focus their efforts – and those of their companies – on improving lives? What actions do you think about in achieving that goal?

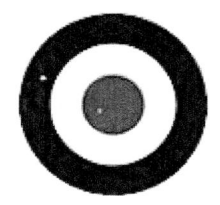

CHAPTER TWO

DEFINE SUCCESS

Defining success – what you want to achieve – is the central goal of any strategy. Using that strategy to mobilize what Clausewitz describes as your "center of gravity" is what makes your marketing strategy and campaign sing.

Executives and military leaders invoke different language to describe success, but it amounts to the same thing. Strategic communication uses language, action, images, or symbols to influence attitudes and opinions to motivate behavior that achieves the desired outcome or, for the military, the "end-state." Let's start with the military's approach that talks about "end-states." It applies to executives but adds clarity to the notion of success.

Bob Giesler served as the Director for Strategy Coordination for the Secretary of Defense. "Any good strategy starts with the desired end-state," he says. "From there, you build strategy, operations, and plans to achieve the end-state. The end-state describes the nature of success because the achievement of goals and objectives that create one state of affairs creates a new one. Military leaders think in those terms. I've worked in both worlds, and I advise corporate CEOs to do so as well. The process produces sharper, more disciplined strategic thinking."[44]

Every Commander develops a "Commander's Brief" that articulates "Commander's Intent." You can draw a parallel in "creative briefs" that executives espouse. These ensure that subordinates or team members coordinate.

---

[44] Interview with Bob Giesler, April 14, 2021.

First, define what you want to achieve. Maj. Gen. (Ret) John Davis reminds: "First, if you don't know where you're going, any path will do. Second, planning always starts with the end in mind. From that flows plans and operations. By understanding the overall intent or goal, you can improvise, be agile, flexible, and still accomplish the goal if things start to fall apart."[45]

Colonel (Ret) Mark Mitchell served as a Special Operations Officer and Assistant Secretary of Defense for Special Operations – Low-Intensity Conflict. The post is the service secretary for Special Operations. Mitchell emphasizes the need to "write down a clear strategic plan. When you write it down, you review it, and your team reviews it, you identify strengths and weaknesses. You crystallize unacknowledged assumptions that need to be made explicit.

Strategic situations for business and the military change. Leaders change, and workers come and go. A written plan provides continuity through these changes. It also enables you to adapt and maintain a competitive edge. It's not just about winning, either. It's about sustaining success."[46] I discuss written strategic plans below.

As noted above, you know that customers maintain brand loyalty. You need a compelling reason for them to switch. What are some of these "compelling reasons?"

The military roots thinking in Operational Art. This is the application of creative imagination to design strategies, campaigns, and major operations, and to organize and employ military forces. Operational art integrates ends, ways, and means across the domains of war.[47]

David Petraeus agrees that's a good description of forging strategy. Still, he notes that both industry and military strategy requires "a nuanced understanding of all aspects of the situation and the missions (tasks and associated purposes) – the ends – assigned to us." A theme of his strategic thinking is to "distill the big ideas that should guide us to make the best use of the resources made available to us to accomplish the missions we were given."[48]

---

[45] Interview with Maj. Gen. (Ret) John Davis, March 18, 2021.
[46] Interview with Colonel (Ret) Mark Mitchell, April 7, 2021.
[47] U.S. Department of Defense, "Joint Operations," 17 January 2017, Incorporating Change 1, 22 October 2018,
[48] Interview with General David Petraeus, April 14, 2021.

Acquiring the Knowledge

Defining success or the desired end-state is step one. But *where* does one acquire the required *knowledge* to get you there? During the 1930s, information on German military strategy was sketchy. George Marshall's planning for World War II began by asking *who* knew how to write an actionable victory plan.

He chose West Point graduate Lt. Col. Albert Wedemeyer for the job. Buried in the Pentagon's War Plans Division, Wedemeyer had a key asset. He had observed the German Army grand maneuvers of 1938 and served as one of two U.S. Army officers who attended the *Kriegsakademie* in Berlin as exchange students.

Wedemeyer knew German military strategic thinking. Still, for Marshall, he worked from scratch. The questions were boggling. What would a war look like? What were each side's strengths and weaknesses? What resources would a win require? Where would we acquire them? Remarkably, the Victory Plan that he produced closely resembled the U.S. and the allies' actual strategy.[49] Wedemeyer epitomizes the value of relying on experience and first-hand knowledge.

General David Petraeus believes in casting a wide net.

> "The only way to accumulate knowledge, in my experience, is to seek it from all possible sources aggressively, but particularly the most important ones. I have often talked about 'marinating' in the details of a particular country or situation to develop a nuanced, detailed, and informed understanding of the details that ultimately comprise knowledge."[50]

---

[49] See: General Albert C. Wedemeyer, Wedemeyer Reports, (New York: Henry Holt & Company, 1958) and John McLaughlin, General Albert C. Wedemeyer: America's Unsung Strategist in World War II, (Havertown: Casemate: 2012).
[50] Interview with General (Ret) David Petraeus, April 14, 2021.

Former US CENTCOM and US SOCOM Commander General Joseph Votel echoes Petraeus.

> "I tried to look at the *New York Times,* the *Wall Street Journal*, and news aggregators. I'd have my classified intelligence briefing. I'd engage with my public affairs officers and my web ops person. I looked at every credible source of information relevant to operations to stay ahead of the curve and maximize the chances of success."[51]

UK General Sir Richard Shirreff emphasizes connectivity and networks. Applying his military experience, he now advises corporate clients to identify networks that connect people, "who can help you get answers and to process and understand the answers. Equally important is looking beyond the boundaries of a company's internal network to third parties. One must avoid the danger of group-think that can prevail inside a company. Turning to outside third parties can provide objective advice and assessments. They can be a rich source of knowledge that informs a successful strategy or plan."[52]

As a commander of the Allied Rapid Reaction Corps, he formed a commander's initiative group. "We brought in free-thinking academics, journalists, people from NGOs, military and intelligence operators, and other experts who brought knowledge of particular issues. They served as a critical friend to the commander, sharpening our thinking and enabling us to focus on obstacles and forge solutions."[53]

Former Under Secretary of Defense (Policy) – the third most powerful post in the Pentagon and today CEO of the space infrastructure company Momentus – John Rood remarks that acquiring the proper knowledge challenges every official who deals with a foreign government. He advises that

> "before you meet with foreign officials, you get the U.S. Ambassador or the regional desks in the Pentagon with expertise in the country to brief you on the individuals you'll meet with, relevant cultural points, and the strategic situation on the ground. They'll describe what they believe to be

---

[51] Interview with General (Ret) Joseph L. Votel, May 5, 2021.
[52] Interview with General (Ret) Sir Richard Shirreff, May 5, 2021.
[53] Id.

> the agenda of the people you'll meet with, their personalities, alliances, politics, and other matters that fill out the picture. You engage with people who know the country or the people you'll engage with. Finding the right person on the ground who is plugged in and has relationships with key people helps a lot. And when you make a foreign visit, you can absorb nuances by just soaking up the environment. Above all, you do a lot of *listening*. There is no substitute for listening. A lot of accomplished people you meet are adept at hiding their true motives or intentions. Acquiring the knowledge you need takes time, patience, and focused attention."[54]

Virgil Scudder, one of the top corporate communication experts whose practice centered on advising Fortune 100 executives, has worked extensively in other nations. He summarizes his approach:

> "When I do work in a country for the first time, I get a local from my client or collaborating organization to walk me through all of the cultural dos and don'ts, local pronunciations, meaning and rank of titles such as Sri or Dato, and a briefing about what locals are especially proud of and offended by. If you kick the analysis to the military side, when the U.S. invaded Iraq in 2003, President George W. Bush didn't know the difference between Sunni and Shia and the tensions between them. His ignorance was costly."[55]

Austin Branch echoes those views, arguing that you need to

> "network with everyone who can provide insight and understanding into a situation. I once formed a strong working relationship with a US AID expert

---

[54] Interview with John Rood, April 15, 2021.
[55] Interview with Virgil Scudder, May 3, 2021.

on water wells. The work provided a powerful way to connect with local populations. Private enterprise is a rich source of information. In Africa, safari companies are well connected. Energy companies tap into broad networks that provide a deep understanding of culture and local politics. They know a lot and what they know is relevant to what the military needs to know. Private companies have a greater ability to move and adapt than the government. It's one reason I've strongly advocated that in any region, our military engage in thoughtful discussions with companies. We can help one another through sharing information."[56]

Lessons from Iraq and Afghanistan

The 2003 Iraq war is a case study for how an initial failure to define winning produces setbacks. War hawks favored ousting Saddam Hussein to block his possessing weapons of mass destruction. Lieutenant General F. John Kelly talked about establishing democracy in Iraq – a different goal.[57] The Department of State offered its own plan, labeled the "Future of Iraq." The project sat on a shelf. Ultimately, the Department of Defense co-opted planning for Iraq.

DoD excels at planning. Yet, the Pentagon failed initially to define a successful end-state or a strategy for achieving it.[58] The military, the White House, the State Department, and Secretary of Defense Donald H. Rumsfeld clashed. Finally, after getting trounced in the 2006 elections, Bush sacked Rumsfeld and put in a

---

[56] Id.

[57] Richard H. Shultz Jr., The Marines Take Anbar: The Four-Year Fight against Al-Qaeda (Annapolis: Naval Institute Press, 2013), 33. See also George Packer, The Assassins' Gate: America in Iraq (New York: Farrar, Straus, and Giroux, 2005), 58–59.

[58] Shultz, The Marines Take Anbar, 34–35. U.S. Central Command commander Army Gen Tommy R. Franks blew off the idea of post-war planning, referring people to Deputy Secretary of Defense Paul D. Wolfowitz.

cohesive team that forged and executed a plan that stabilized Iraq until the U.S. pulled out in 2011.[59]

One reason it worked was that the U.S. forged a clear vision. Bush appointed General David Petraeus to command ground forces and Ambassador Ryan Crocker to captain the diplomatic front. They formed a great team. Most media reporting discussed the Iraq Surge, an operation to stabilize Iraq by defeating Al-Qaeda in Baghdad and creating breathing space so that Iraqi political leaders could set up a sustainable government.[60] We looked at Petraeus's views on that earlier.

Strategies that worked in Iraq, an urban nation comprised of three major ethnic groups – Shia, Sunnis, and Kurds – proved more problematic in tribal Afghanistan. Afghan's rural culture favors decentralized power. The population includes a kaleidoscope of ethnic groups, clans, tribes, families, and villages. The Special Inspector General for Afghanistan Reconstruction (SIGAR) blasted the failure to come to terms with this reality. SIGAR criticized the military's failure to stabilize insecure and contested areas, lack of military and civilian coordination, and, failing to forge a cohesive *political* strategy for winning.[61]

Lt. Gen. (Ret) Frank Kearney served as the Deputy Combatant Commander at the United States Special Operations Command. In his view, "we didn't define the political end-state that was acceptable to NATO, the U.S., or the Afghans. We never built a plan around achieving that end state. It was a strategic failure."[62] General (Ret) Sir Richard Shirreff concurs, declaring:

> "From my NATO perspective, while the agreed Allied strategy was that we should build up Afghan security forces to hand over responsibility for security to the Afghan government, what was missed was the need to build up and maintain the institutions of the state – governance, statecraft, competent ministries, cleaning out corruption so that the government served the people, was *seen*

---

[59] Thomas E. Ricks, The Gamble: General Petraeus and the American Military Adventure in Iraq (New York: Penguin, 2009), 37–40.

[60] Thomas E. Ricks, The Gamble: General David Petraeus and the American Military Adventure in Iraq, 2006-2008 (New York: Penguin, 2009).

[61] Stabilization: Lessons from the U.S. Experience in Afghanistan (Arlington, VA: Office of the Special Inspector General for Afghanistan Reconstruction, 2018).

[62] Interview with Lt. Gen. (Ret) Frank Kearney, April 13, 2021.

> and *believed* to serve the people and had the credibility to be sustainable."⁶³

Flag and senior military officers, intelligence and Pentagon officials interviewed for this book, on- and off-the-record, expressed different views on why we lacked a cohesive, actionable grand strategy for defeating the Taliban. Still, all agreed we lacked such a strategy. Their dire predictions about the knock-on consequences came sadly true in August 2021.

Admiral Stavridis identifies four lessons that the Iraq and Afghanistan wars can teach executives.

> "First, understand your objectives. Both nations were multi-ethnic and multi-religious. Executives need to understand comparable nuances within their target customer bases. Second, be realistic in what you think you can accomplish. The US encountered huge challenges in both nations on that score, and business confronts them every quarter. Third, think through how evolving technology will affect your ability to gain market share and win over target audiences. Somebody came up with the idea of naming a car Nova and selling it to Latin America. *NoVA* in Spanish means *won't go*. Guess what? Novas were not the hot seller in Spanish-speaking countries. Finally, you must understand the language, history, and culture of target audiences. Otherwise, you're flying blind. Your end-point if that happens is a brick wall."⁶⁴

The Drug Wars and Centers of Gravity

Success requires that you mobilize support in what Clausewitz refers to as *centers of gravity*. These are the core interests that you have to satisfy. In wartime, the will of the people always matters. Abraham Lincoln and Franklin

---

⁶³ Interview with General (Ret) Sir Richard Shirreff, May 5, 2021.
⁶⁴ Interview with Admiral (Ret) James G. Stavridis, June 2, 2021.

Roosevelt understood that. It's why each made certain that the other side fired the first shot, at Fort Sumter and Pearl Harbor. Voters would not support the U.S. starting a war. They rallied to the defense of the Union. During the 19th century, the great Prussian leader Otto von Bismarck battled to unify Prussian states into a unified Germany. Harvard historian Graham Allison splendidly describes his manipulation of France to provoke its leader into starting a war that achieved that result.[65]

Joe Biden had long disdained the war in Afghanistan. He drew a firestorm of criticism for the execution of withdrawal from Afghanistan in August 2021, but one reason he felt comfortable with the decision to withdraw was that overwhelming numbers of voters in both parties decided that twenty years was long enough to fight a war.

The Drug Wars illuminate the need to satisfy your *centers of gravity*. Pursuing the impossible dream makes for a catchy song but do that wantonly in real life and you'll hit a brick wall. Centers of gravity vary depending on objectives. Carl von Clausewitz's conception of grand strategy in his book *On War* revolves around his views on the topic. He describes it as a point in the enemy's organism – military, political, social – that collapses the enemy's national will if lost or defeated. He believed the right strategy aims to defeat an enemy's center of gravity, as that forms the basis of an opponent's power at the operational, strategic, and political levels.[66]

Mexico's Challenge

Mexican President Felipe Calderon fearlessly took on the entrenched drug cartels. Victory required dependable law enforcement and military, persuading the Mexican people that the war was worth the cost. He failed to on both counts and paid the price.

Vicious and ruthless, the cartels littered the country with chopped-off heads and bodies hanging from traffic overpasses. They had unlimited resources. Drug profits may reach $64 billion a year.[67] Law enforcement sources quoted $39 billion in their interviews for this book. Whatever the figure, it's enormous. Compare that to the brouhaha over money reserves that the Islamic State

---

[65] Graham Allison, Destined for War, (Boston: Mariner Books, 2017), p. 265
[66] J.J. Graham, commenting on Clausewitz, On War, supra, Kindle Location 4343/4382. See also: J.F.C. Fuller, The Conduct of War, 1789-1961, supra p. 69.
[67] S. Sered, M. Norton-Hawk, Can't Catch a Break (Berkeley: U. of California Press, 2014)

reportedly has stashed away – several hundred million dollars. ISIS's wealth is small potatoes compared to the cartels, whose violence has killed 200,000 civilians in Mexico.

The drug lords possess virtually unlimited resources. They can fund any activity. When the Zetas cartel wearied of fighting Mexican Special Forces, they *hired* them.[68] Only the Mexican Marines have measured up. But what Calderon really lacked was active popular support.

A 2008 survey conducted by *Centro de Investigacion y Docencia Economicas* revealed that 79 percent of Mexicans viewed drug trafficking and organized crime as a concern.[69] But Mexicans viewed their *government* as corrupt. Hence Calderon lacked the legitimacy a leader needs to wage war. He articulated no clear rationale. He showed no strategic clarity. He never explained how the war could end, or why Mexicans should buy into it.

Mexicans responded by electing Enrique Peña Nieto – Mexican presidents serve a single term – as Calderon's successor. They capitulated to a mirage. The smooth-talking Nieto backed off from the fight. Critics had long worried that Nieto's Institutional Revolution Party (PRI) was in bed with the Sinaloa cartel. Until National Action Party (PAN) Vincente Fox's election in 2000, the PRI had held a near-monopoly on Mexican power. Many believed that the relative peace that marked its politics stemmed from an unwritten understanding between the PRI and the cartels of living and letting live. Fox pursued trade and economic policies. Calderon, also a PAN member, put fighting drugs first.

The smooth-talking Nieto was a piece of work. Married to a wealthy woman, the handsome President was a Hollywood talent agent's dream. He looked like a star and pranced around like one. But when U.S. prosecutors put the notorious Sinaloa cartel leader Joaquin Guzman Loera, a.k.a. El Chapo, on trial, a darker portrait surfaced. Witnesses accused Nieto of pocketing a $100 million bribe from the crime lord.[70] In the meantime, Mexico's drug problem had worsened. It's not improving under Nieto's successor, Andres Manuel Lopez Obrador, who shows little interest in challenging the cartels.

---

[68] See: "Strategic communications and cyberspace in Mexico's Drug War (co-authors: James Farwell, Darby Arakelian and Antoine Nouvet), in Open Empowerment: From Digital Protest to Cyber War (R. Muggah & R. Rohozinski, Ed)(Ottawa: SecDef Foundation, 2016).

[69] "CIDE Presents the Survey Results, Mexico, the Americas and the World," *Protocolo*.

[70] Alen Feuer, "Nieto Took $100 Million Bribe, Witness at El Chapo Trial Says," *New York Times*, January 15, 2019: https://www.nytimes.com/2019/01/15/nyregion/el-chapo-trial.html

Perhaps surprisingly, Obrador and President Donald J. Trump enjoyed a cooperative relationship, although they focused on border issues, not the drug wars. At this writing, it is too early to judge how President Joseph Biden and Obrador will get along. Obrador is at heart a left wing authoritarian and his agenda seems more focused on amassing personal power. The Biden administration has swung left on U.S. domestic policy, but in international affairs, it continues the traditional U.S. posture as a champion of democracy and political freedom.

Lessons for Executives

The stakes for you as an executive don't usually involve life or death. But sometimes they may. As Retired British Army Colonel Stephen Padgett OBE, former commander of British troops in Afghanistan and Britain's defense attaché there, and today the CEO of Britain's National Horseracing College that educates thoroughbred horse trainers, jockeys, and support staff, points out, "a horse weighs half a ton, and when you're a jockey riding in a crowded field of twenty horses, you're well aware of the genuine risk to life and limb."[71]

You must maintain a grip on your centers of gravity. Apple's center of gravity rests on its ability to project the image of a cutting-edge company that opens new vistas of knowledge. Nike's center of gravity is athletes who agree sports improve their lives. Nike's inspiring narrative – I come back to Nike throughout this book as I find its approach is so outstanding – appeals to our innate desire to excel.

Harry's Razors illustrates how innovative thinking that zeroes in on a well-defined goal of success can pay off.

The Hope Diamond of Razor Blades

Harry's Razor's success required the same imagination and disciplined thinking that military combat demands. Harry's did not need to corner the market in razor blades. It just needed to get its share. It devised an ingenious strategic communication plan. Let's take a look.

"This thing might just be the Hope Diamond of razors," *Gentlemen's Quarterly* trumpeted in reviewing Harry's Razors "Winston" razor blade. This article compared the startup company that makes razor blades for men to the famous

---

[71] Interview with Colonel Stephen Padgett, O.B.E., March 22, 2021.

jeweler whose diamonds have adorned stars like Dame Helen Mirren, Julie Andrews, Madonna, and Natalie Portman.[72]

One might wonder about the comparison. Reportedly, the Hope Diamond carried a curse from Louis XIV to an American heiress. The curse holds that whoever owns the 45-carat diamond is ill-fated for life.[73] Weeks after a French merchant sold it to the Sun King, a pack of wild dogs mauled the merchant to death. King George IV got hold of it and wound up with a mountain of debt that forced him to sell the diamond. Suicide, murder, and bankruptcy afflicted subsequent owners.[74]

Bold and irreverent, Harry's Razors proudly quoted GQ on its website. Founded in 2012, owners Andy Katz-Mayfield and Jeff Raider believed they could take on Gillette, the razor blade market's 800-pound gorilla in the $2.4 billion shaving industry. They launched a bold subscription service that garnered 100,000 email addresses within a week.[75] Harry's Razors had innovative marketing that stressed personal service and a top-tier product. It made consumers who wanted a personalized, tailored product its center of gravity. Entering the market, Harry's moved fast and decisively, catching Gillette off-guard.

Customers define its marketing strategy. The company continuously interacts with them. As a customer myself, I can attest to the customer service and blades. Harry's Razors delivers. By 2016, it had attracted two million customers[76] and expanded its product line with Flamingo, a women's skincare brand.[77] Harry's Razors and competitors like the Dollar Shave Club, another subscription service,

---

[72] Adam Hurly, "The Best Razor for the Smoothest Shave," *Gentlemen's Quarterly,* November 3, 2016: https://www.gq.com/story/best-razor-for-smooth-shave.

[73] Stefan Andrews, "Hope Diamond is thought to carry a curse from Louis XIV to an American heiress," *Vintage News*, December 15, 2017:
https://www.thevintagenews.com/2017/12/05/the-hope-diamond/

[74] "The Curse of the Hope Diamond," *Thoughtco.com*, March 20, 2020: https://www.thoughtco.com/the-curse-of-the-hope-diamond-1779329

[75] "Harry's shows it's not the biggest marketing budgets that win," *canova.com*:
https://www.canva.com/learn/harrys-shows-its-not-the-biggest-marketing-budgets-that-win/

[76] "Our story," Harrys.com. Harry's marketing team focuses on new products; getting in front of new and existing customers; thinking about advertising direct sales to its website; and a large in-house creative team.

[77] Michael J. de la Merced, "Harry's Raises $112 Million to Move Beyond Shaving," *New York Times*, February 15, 2018: https://www.nytimes.com/2018/02/15/business/dealbook/harrys-shaving-financing.html

disrupted the industry and created a new business model for men's grooming.[78] They developed a strategy and pulled out the stops.

Gillette Pays for Its Hubris

Gillette dismissed the competition. The big dog depended upon long-term brand loyalty and a conviction that it owned the best product. I was like a lot of folks who junked the brand. Its razors were expensive. Gillette was a walking excuse for growing a beard. I came across a Harry's Razors ad, took a chance. and found them as good Gillette but less expensive. I loved the personal service.

Writing in *Inc*, John Warrillow echoed my feelings in a "Dear Gillette" Op-Ed: "With no other solution, we buy the same blades every few weeks because we have better things to worry about. Until one day something shocks us back to reality and the insanity of paying $45 for blades."[79] Gillette's form letter reply was babble. Warrillow said it well. Gillette's had a weak rationale for its product. Harry's Razors and Dollar Shave Club exploited that and won big.

Gillette had the resources to add muscle to its marketing. But Harry's had bold leaders who seized – and continue to build – market share before the behemoth could stop them. Harry's had a clear-eyed view of success and zeroed in on doing whatever it took. It succeeded.

Innocent and the Three College Guys

Innocent Drinks is a healthy smoothie drink sold in the British market. It had no advertising dollars. Its founders defined success as getting into the marketplace and using word of mouth to jump-start sales. They recognized that the British place a high value on environmentally sound, healthy drinks. So they targeted audiences who wanted the product as Innocent's center of gravity. It defined success as market positioning to attract and expand a sustainable customer base. Its clear vision, message discipline, and high-quality product caught the market by surprise. Success required a steady build. But like the movie said, build it and they will come. Customers came.

---

[78] "Harry's shows it's not the biggest marketing budgets that win," *canova.com:* https://www.canva.com/learn/harrys-shows-its-not-the-biggest-marketing-budgets-that-win/

[79] John Warrillow, "Dear Gillette, You Took Advantage of My Loyalty and Now I'm Gone for Good," *Inc*,

How did they do it? Three Cambridge graduates, Richard Reed, Adam Balon, and Jon Wright were friends at St. John's college. On a snowboarding holiday, they came up with the idea for Innocent as a company that would make healthy smoothie drinks. They spent six months working on smoothie recipes. They used 500 pounds sterling worth of fruit. They made the drinks in a small kitchen in a shared house in West London and then sold them from a London music festival stall. They asked people to put the empty bottles into a "yes" or "no" bin, in answer to the question: "Should we quit our jobs to make smoothies?" "Yes" carried the day in a landslide.[80] The off-beat strategy was stood apart.

Raising capital was tough. They used up their savings and maxed out their credit cards.[81] They sent an email to friends asking if anyone knew a venture capitalist. One friend knew a venture capitalist, Maurice Pinto. Pinto liked the idea and invested 250,000 pounds sterling.[82] Innocent's premise was that a company rooted in ethical values, natural ingredients, and a superior product could break into a tough market. It promised to donate 10% of profits to charity. The high-end boutique grocery Waitrose took a flyer and gave them shelf space. That got Innocent on track. But, lacking ad money, how could they bump up sales?

One partner, Richard Reed, came up with a solution. "We had to make sure the smoothies sold," he says. "The only way we could guarantee that was to go into the stores and buy our own products. So that is what we did." He smiled. "It was largely an exercise in faking it 'till you make it.'"[83] The drink proved a hit. Major supermarket groups picked up Innocent. It took off. As the company matured, it used slogans such as "Tastes good. Does good." It persistently worked to strengthen its hold on its center of gravity.

One marketing campaign followed the story of Joseph, a local boy aided by family donations from the Innocent Foundation. The narrative resonated. Working with NGOs to create a secure future for farmers enhanced its stature in environmentally sensitive Britain.[84] Then came rough sledding. In 2008, a

---

[80] Chris Tryhorn and Mark Sweney, "Smoothie Operators tread familiar path to lucrative deal," *Guardian*, April 6, 2009: https://www.theguardian.com/business/2009/apr/07/innocent-smoothies-coca-cola

[81] Will Smale, "How smoothie brand Innocent became a bestseller," *BBC.com*, April 9, 2018: https://www.bbc.com/news/business-43542605

[82] Id.

[83] Id.

[84] Loulla-Mae Eleftheriou-Smith, "Innocent focuses on emotion and charity in marketing overhaul," *campaignlive.co.uk*, December 9, 2013:

market downturn forced them to find a new investor. Coke stepped up. Reed beams at the result. "For me, it is a fairytale," he says. "We all did better than we thought, not a single person lost their job, and the relationship [with Coke] is brilliant. And Coke is committed to Innocent's ethical ideals, including giving 10% of its profits to charity."

The Diaper Wars

Who would suspect that information warfare would underlie competition for the sale of baby diapers? The answer is: anyone who understood that billions of dollars were at stake.[85]

Pampers went from owning the diaper field to facing stiff competition from Huggies. Huggies were less expensive, fit better, kept babies dry. The Pampers team did in-depth research and testing. They uncovered the challenge. The data pointed to a solution. It revealed that toddlers need different diapers at different stages of growth. Pampers tailored other products to each step. It drove a narrative that positioned it as a partner with moms in fostering their children's happy and healthy growth. Success meant repositioning Pampers to satisfy the requirements of moms concerned about the healthy development of their children.

Pampers center of gravity was a group of moms who put those priorities first. This wasn't Special Operations thinking. It was good, clear, well-executed strategic thinking that aimed to regain a lost edge in the market and sustain a lead by understanding that a mother's concern for their child's healthy growth was a pivotal center of gravity to success.

Values and Centers of Gravity

Corporate marketing expert Jim Stengel does not use the notion of center of gravity in his respected book Growth. He argues that successful companies position their culture as a center of growth. He asks: Do they stand for the correct values? That applies to the military and corporate worlds. Sir Richard Shirreff declares: "Values-based leadership is fundamental to success. It is about

---

https://www.campaignlive.co.uk/article/innocent-focuses-emotion-charity-marketing-overhaul/1224153

[85] For a detailed analysis, see Jim Stengel, Grow, supra, p. 167-189.

inspiring people to do willingly and well what the leader wants them to do, whether in business or the military. Core values are the bedrock for success and are critical to building the mutual respect and trust upon which empowerment depends."[86]

Stengel's focus is on business. He argues that as executives, you must answer critical questions rooted in values. The most critical is whether your vision and mission are to improve the lives of people. In short, corporate culture is a center of gravity. The demand for a particular service or product is a center of gravity.

IBM forgot that, and the laptop computer business passed the company by. In the nick of time, IBM recognized the demand for its data analytics and consulting. It shifted course and rooted its business in its big data Watson software. You can see IBM's approach in ads with a narrative of "Let's put smart to work" and "Problems inspire us to fix things, to move the world forward." I've cited four ads in the footnotes that you can link to on YouTube.

The first addresses IBM and COVID-19. I find it is the most persuasive. It hits all the right notes for what IBM offers: big data to rethink health care challenges and solutions that working smarter produces. IBM's ads may lack the emotional drama of a Nike ad, but they're well calibrated to its audience. "Smart loves problems" stands out for defining why people would pay attention to IBM. The other ads are a bit cute for my taste but skillfully employ wit and humor to illustrate IBM's message. All these ads elevate IBM's visibility and create memorable images.

The notion of identifying a center of gravity – the beating heart of your company and its bedrock – is central. It marks their path forward. Those are the basics in determining what constitutes success. Do this right, and you're on your way.

---

[86] Second interview with General (Ret) Sir Richard Shirreff, May 6, 2021.

Discussion Questions

1. For your project or campaign, how do you define success or a winning "end-state?"

2. What are your centers of gravity?

3. How does your strategic communication persuade and motivate behavior from your center of gravity that produces success?

4. What are the key elements that make your strategic communication work?

5. Not everyone has a big budget for marketing or advertising. Innocent Drinks is one example. In his book, The Tipping Point,[87] social psychology journalist Malcolm Gladwell cites the example of Hush Puppy shoes, which made a huge comeback through word-of-mouth and no advertising. What lessons do you draw from these success stories?

6. What core values for yourself and as an executive do you most respect?

7. How do you relate core values to a successful plan for strategic communication or marketing?

---

[87] Malcolm Gladwell, The Tipping Point, (New York: Little, Brown 2000).

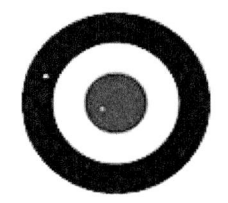

CHAPTER THREE

WHAT OBSTACLES MUST YOU OVERCOME?

You – and the military – need to know the competition and the strategic area in which competition takes place. Once you've defined what success means, you will need to identify the obstacles to your success. The general precept is "know your enemy" – or competitor. That means do your homework, which includes cogent target audience analysis.

Here are essential considerations.

1. Identify your competitor or enemy.

Identifying the enemy can challenge the military commanders. Identifying Taliban members in Afghanistan, Al Qaeda in Iraq, and the Viet Cong or North Vietnamese during the Vietnam war often proved tricky, as they blended in with the population. Enemies often avoid showing themselves. You need dependable ways to identify enemies. Intelligence collection is vital. Understanding the enemy can prove tricky. What motivates, inspires, threatens, or frightens an enemy? What coalitions does the enemy belong to? What is the nature and composition of such alliances? Understanding these considerations enables you to identify vulnerabilities.

As an executive, you can skip over this obstacle. You can easily identify competition. Less obvious, says David Patterson, is which competitor offers the best opportunity to compete against and win.[88] If you design a new shirt, is Brooks Brothers, Saks Fifth Avenue, or a regional brand the easiest target to raid for market share? UNTUCKit's Wrinkle-Free Douro Shirt and the men's clothing subscription service Bombfell are designed to be worn untucked. They're not competing in style or price-point against SAKS Fifth Avenue or J. Press. They tailor their advertising to avoid competing for customers of the latter two. Chivas Regal scotch flopped in making its debut in the market as a lower-priced brand. The company fired the ad agency. The new agency repackaged the same whiskey as premium scotch. Snob appeal did the rest. Chivas targeted a select share of the whiskey market and zeroed in on that. It understood the competition.

2.   Know the strengths and weaknesses of the enemy or competition – as well as your own.

The Chinese strategist Sun Tzu said, "If you know the enemy and know yourself, you need not fear the result of a hundred battles. If you know yourself but not the enemy, you will also suffer a defeat for every victory gained. If you know neither the enemy nor yourself, you will succumb in every battle."[89] Mao Zedong stated, "Some people are good at knowing themselves and poor in knowing the enemy, and some are the other way round; neither can solve the problem of learning and applying the laws of war."[90]

Both military leaders and business executives need to understand their strengths and weaknesses and those of competitors or adversaries. I've had the pleasure of working closely for several years with George Beebe, who held the civilian equivalent of one-star rank in the Central Intelligence Agency as head of the agency's Russia Analysis and later advised Vice President Dick Cheney on Russian affairs. Beebe argues that one cannot overstress the importance of understanding both the strengths and weaknesses of an adversary or competitor and their appeal to target audiences.

"I call this *analytic empathy*," Beebe says, "and it's one of the most fundamental duties of intelligence officers and anyone who deals with foreign affairs. You want to walk around in their shoes. Get a feel for what their world looks like. At

---

[88] Interview with J. David Patterson, April 7, 2021.
[89] Sun Tzu, The Art of War, trans. Lionel Giles (Seattle, WA: Amazon Classics, 2017), Kindle Loc. 727/3205.
[90] Mao Tse-tung, Selected Military Writings of Mao Tse-tung (Peking, China: Foreign Language Press, 1963), 88, as quoted in Michael I. Handel, Masters of War: Classical Strategic Thought, 3d ed. (London: Taylor and Francis,
2005), 36.

a minimum, that will open your eyes to what's coming and avoid being blindsided."[91] He adds: "This exercise is equally important so that we understand our partners and allies, their agendas, and how most effectively to engage with them."[92]

In Beebe's experience,

> "when you're trying to deal with such parties, you need to know what's possible and how you get to the desired outcome. That requires understanding their perceptions of a situation. Unless you know how they understand their interests, it's hard to judge what makes them strong or weak and what realistically they can do. This is not easy for many Americans because the reality is that too many Americans don't feel the need to understand foreign cultures."[93]

National security examples furnish a good starting point for understanding this.

In 2020, China recognized that the COVID virus forced it to confront enemies at home and abroad. China's strategic communication has consistently pursued one overwhelming goal: regime preservation. All its actions keep this objective center stage. Rooting narrative, theme, and message in nationalistic appeals, Beijing has worked to persuade its population that it brought the virus – one it maintains was transmitted from animal to humans[94] – under control. It drove a narrative that placed the health and safety of Chinese people first. It has succeeded admirably. President Xi Jinping and his team understand their citizens. They know they run a repressive regime. They realize that their claim to legitimacy requires creating prosperity for consumers and ensuring public health. It's a sensitive balance.

The theme that drives Chinese Communist Party (CCP) propaganda is patriotism. This theme flows from a storyline that alleges that foreign nations exploited the 19th-century Opium Wars to bully the Chinese people. In 1949, the

---

[91] Interview with George Beebe, May 2, 2021.
[92] Id.
[93] Id.
[94] See: Nicholas Wade, "The origin of COVID: Did people or nature open Pandora's Box at Wuhan," *Bulletin of the Atomic Scientists,* May 5, 2021: https://thebulletin.org/2021/05/the-origin-of-covid-did-people-or-nature-open-pandoras-box-at-wuhan/. Wade clearly believes it came from a laboratory accident.

CCP defeated imperialist influence and liberated the country. The narrative is that by 2049 China will emerge as globally supreme economically, wiping away the stain of past humiliation and reclaiming its rightful place as the most powerful nation. The CCP calls this vision "the China Dream." The current narrative substitutes an *internationalist* story that united the oppressed in China and the rest of the world with a *nationalist* tale that sets the Chinese people against the rest of the world."[95]

Abroad, a different challenge confronts the CCP. China has adopted a sophisticated, inter-disciplinary, and multi-dimensional approach to security. China weaves political, diplomatic, economic, and military strategies, operations, and tactics into a relatively cohesive grand strategy to realize the China Dream. The dream envisions ending a rules-based international order comprised of sovereign nations, freedom of speech, and democracy and creating a new global system that forces other countries into the role of economic tributaries.

Its major initiatives include promoting Huawei's 5G Internet standard, the Belt & Road Initiative, and a "Thousand Talents" program that harvests intellectual property from unsuspecting academic institutions in other countries. Military notions of "unrestricted warfare" and the "Three Warfares" that aim to achieve victory without armed conflict integrate with those into a cohesive grand strategy.

Of course, not even a superpower like China can create foolproof strategies. China has weak points. Its economy is more tenuous than may appear. Imaginative efforts to escape Internet censorship attest to resistance to state crackdowns on freedom of expression. China's leadership feels insecure about their legitimacy in the eyes of their compatriots. China's handling of COVID blew up in its face and could sidetrack the 2049 vision. An invasion of Taiwan might succeed militarily but could have devastating consequences for its international credibility and ability to exert global influence.

The U.S. exploited credibility weakness well in fighting ISIS. Our communication stressed that foreign fighters from Europe and the U.S. got better food and living conditions than Middle East recruits. Influence operations highlighted the disparity, creating tensions and morale problems among the terrorist recruits. ISIS fighters were good bullies but, mostly, they proved an indifferent military force. We communicated through words and action that ISIS would lose, then proved the point by beating them on the battlefield. It will be interesting to see how the Taliban fares in fighting ISIS in Afghanistan.

---

[95] Clive Hamilton, Silent Invasion, (Sydney: Hardie Grant Books, 2018), p. 19-20.

In Somalia, lack of cultural understanding helped produce the Blackhawk Down fiasco. Naval War College strategic studies expert Jonathan Stevenson pointed out the trap of failing to think things through up front. Clan leader Farrah Aidid turned Somalia into a live-fire simulation of the post-apocalypse after the American commandos hit the ground. It began when Admiral Jonathan Howe ordered Somalis to turn over their weapons.

The National Rifle Association could have drafted the Somali response. Somalis asked why they should disarm while the Second Amendment protected U.S. gun owners. The Somalis said, "My gun is to protect myself, my family, and my property."[96] Howe had done too little cultural research. Somali leaders made him look like a fool.

Like those who have served with him, I've long held General Joseph Votel in high esteem, since meeting him through Special Operations. Votel stresses the need in dealing with foreign audiences "to listen, understand, and respond. You have to understand what they're telling you, to grasp their perspective and how they see things before you try to solve problems that affect them. It's not always easy because Americans generally want to be helpful. We want to try and solve problems. What you're trying to do is build credibility. You're trying to build a connection. You're trying to build mutual understanding. You're showing you are responsive to their needs and that we will earn their trust."[97]

The Somali experience teaches that you need to think through the knock-on consequences of a decision. The "Blackhawk Down" incident was militarily successful but a political failure. That made President Bill Clinton gun-shy about involving the U.S. in local conflicts. Clinton wasn't interested in foreign policy, anyway, until getting caught with an intern refocused his attention to the Middle East during the closing days of his term. Those who participated in his regular Friday night staff conferences in the White House residence told me that when a national security issue cropped up, he referred the matter to his National Security Adviser.[98]

The bitter fruits of Clinton's hands-off attitude included the massacre of 8,000 Bosnian Muslims at Srebrenica and other Serb-sponsored genocide. The Hutu massacre of Tutsis in Rwanda shocked the world. Strong Presidential leadership – again by Clinton – could have avoided both debacles, especially in Rwanda,

---

[96] See: Jonathan Stevenson, <u>Losing Mogadishu: Testing U.S. Policy in Somalia</u> (U.S. Naval Institute Press, 1995), p. 74.
[97] Interview with General Joseph L. Votel, May 5, 2021.
[98] Off-the-record interviews with three individuals who participated weekly in the conferences.

where a small coterie of Hutu extremists instigated the slaughter. Clinton later said he regretted his mistake. He's adept at issuing facile apologies to excuse his failures. That hardly excuses his poor leadership. The relevant point here is that defeat in one campaign can dramatically choke off sensible, imaginative initiatives in subsequent ones.

I was paired at the US STRATEGIC COMMAND with British Colonel Sandy Wade. Sandy is a sophisticated, decisive guy who had commanded British forces in the Balkans in 2003-2004. Looking back to the time before the Stabilisation Force in Bosnia and Herzegovina (SFOR) on what NATO forces refused or were prohibited from doing to stop the genocide, he observes that

> "leaders have to think through the consequences of inaction as well as action, and to understand why and how their opponent might be defeated. The failure of NATO forces to detain or apprehend Serb leaders responsible for committing war crimes was a failure to communicate strategically. The passive posture of the forces, mandated by their civilian leadership, signaled to the Serbs that NATO would not stand in their way. It was a terrible political decision, and the lesson learned applies to the military and other areas of endeavor."[99]

Wade notes the irony of deploying so-called peacekeepers. "Nations who do so want to keep their soldiers out of direct armed conflict, in which they can sustain casualties until there is peace. But if you already have peace, who needs military peacekeepers?"[100] The lesson is to pay heed to the context in which decisions are reached.

Bob Giesler observes: "It's pivotal to collect and properly analyze the right information and intelligence," he says, and "then put that to work." He compares military failure to think through the consequences of a strategic communication plan to industry challenges.

Giesler's thinking is a good link to the challenges that beset executives. After working for the Pentagon, he became a high-ranking executive with a major defense company.

---

[99] Zoom interview with Colonel (Ret) Sandy Wade, March 19, 2021.
[100] Id.

> "The key to competing lies in understanding your competitor's failings and compare that to your strengths. Never bad-mouth a competitor. That's bad ethics and bad business sense. But you can persuade a client prospect to ask hard questions about how competitors stack up against one another. One big corporate competitor had a habit of bidding their top talent to get a contract. Within a year, they would yank out the top folks and substitute cheap talent. It was bait and switch. They failed to think through how their communication, which exaggerated promises, would play out. We nudged the client into examining the past performance of competitors. They detected the game our competitor was playing and recognized that we kept that talent on the job when we bid top talent. We won the contract."[101]

Executives can spot weak points in the competition's appeal, stories, narratives, themes, or messages more easily than the military. Nike is the giant among athletic apparel manufacturers. Adidas trails but is a powerhouse. Athletic wear startup Under Armour ingeniously finessed the issue and defined a lesson you should imprint on your brain.

Instead of going head-to-head, UA founder Kevin Plank identified a new niche in the market, a stretch tee shirt called "the shorty" worn as an undergarment that absorbed sweat.[102] It was a simple, single-minded idea that suited what Plank termed a "blue ocean" strategy.[103] W. Chan Kim and Renee Mauborgne have written a book advocating the idea.[104] They argue that startups should expand market boundaries by moving into uncontested market spaces. They urged innovation as the tool to disrupt the market and leap forward.

---

[101] Interview with Bob Giesler, April 14, 2021.
[102] The description of Under Armour marketing draws partly on Effy Pafitis, "What Can Be Learnt From Under Armour's Marketing Strategy?", *Starting Business.com,* September 30, 2020: https://www.startingbusiness.com/blog/marketing-strategy-under-armour.
[103] See: "Under Armour Marketing – Sailing into a big, blue ocean of opportunity," *Brand Insight Blog*: https://bnbranding.com/brandinsightblog/under-armour-marketing/.
[104] W. Chan Kim and Renee Mauborgne, Blue Ocean Strategy, (Cambridge: Harvard Business Review Press, 2005, revised 2005).

Kim and Mauborgne's book is required reading. I agree strongly with their view that the best way to beat the competition is to stop trying to beat the competition. The notion defines a strategic view about achieving success. Plank offers one example; there are many others.

Cirque du Soleil created a new market in the circus world, a declining space, by reimagining what a circus could be. Traditional circuses spent money on expensive clowns and highly criticized animal shows that raised their cost structure without much altering the circus experience. Their costs rose, but not revenues. Circus demand was declining. Cirque du Soleil discarded expensive elements of a traditional circus and combined the thrills and fun of the circus with the intellectual sophistication and artistic richness of theater. It created an original product that attracted traditional circus fans and new ones.[105]

Yellowtail, an Australian wine, did the same thing. It recognized that many wine drinkers knew nothing about wine and found searching for wine intimidating. It realized that Americans prefer a sweeter taste. It produced wines with a bright yellow label and a Kangaroo into supermarkets and other stores, where it brought a broad group of new non-wine-drinkers into the market. It also appealed to jug wine drinkers looking to move up.[106]

Those of us who like good claret might not care for Yellowtail – it's plonk – but it blew away the competition. The winery's owner, Casella Wines, held down costs and marketed an easy-drinking, easy to select soft wine. It eased selection by producing only two wines: a Chardonnay and a red Shiraz. These held down costs for the producer and the buyer and provided a fun experience to its target audience.[107]

Kim and Mauborgne call their strategy *value innovation.* You make the competition irrelevant by creating a leap in value for buyers and your company and opening up uncontested new market space.[108]

Kevin Plank had the same market insight. That was no guarantee of success. He had his ups and downs. But he built a fifteen billion dollar storybook success from scratch. He might not have seemed a likely star; Georgetown Prep threw him out after he failed two classes. But athletes loved the shorty. Plank touted his designs as "innovations to perform."

---

[105] Id., p. 4, 10, 14, 18.
[106] Id., p. 31.
[107] Id., p. 32-35.
[108] Id., p. 12.

Word of mouth and $40,000 of credit card debt got him started. He operated out of his grandmother's home. Here we see another lesson: you don't need a fancy office to launch a successful business. Deals with Georgia Institute of Technology and North Carolina State University gave UA liftoff. Then came a third lesson: Plank waited until his first product proved a success and his company was established before introducing new designs. He took it one step at a time.

In 2016, UA entered the shoe market with its SpeedForm Gemini 2 Record Equipped, a smart shoe with a built-in sensor to store and track data. Partnerships with star quarterbacks Tom Brady and Cam Newton elevated Under Armour's visibility.[109] Other partnerships with sports teams and colleges promoted the brand across different sports. Celebrity endorsements from Michael Phelps[110] and Dwayne Johnson further raised visibility. Product placement in *Any Given Sunday*, director Oliver Stone's homage to the NFL, and persuading Dolphins' quarterback Dan Marino to wear UA's shirt, raised visibility.

Echoing Steve Jobs' gutsy move to bet the farm on the *1984* ad, Plank invested all the company's savings – $25,000 – in a single ad for *ESPN* magazine. That tactic generated $750,000 in earnings.

By 2005, UA was sold in 2,000 stores. UA went public and grew into a "unicorn" – a startup that achieved a value of a billion dollars. It refined its message to the somewhat arcane slogan "Protect the House" – like the first one, more style than substance. As before, UA oriented itself towards Gen Z men.

UA rooted its appeal in strong values: *Stand for Equality, Stay True, Think Beyond.* It stresses environmental sustainability. It publicizes charitable endeavors and mobilizes customers to join in. It fosters customer interaction that builds long-term loyalty. UA later sharpened its image, but it has always played off a theme that echoes Nike's: *Under Armour makes you better through its performance.*

Recognizing that its initial appeal was too oriented towards men, UA deftly course-corrected through its "I Will What I Want" campaign,[111] to make women

---

[109] Shoshy Climent and Mary Hanbury, "Here's how Under Armour went from a new hotshot sportswear brand taking on Nike to having a wholly uncertain future," *Business Insider*, November 15, 2019: https://www.businessinsider.com/under-armour-history-to-uncertainty-2019-8

[110] See: "Michael Phelps: Earn Your Armour," https://www.youtube.com/watch?v=kTG6rfhejsQ.

[111] "Misty Copeland: I Will What I Want:" https://www.youtube.com/watch?v=zWJ5_HiKhNg; Gisele Bundchen: I Will What I Want:" https://www.breitbart.com/politics/2021/08/25/white-

feel empowered, valued, and respected. It named ballet dancer Misty Copeland, basketball star Bella Alarie, and model Gisele Bündchen – quarterback Tom Brady's glamorous wife – as brand ambassadors. Bundchen's ad drew 3.6 million views. The message to women was about overcoming adversity. The payoff: a 900% increase in its association with the term "stylish" and a 730% increase in its link to the word "empowering." The campaign drew five *billion* worldwide impressions.

Under Armour had a terrific narrative. But later, delivery fell short. The shoes set off alarm bells. UCLA athletes refused to wear the shoe – the school's official shoe – complaining that the bottoms were peeling off. Others blamed the suits designed for the US speed skating team for slowing down Olympic skaters at the 2014 Olympics in Sochi, Russia. Here we see a fourth lesson: UA had a gap between what it promised and delivered. That's toxic – you want to market aggressively, but deliver what people expect.

Younger customers felt the styles weren't fashionable enough. Lack of brand clarity kept UA from differentiating itself from Nike and Adidas. Kevin Plank stepped aside as CEO in 2017 over legal issues.[112] Five top executives left.

Still, UA has proven resilient. UA's story shows that to stay on top, you have to keep fighting. More recently, it recalibrated its message under the more sophisticated and relatable theme "The Only Way is Through."[113] I love the ads, which seem inspired by Nike's theme of heroic sacrifice and discipline. UA's message is that we must surmount ourselves, push through when our bodies say "enough," and take control.

In one ad, German runner and fitness influencer Imke Salander declares that working out is "all about the grind," and that she doesn't listen to the voice insider her head that says "stop."[114] She pushes through to become the best version of yourself. In "Rule Yourself," an ad of startling, dramatic images, UA argues that "you are the sum of all your training," and exhorts athletes to "rule yourself."

---

house-closes-puppy-bill-signing-to-the-press-as-afghanistan-debacle-continues/; and Bella Alarie: Under Armour:" https://www.youtube.com/watch?v=EBcSKgZCoOU

[112] Shoshy Climent and Mary Hanbury, "Here's how Under Armour went from a new hotshot sportwear brand taking on Nike to having a wholly uncertain future," supra.

[113] Imke Salander, "The Only Way is Through:" https://www.youtube.com/watch?v=2zw6fXixWdc; and "Under Armour: The Only Way is Through," https://www.youtube.com/watch?v=wx-kvJlKvJI; and "The Only Way is Through," https://www.youtube.com/watch?v=55kJywFUkj8.

[114] The copy closes resembles a Nike ad that talks about the same ideas in the same language.

Nike has the resources to do everything. UA focused its resources. UA redirected its appeal to athletes and worked to strengthen the brand, rather than relying upon sports partnerships for credibility. UA's ads lack the inspirational, emotional impact of NIKE's, but they present a compelling message through brilliantly conceived and executed ads that you can't take your eyes off. "Will Makes us Family,"[115] advocating that "you can make it if you try" sums up UA's tough spirit and its values.

Message discipline and clear ideas matter. You may have hit on a unique, innovative product or approach, but don't trick yourself into thinking you can do everything. I've advised a startup with an innovative technology whose initial third-rate management team spread itself too thin. They squandered money and tried to market ideas that strayed from core strengths. The team was a fiasco – for themselves, the company, and their hapless investors.

Budweiser, the self-styled King of Beers, has lost its crown as Stella Artois, which most beer drinkers tell me is a better beer, cut into its market. Bud no longer ranks among the top three best-selling beers in the U.S.[116] But I cite Stella Artois for its out-of-the-box thinking in responding to COVID. Anheuser-Busch owns Budweiser, Corona, and Stella Artois. All three sell well and enjoy strong resilience. During the pandemic, Corona and Bud more or less stuck with their traditional marketing.

Budweiser has made its mark through powerful emotional appeals, notably with ads invoking its iconic Clydesdales. Corona prospered through its iconic amber color, distinctive long-necked bottle, emblematic golden crown, and wedge-of-lime ritual.[117] The apparent similarity between COVID and Corona gave executives a scare, but sales held steady. As a large, trusted brand, it maintained customer loyalty.[118]

Stella Artois confronted a different challenge. Stella positions itself as a premium brand that built upon connecting people and bringing them together. Famous for

---

[115] "Under Armour: Will Makes Us Family," https://www.youtube.com/watch?v=3-Cpw7eZwAg
[116] Mark Snider, "Budweiser falls from top three U.S. beer favorites," *USA Today*, January 23, 2018.
[117] Mike Teasdale, "What do booming sales for Corona beer say about brands?", *WARC.com*, January 29, 2021: https://www.warc.com/newsandopinion/opinion/what-do-booming-sales-for-corona-beer-say-about-brands/en-gb/4041.
[118] Nat Ives, "Echo of Coronavirus Didn't Keep Beer Drinkers From Corona," *Wall Street Journal*, December 21, 2020: https://www.wsj.com/articles/echo-of-coronavirus-didnt-keep-beer-drinkers-from-corona-11608590773.

its "9-step ritual" in serving this Belgian Pilsner,[119] which traces its founding to 1366 in the city of Leuven, Belgium, The pandemic shut down bars and restaurants and sent people into isolation. Social distancing kept people at home. Restaurants operate differently. Over 60% of breweries slowed production.

Stella Artois (the brewer instructs bartenders to use both names; nobody says, "have a Stella") had showcased its quality and craft. It used videos, murals, billboards, and posters. It sponsored events and pop-up stores. Point-of-purchase displays were prominent. During the height of COVID, it devised an imaginative strategy that played to its core strengths.[120] It partnered with Netflix's "Love is Blind" stars Lauren and Cameron Hamilton to launch a contest. Couples who got engaged during COVID earned the chance to win an all-expenses-paid wedding. Social media encouraged loyalists to share images, stories, and recordings of their engagement. "Stella Artois Digital Cheers" beat the social distancing blues by inviting loyalists to share a beer on Facetime. The tagline was *Even when we can't be with each other… we find a way to be together.* The company hosted "Stella Sessions" at home through Instagram with hosts like Eva Longoria and celebrity chefs.

Stella Artois teaches that when circumstances throw your marketing strategy into chaos, there's always another play. This company identified a host of them and played to win.

Taking on a Bigfoot who holds a tight grip in the market can be tough, so you need to take the measure of one if you want to challenge it head-on. Virgin's Richard Branson's team created Virgin Cola. He insists it's better than Coca-Cola. He understood that taking on Coke was no mission for the faint-hearted. He recognized that public relations can get you a long way.

Talk about a showman. Win or lose, he's got brass balls. He knows how to make a point. "Believe it or not," he told *Inc.* magazine at the time he launched Virgin

---

[119] Stella Artois has 6,000 people on board to train bartenders and restaurants how to use the ritual. The steps include (i) a clean glass, (ii) letting the first few drops run from the tap to obtain the purest taste, (iii) holding the glass at a 45-degree angle and slowly straighten it as the beer pours, (iv) raising and lowering the glass to create the foam head, (v) removing the chalice from the tap, (vi) shaving off excess foam, (vii) measuring to ensure the foam is two-fingers thick, and (ix) serving the beer on a coaster with a drip catcher at the base. "Stella Artois: Pivoting in the Face of a Pandemic," *BCIT Marcom*: https://bcitmarketing.ca/stella-artois/.

[120] See: "Stella Artois: Pivoting in the Face of a Pandemic," *BCIT Marcom*: https://bcitmarketing.ca/stella-artois/. This section draws upon this excellent description of the company's COVID response.

Atlantic airlines in 1984, "I was actually quite shy."[121] Sure, and James Bond is a shy, retiring bureaucrat.

In Britain, his Branson cola outsold Pepsi and Coke. He wanted to boldly introduce it in the US. Brashly imitating World War II German General Erwin Rommel, he drove a tank through Times Square in New York, running over Coca-Cola cans and pretending to unleash a fire barrage at a Coca-Cola sign. The sign had been wired with explosives. When he fired, the explosives detonated.[122] It appeared he had blown up Coke. As *Inc* noted, you might not get away with that stunt today. But it worked quite well then.[123]

Branson pulled off another funny stunt with *Baywatch* star Pamela Anderson in creating a cola bottle that reflected her curvy body. Branson did product placement on the television show *Friends*. A great video, "Richard Branson's secret war on Coca-Cola," captured the campaign.[124] Making a splash is a great way to drum up publicity, elicit a smile, and cause people to pay attention. Branson cut into Coke's market share in the U.S.

Somehow, Branson suggests, Coke managed to persuade retailers to take Virgin Cola off the shelves, forcing Virgin to halt production.[125] Branson offers an important lesson. Virgin Cola may be a better product but challenging the major market player requires you to be, as he put it, "markedly better, not just better" than the competition.[126] For those sorry to miss out, reportedly Virgin Cola is available for the adventurous in Afghanistan. Bring along a bulletproof vest.

3. **Know how the enemy or competition sees itself**.

In a military conflict, the enemy usually sees itself through different eyes than we do. General Petraeus stresses the importance of "understanding that it matters a great deal which one's enemy or competitor is, sees us, and sees itself. Such issues can be of central importance in what often is a contest of wills and

---

[121] Oscar Raymundo, "Richard Branson's most explosive publicity stunt," *Inc.* (no date): https://www.inc.com/oscar-raymundo/richard-branson-most-explosive-publicity-stunt.html

[122] His video "I fired the gun and the Coke sign exploded" can be viewed on YouTube. https://www.youtube.com/watch?v=KcTZMJFiIgo&t=4s

[123] Id.

[124] Richard Branson's Secret War on Coca-Cola," https://www.youtube.com/watch?v=KcTZMJFiIgo

[125] Id.

[126] Id.

also in seeking to deter a would-be adversary from taking provocative or dangerous actions."[127]

By any measure, Usama bin Laden qualified as a terrorist. But he did not consider himself one. He saw himself as a good Muslim battling to reclaim Muslim lands – *dar al-Islam*.[128] He instigated the 9/11 attack over the objections of the Al Qaeda *shura* – the organization's governing body.[129] Al Qaeda members view themselves as champions of the correct interpretation of Islam. That governs their tactics, which include killing individuals we consider to be civilians. The *Law of Armed Conflict* bans killing civilians. Whether Al Qaeda's targets are in Israel, Algeria, or elsewhere, their rationale is that the civilians they target support or constitute part of the enemy's military forces.

As Al Qaeda receded from view in Iraq after the 2003 Iraq War, ISIS – the Islamic State – surfaced. ISIS is a genocidal organization. But as Graeme Wood points out, the appeal of ISIS, rooted in establishing a new Caliphate and a particular – and valid – interpretation of Islam that favors slavery and justifies genocide.[130] Its appeal has been to Sunnis.

In June 2014, ISIS captured Mosul and shook the Iraqi government to its foundations. That should have surprised no one. Sunnis had long oppressed the Shia minority. When the U.S. ousted Saddam, it overturned the balance of power in Iraq. Shiites asserted their majority status aggressively, alienating Sunnis and opening the door to ISIS propaganda.

Countering violent extremist movements like Al Qaeda and ISIS requires understanding why their ideas appeal to their audiences. The question is not why they fail to understand our views – they don't care. The question is what

---

[127] Interview with General David Petraeus, April 14, 2021

[128] See: Ahmed S. Hashim, "The World According to Usama Bin Laden," *Naval War College Review*, Vol. 54 No 4 (Autumn 2001), pp. 11-35: https://www.jstor.org/stable/pdf/26393869.pdf.

[129] See: Adrian Levy and Catherine Scott-Clark, The Exile: The Stunning Inside Story of Osama Bin Laden and Al Qaeda in Flight," (London: Bloomsbury, 2017). Bin Laden's cohorts jumped on board after the attack but correctly understood that the attacks would alienate the world. The distinguished scholar and expert on Al Qaeda, Fawaz Gerges, has pointed out that had the U.S. avoided the 2003 invasion of Iraq, Al Qaeda's credibility in the Muslim world would have been destroyed. Interviews with the author, February 2017; see also: Fawaz Gerges, The Far Enemy (Cambridge University Press, 2009) and Fawaz Gerges, Journey of the Jihadist, (New York: Harcourt, 2006).

[130] Graeme Wood, "What ISIS Really Wants," *Atlantic*, March 2015: http://cfcollegefoundation.ca/wp-content/uploads/2016/08/150219-What-ISIS-Really-Wants-The-Atlantic.pdf.

motivates their supporters. We turned around a fiasco by discerning how to exploit social, cultural, philosophical, and political differences between tribes in western Iraq and Al Qaeda. We reached out to them on their terms. We respected their values, treated them as equal partners, and demonstrated staying power.

Amazon started as an online book-seller. That's how their competitors long viewed it. Amazon views itself differently. It yearns to be the largest retailer in the world. In 2021, it offered over 330 million products that other companies sell. It arranges shipment of products purchased on the Web. Today it sells over a third of all products sold or bought online in the U.S.[131] Soon it will open retail stores.[132] Top customer service, fast delivery, and access to a vast market draw customers. Its Web services division powers Netflix and the C.I.A. Amazon Founder Jeff Bezos sees his company as disruptive because people think they're getting something for free.[133] The company earns $14 billion just from Amazon Prime fees. Other divisions are also highly profitable.

Streaming services like Netflix, Amazon, Hulu, Disney, and Apple have forced the motion picture industry to rethink what they produce and distribute. Netflix uses AI to pick scripts it produces. This approach has upended what films are made, budgets, and channels for reaching audiences.

Ben Fritz has described this revolution in The Big Picture.[134] He explains how Hollywood tradition is collapsing, replaced by a new business model. The shift has riled show biz. Scarlet Johansson's high-octane suit against Disney for streaming *Black Widow* at the same time the studio released the film in theatres epitomized the radical shifts that the pandemic and shifting viewer tastes have brought about.[135] That the suit was settled does not alter the existence of the tectonic shift that is taking place.

---

[131] Charles Duhigg, "Is Amazon Unstoppable?", *New Yorker*, October 10, 2019: https://www.newyorker.com/magazine/2019/10/21/is-amazon-unstoppable

[132] Sebastian Herrera, Esther Fung and Suzanne Kapner, "Amazon Plans to Open Large Retail Locations Akin to Department Stores," *Wall Street Journal*, August 19, 2021: https://www.wsj.com/articles/amazon-retail-department-stores-11629330842.

[133] Lucy Handley, "Amazon is seen as so disruptive because people think they're getting something for free," *CNBC.com*, June 18, 2018: https://www.cnbc.com/2018/06/18/amazon-is-disruptive-because-people-think-they-get-something-free.html

[134] Ben Fritz, The Big Picture: The Fight for the Future of Movies, (New York: Houghton Mifflin Harcourt, 2018).

[135] Joe Flint and Erich Schwartzel, "Scarlett Johansson Sues Disney over 'Black Widow' Streaming Release," *Wall Street Journal*, July 29, 2021: https://www.wsj.com/articles/scarlett-johansson-sues-disney-over-black-widow-streaming-release-11627579278. She complained that streaming

Until COVID-19 closed theatres, towering giant Disney took a risk out of movies by focusing on tentpole films, especially about superheroes. Its decisions to acquire George Lucas's Lucasfilm and Marvel Entertainments created goldmines. Disney's model enhanced profits by using its vast resources to distribute films produced by third parties. The Hollywood shift to tentpole franchises like *Spider Man* marked Fritz's analysis.

COVID introduced a radical new shift to cable streaming. Big name Hollywood stars who used to shy away from streaming or television are embracing it, and streaming services like Netflix are paying what studios have been used to forking up. For example, Leonardo DiCaprio received $32 million for his star-turn in Adam McCay's extraordinary satirical film, *Don't Look Up* (the real gag is that in reality events would probably play out pretty closely in Washington to the way the movie comically depicts the action). As traditional cinemas struggle to attract audiences, the big names have discovered – and like – streaming.[136] Welcome to the Brave New World.

Innovative entrepreneurs don't have to kowtow. The direct-to-consumer innovators like eyeglass company Warby Parker, Dollar Shave Club, BarkBox, Blue Apron, and Casper are showing they can flourish with savvy strategy and promotional campaigns that capitalize on "blue ocean" gaps in the market.[137] Warby Parker and its competitors realized that one Italian company, Luxottica Group S.p.A., made a good many of the frames sold by opticians and optical retailers. The mark-ups are astronomical. The rebels saw how to combine lower prices with personalized service that let you try on glasses online as well as providing a right to return glasses. They see themselves as disruptors and they've made a huge dent.

---

deprived her of compensation tied to box office performance possible only with an exclusive theatrical release. The suit upended Hollywood, although the parties eventually settled.

[136] Brooks Barnes, "Hollywood Tests the Limit of Marquee Names a Single Film Can Hold," *New York Times*, December 26, 2021: https://www.nytimes.com/2021/12/26/business/movies-stars-hollywood.html. During the 2021 Christmas season, only the new *Spiderman* movie did well at the box office. Well-reviewed films like *West Side Story*, directed by Steven Spielberg, a sequel to *The Matrix,* and other films were flat. Distinct reasons may explain the box office failure of each, but this much seems clear, especially in the COVID era: audiences feel increasingly more comfortable – and secure – watching movies on a big screen smart television at home.
[137] See Lawrence Ingrassia, Billion Dollar Brand Club (New York: Henry Holt and Co., 2020).

4. Understand the language the enemy or competition uses to promote its narratives, themes, and messages.

Al-Qaeda has a strong narrative that appeals to its target audiences. It goes like this: A thousand years ago, infidels sacked Damascus, repressed Islam, killed Muslims, stole their treasure. Today they're back, repeating their infamy. Al-Qaeda propagates the theme that every Muslim must stand up for Islam and repel the foreign invasion.

Its message is that good Muslims must kill or eject the infidels. ISIS added two powerful arguments: restore the caliphate, the spiritual leader of Islam, and eliminate the national boundaries between Iraq and Syria drawn by colonial powers through the Treaty of Lausanne. The Taliban has extolled religion and nationalism and contrasted its reputation for integrity – however harsh its values – with the corruption that riddled every central government until Kabul fell in August 2021.

Our military has struggled in Middle East wars. The strategic situations are inherently vexing. In Afghanistan, it's proven untenable, a lesson that great powers learned in the 19th century, and Russia learned the hard way in the 20th century. Except for the U.S. Marines, we're not adept at engaging with foreign cultures on their terms, taking into account their history, culture, social hierarchies, values, hopes, and fears. And we've paid the price.

Here's a concrete example from Afghanistan that *New York Times* reporter Craig Whitlock identified that drives the point. A US military PSYOPS team designed a soccer ball featuring the flags of other countries, including Saudi Arabia. Its flag depicts the Koranic declaration of faith in Arabic script. They distributed the balls expecting plaudits. Instead, Afghans thought putting holy words on a ball to be kicked around was sacrilegious. The U.S. military had to issue a public apology.[138]

Language helps executives to navigate an easier path. Jack Daniels proclaims that "every day we make it, we'll make it the best we can," playing into its history of making a classic Tennessee Whiskey matured in handcrafted barrels. This language summons tradition, heritage, and intense story-telling, all relatable to the liquor company's target customers who see themselves as ruggedly

---

[138] Craig Whitlock, The Afghanistan Papers, (New York: Simon & Schuster, 2021), p. 68-69.

independent and part of a tradition that has included such wide-ranging adherents as Frank Sinatra and Winston Churchill.[139]

Slogans sum up company narrative and messaging. The best ones are consistent; different; short and simple; timeless; and stand alone.[140] The classic ones stick with us: Lay's potato chips "You can't eat just one;" The California Milk Processor Board's "Got Milk?;" Wheaties "Breakfast of Champions;" Mastercard's "There are some things money can't buy; for everything else, there is Mastercard;" State Farm's "Like a good neighbor, State Farm is there;" Red Bull's "Red Bull gives you wings;" Capital One's "What's in your wallet?"; Air BnB's "Belong Anywhere;" and, BMW's "the Ultimate Driving Machine."

5. Understand how credible and persuasive the enemy or competition is to your target audience.

The military grapples with this in every operation. During the Vietnam War, Communists suffered a severe military setback on the ground during the 1967 Tet Offensive. But when CBS anchorman Walter Cronkite pronounced the war a loser, this nation's will to fight eroded. Cronkite was a fine journalist, but he misjudged the facts. Communist propaganda persuaded him. Cronkite's high standing shifted American perceptions. His words helped force Lyndon Johnson from office and undercut U.S. efforts in Vietnam. Whether we or, more accurately, South Vietnam could have prevailed will be debated for generations.[141]

NIKE's approach exudes a compelling message that resonates emotionally. The power is evident in the language its advertising invokes and the visual vocabulary of its videos and ads. Apple's wit and IBM's stolid perseverance – even though critics have suggested better options exist in the market than its Watson data analytics – have driven clear messages that resonate. Coca-Cola and other successful soft drink manufacturers conjure up cheerful, rewarding

---

[139] See: Kim Bhasin, "It Took Brilliant Marketing To Turn Jack Daniel's Into The World's Most Popular Whiskey," *Business Insider*, January 10, 2012: https://www.businessinsider.com/jack-daniels-marketing-history-biggest-whiskey-brand-2012-1; and Fortune Editors, "Jack Daniel's marketing magic," *Fortune,* December 8, 2011: https://fortune.com/2011/12/08/jack-daniels-marketing-magic/

[140] Rachel Burns, "63 Iconic Company Slogans and Taglines," *ActiveCampaign.com*, February 9, 2021: https://www.activecampaign.com/blog/company-slogans.

[141] See: Lewis Sorley, A Better War, supra, arguing our side could have prevailed had Presidents Lyndon B. Johnson and Richard M. Nixon, and the Congress, comprehended the true strategic situation in which North Vietnam was losing, and Gordon M. Goldstein, Lessons in Disaster, (New York: Henry Holt & Co, 2008), arguing that the war was not winnable.

lifestyles through a combination of music, language, and images. Mercedes and Porsche adroitly appeal to pride, the psychological reward for achievement, glamour, and excitement, to sell probably every vehicle either manufactures.

6. Avoid mirror imaging.

Too often, the U.S. acts as if other cultures behave the same way that we do, espouse the same values, employ the same language. That's delusional. Middle Eastern regimes tend to be monarchies for religious and historical reasons. The legitimacy of the Kings of Saudi Arabia and Morocco is rooted in their direct descent from the Prophet Muhammed. Citizens may want the government accountable and responsible, but they may look to ways besides the ballot box to secure it. In Saudi Arabia, Crown Prince Mohammed bin Salman has put himself in line to succeed King Salman. Still, in the past, Saudi tribes selected the new monarch by carefully balancing tribal interests.[142]

Former Under Secretary of Defense (Policy) John Rood is among the smartest Pentagon officials I've worked with. He agrees that mirror-imaging is a problem for Americans. How should we address it? He argues,

> "One key is to think like an analyst. Try to put yourself in the shoes of the person who lives in a foreign country. Try to understand their motivations or behaviors and what triggers them. You have to immerse yourself and take a clinical approach that sets aside your own biases and views others objectively. Once you confront the reality of who they are, you can better evaluate whether a strategic plan is working and make relevant adjustments. The military does this much better than it used to. Ironically, many executives find it difficult to walk away from a course of action that they insisted was the right way. That mindset hurts them and their organizations because it blinds them to a bias as to what works or doesn't work."[143]

---

[142] See, e.g., Robert Lacey, Inside the Kingdom: Kings, Clerics, Modernists, Terrorists and the Struggle for Saudi Arabia, (New York: Viking, 2009).
[143] Interview with John Rood, April 15, 2021.

United Kingdom Colonel (Ret) Mark Neate adds:

> "The most critical factor in avoiding mirror imaging is self-awareness. You need to recognize how the other person interprets what you say or do. Communication is what the audience hears, not what you say. Red teaming strategies and operations afford the opportunity to put your ideas and the language in which you articulate them, as well as your actions, to the test. You can gain invaluable insights into how other people will react. Many companies don't think about *red teaming*, but it doesn't matter, as long as they conduct in-depth research that provides the same information. Conducting this work maximizes chances of success and minimizes the chances that a strategy will produce a train wreck."[144]

Rood's views align with General Votel's point that you want to do "whatever it takes to understand who you're dealing with, what's controlling your messages, what's the big idea that you're conveying to them? And you want the consistency of engagement. You want to make certain that everybody on your team is saying the same stuff."[145]

Malaysia

The Malaysian Rebellion during the 1950s showed the confluent importance of language and the need to understand the weakness in the enemy's message. Sir Robert Thompson helped defeat an anti-colonial-driven insurgency led by Communists. A key to Britain's successful communication strategy lay in the recognition that Malays wanted independence from Britain. His campaign promised Malays their autonomy. This decision proved decisive in separating insurgents from the population. The Brits made nationalism work for them.[146]

---

[144] Interview with Colonel (Ret) Mark Neate, April 15, 2021.
[145] Interview with General (Ret) Joseph L. Votel, May 5, 2021.
[146] See: Sir Robert Thompson, Defeating Communist Insurgency: The Lessons of Malaya and Vietnam (New York: F.A. Praeger, 1966). Thompson's five basic principles of counter-insurgency have achieved the status of catechism. See also: John A. Nagl, Learning to Eat Soup with a Knife:

British General Sir Gerald Templar changed the vocabulary in describing rainforest people. They had been referred to as "Sakai," or slaves. He ordered British troops to refer to them as "Orang ulu" – "people of the campaign."[147] The British rebranded the Malayan Races Liberation Army as the *Communist Terrorist Organization*. The strategy cut the legs out from under Communist efforts to make a nationalist appeal. Indeed, showing the populace that the Communists, led by the Chinese, were not Malays and did not have their interests at heart finished their chances.

A Commercial Parallel

The U.S. automobile industry provides a converse illustration. Car executives made pilgrimages to encourage the Japanese to buy American cars. They overlooked that the Japanese drive on the left-hand side of the road, while the steering wheel in American cars sits on the American passenger side. American executives expected the Japanese to think like Americans. Toyota, Nissan, and other thriving Japanese manufacturers were delighted. Perhaps they served apple pie at company outings to honor such arrogance.[148]

7.   What channels of communication do the enemy or competition use?

The general rule for the military (and in politics) is to counter-attack, using the same channel to attack. Companies rarely attack one another. The most they do is offer tame, implicit comparisons on price, quality, and service, or poke fun at one another. The Federal Trade Commission Act prohibits deceptive or misleading advertising. Hard-hitting comparative or negative ads that you see in political campaigns take advantage of First Amendment rules. These rules don't apply to the commercial world. Harry's Razors does that implicitly. Apple's marketing strategy gives everyone a good time comparing Apples to PCs with witty commercials that depict Apple as hip and cutting-edge.

"The Pepsi Challenge" was friendly and illustrated how using multiple channels can disrupt a market. Pepsi's strategy was to conduct taste tests to prove that people liked Pepsi more. A Pepsi emissary set up a table with two white cups in

---

Counterinsurgency Lessons from Malaysia and Vietnam, supra, which discusses various insurgencies including Malaya.
[147] Steve Tatham, Losing Arab Hearts and Minds: The Coalition, Al Jazeera, and Muslim Public Opinion, (London: Front St. Press, 2006), and John Nagl, Learning to Eat Soup with a Knife, supra.
[148] See: Herbert Jack Rotfeld, Adventures in Misplaced Marketing, (New York: Praeger, 2001).

a mall and other public locations. Shoppers were invited to test both colas and select their preferences. Pepsi won that contest. This public outreach supported a clever ad campaign.[149]

PepsiCo CEO John D. Sculley explained Pepsi's thinking and how it pulled off the campaign.[150] He said:

> "We began The Pepsi Challenge in San Antonio, a market…in which we were outsold 9 or 10 to 1. We were looking for Pepsi, having found it had a slight preference over Coke as long as you didn't tell anybody what the product was. The history of Pepsi was that if you wanted to serve your family or friends a Cola drink, and you had Coca-Cola in your refrigerator, you would typically walk out to the living room with a bottle of Coke and pour it in front of them and put the bottle of Coke down next to the glass. If it were Pepsi, you would go out to the kitchen, you would pour it in the kitchen, and only bring the glass out and hope they didn't ask what was in it."[151]

Pepsi ads captured the surprised expression of Coke drinkers when they discovered they preferred Pepsi. Pepsi's campaign disrupted Coke's dominance, built up the morale of Pepsi organizations, and helped propel a campaign that changed the market. In <u>Blink: The Power of Thinking Without Thinking</u>,[152] Malcolm Gladwell argues that the results may reflect the bias of Americans for sweeter drinks. In any event, taste tests helped Pepsi make a case for its cola.

Coke reacted with horror. First, it sued Pepsi and claimed Pepsi's ads were unlawful. Coke created an advertisement with two chimpanzees doing the same test. The press laughed. Undeterred, Pepsi went into markets where Coke was

---

[149] See: "Pepsi Challenge:" https://www.youtube.com/watch?v=ghMYzo0rgrw; and "Pepsi-Coke Blind Taste test:" https://www.youtube.com/watch?v=8olGvgs9FnM. This drew over 2.3 million views.

[150] J.D. Sculley, "How the Pepsi Challenge" disrupted Coke's dominance:" https://www.youtube.com/watch?v=ivumtJZ6fiU

[151] Id.

[152] Malcolm Gladwell, <u>Blink: The Power of Thinking Without Thinking</u>, (New York: Little, Brown & Co. 2005).

less intense and built up its business. Pepsi's success teaches that persistence, adaptive innovation, and capitalizing on strengths rooted in a slight preference for its products can pay off. A hunger to beat Coke motivated Pepsi's team.

The campaign opened up new ways to market its product, such as putting disruptive pricing on 2-liter bottles. Year after year, Pepsi spoofed Coke. Pepsi's lesson: adaptive innovators are adaptive business builders who innovate and try unconventional tactics to win.

As an executive, you need to select the channel that works best. The direct-to-consumer companies didn't have money for advertising and rightly have focused on the Internet. Major brands cover all the bases. Targeting audience analysis and resource availability will reveal what channels are best suited for reaching suitable targets.

8. What unique obstacles characterize a particular kind of competition or conflict?

The battlespace for companies and the military is global. Every living room is one. Any individual with online access – that's most people – can be a journalist and influencer. Every competition features unique characteristics. You need to identify them and make them work for you or risk getting blindsided.

In the 2014 Israeli-Palestinian armed engagements, Palestinian teen blogger Farah Baker stunned confident Israelis as she cut through the media noise using just her cellphone to communicate her take on Israeli attacks. Her reports cast a shadow over the legitimacy of Israeli attacks. Not to be outdone, the Israeli Social Media Department established a YouTube channel to refute Baker's slant.[153] Both sides used state-of-the-art technology to crash through traditional media barriers and get out their narratives.

Information dominance decided the outcome of the first battle for Fallujah, Iraq, in April 2004, won by insurgents. It helped to do so for the second one in November 2004, won by the Coalition. In each case, planning and adaptable, resourceful tactics paid off. Elliot Higgins, a video game user, crowd-sourced the 2014 shootdown over Ukraine of flight MH-17 to pin fault on Russia. Until then, the Russians expected they could control the flow of information. Higgins threw Putin's efforts off-balance.[154]

---

[153] David Patrikarakos, War in 140 Characters (New York: Basic Books, 2017), Chapter Two, p. 45.
[154] David Patrikarakos, War in 140 Characters, supra., p. 144.

In his classic book, Here Comes Everybody,[155] Clay Shirkey shows how the Internet has transformed how we communicate and empower the individual to reach audiences by passing traditional gatekeepers such as television networks and major newspapers. This book is a roadmap to understanding social media and how it has disrupted the news media space, making every individual a potential journalist.

Leveraging influence over audiences in a globally connected, networked planet has opened up opportunities *and* erected barriers. China and other authoritarian states are asserting control over the Internet to empower dictators. Evgeny Morozov's witty book, The Net Delusion, details this dark development.[156] Still, the Internet has empowered opponents of authoritarian regimes in Europe, notably protestors who led the pro-democracy "color" revolutions.

Violent repression does not often directly threaten corporations. Yet other obstacles confront their marketing strategies. Competitors who enter a market first – especially with a blue ocean strategy – start with an advantage. Still, talented leaders can take a page out of military playbooks to employ the information aspects of Operational Art to venture into new markets to seize and maintain market share.

Avis built a reputation off its second-place status to challenge the big dog, Hertz. Marketing expert Adam Morgan shrewdly observes that Target shot down the canard that its lower retail prices meant inferior quality. Target worried that customers would view it as a low-rent operation, but it fired back point-blank at doubters. Target argued that just because you don't have money doesn't mean you don't have a taste.[157] Target is prospering.

9. Avoid hubris.

At seminars for prospective authors, teachers start with tough-love advice: "First kill your children." They're not blood-thirsty. Their point is that writers must objectively assess what works and be prepared to delete favorite things. In short, know when to fold.

The U.S. government withdrew its forces from Afghanistan The exit drew heavy criticism, but in deciding whether to exit, it asked prudent questions: Is a 20-year

---

[155] Clay Shirkey, Here Comes Everybody: The Power of Organizing without Organizations, (New York: Penguin Press, 2008).
[156] Evgeny Morozov, The Net Delusion, (New York: Public Affairs, 2001).
[157] Adam Morgan, Eating the Big Fish, (Hoboken: John Wiley, 2009), p. 86.

war winnable, and if so, how? If not, how does this end? What's our exit strategy? The exit affirmed an old truism: war is hell.

10.   No one likes to admit failure.

It happens to the best of them; not every marketing plan succeeds. Jim Stengel relates that Procter & Gamble called it quits with Clarion, which manufactured Cover Girl cosmetics, after concluding the product had lost contact with customers. P&G stood by Max Factor, which it revitalized. Stengel's analysis presents a classic case study about facing up to the realities of a product that wasn't cutting it versus one that did.[158]

Ford's Edsel is arguably the most famous example of a company that resigned itself to reality by canceling production of the failed vehicle. IBM was in dire straits during the 1990s. Its historical focus was on hardware and software. The market passed it by. IBM reinvented itself as a consulting company under the banner of building a smarter planet. It faced up to its crisis, sold its PC business to the Chinese company Lenovo,[159] regained its financial strength, and went on to become a storied business success.

---

[158] Jim Stengel, Grow: How Ideals Power Growth and Profit at the World's Greatest Companies, (New York: Crown Business, 2011).
[159] Glenn Rifkin and Jenna Smith, "Lenovo makes break with IBM brand," *New York Times,* April 20, 1006.

Discussion Questions

1. What are your unique strengths and weaknesses? Are you respecting Sun Tzu's mandate to know both your enemy (competition) and yourself?

2. How does the competition see itself? How does that factor into your strategic thinking?

3. Do you have the *required* resources to succeed? Think about Kevin Plank starting out in his grandmother's house as he built Under Armour into a billion-dollar success story.

4. What unconventional approaches can help you overcome scarce resources? Think about Stella Artois' success and why its campaign worked.

5. Does your competitive analysis factor in what former CIA official George Beebe termed "analytic empathy?" Are you getting a *feel* for what it's like to stand in the shoes of your competitors?

6. Are you sensitive to cultural nuance? Consider the effort to persuade Somalis to lay down their weapons – which its culture would never sanction – and their response, citing the U.S. Second Amendment.

7. Have you thought through the knock-on consequences of your proposed strategy and messaging? Think about what happened in Rwanda, Under Armour, and Ford's Edsel?

8. What "blue ocean" gaps exist in the market you want to enter? How can you exploit them? How do you capitalize on "blue ocean" gaps by reducing your costs and increasing customer value?

9. Is your strategy to make an existing solution better, or to identify an alternate solution for the same problem?

10. What language seems most like to strike a responsive chord with your target audiences? By that, we mean what will appeal to emotions and motivate behavior?

11. Is your product demonstrably better than the competition's – and how can you show that?

12. Do you have backup plans in case a disaster such as a pandemic strikes, and forces you to rethink your marketing strategy?

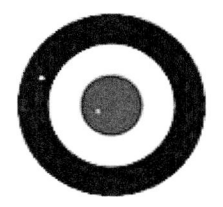

CHAPTER FOUR

UNDERSTAND YOUR TARGET AUDIENCE

The social norms, values, customs, shared beliefs, and behavior in society influence how people judge a military organization or company and their services or products. Understanding a target audience's cultural norms and values sets the foundation. Is the target audience interested and engaged? If so, how? The answers help you prioritize resources, required action, operational phases, milestones, and timeframes.

A wide range of tools can help you understand target audiences. Public opinion surveys, focus groups, mall testing, and dial groups provide keen insights.

In the age of social media, psychographic research is fast evolving to provide cutting-edge insights. It relies upon demographic information such as gender, age, income, marital status, choice of consumer products, lifestyle, and other data that enable marketers to assemble a personal profile on your opinions, attitudes, beliefs, and preferences.

The Marine Corps approaches cultural issues systematically. It works to understand the culture, society, political dynamics, social taboos, and values. We looked at Iraq and Afghanistan earlier. They are poster children for the failure – in Iraq, at least initially – to conduct that analysis. Admiral Stavridis emphasizes the need to root any military or business organization in strong values:

"democracy, freedom of speech, freedom of education and assembly, gender and racial equality, environmental consciousness. Those are our values."[160]

Former U.S. Ambassador to Latvia Brian F. Carlson, an expert on strategic communication, argues that executives face similar questions.[161] Who comprises the target audience? What do they think about a subject on which you wish to engage? Why do they think or feel that way? What do keywords mean to them? Where do they get information on this subject? Who do they trust? Who do they listen to or follow? Are there gatekeepers whose "permission" or encouragement is required before an audience acts or changes behavior?

Nike Gets It

Nike merits additional comment. Money counts, but intelligent thinking drives Nike's success. Nike's narrative, themes, and messages are rooted in well-defined values. Universal themes can move targeted audiences. Its ads are inspired, inspirational, motivating. I talk about Nike throughout this book to illustrate different points because the company stands out. But you need not be big to learn from Nike.

Steve Jobs put it this way:

> "Nike honors great athletes and great athletics."[162] Its message is that sports have the power to move the world forward and improve lives through sports. Nike's marketing tailors itself to diverse cultural idiosyncrasies. It uses multiple channels of communication. All exemplify the vision of Nike founder Bill Bowerman that success is something you need to earn through heroic discipline and hard work to overcome laziness, sloth, and doubt.[163] "This is the grind," a Nike video declares over the image of an exhausted runner pushing himself. Nike implores us "to find our greatness, to be a lion, double down, treat the

---
[160] Interview with Admiral (Ret) James G. Stavridis, June 2, 2021.
[161] Interview with Brian Carlson, April 4, 2020.
[162] https://www.youtube.com/watch?v=keCwRdbwNQY
[163] https://www.youtube.com/watch?v=doYqzS39Gpg

> laws of physics as merely a suggestion and get after it."[164]

Marketing expert Graham Newell observes that Nike sells tenacity.[165] He identifies six threads that run through the Nike messaging: Be first to the challenge. Rise early. Take on a tough challenge. Get into the zone – that place where you reach your stride. Break through the pain that causes hesitation and rededicate yourself. Make the supreme effort that carries you to victory.

Let's look at its *Da Da Ding*[166] campaign in India, connecting Nike with young women. It stylishly builds upon Bollywood culture. Rapper Gizzle composed a hit song and created a dazzling music video entitled *Da Da Ding*. When I was producing political ads with my long-time editor at Red Car in Los Angeles, a top editing house, another editing team was cutting two Nike ads. Politicals are hardly competitive with million-dollar Nike ads, so they graciously allowed me to view their approach.

The editing was brilliant and imaginative and used frame-by-frame cuts to accentuate the dynamic camera work. It was no surprise that Nike ads have made such an impact. The *Da Da Ding* video showcased female athletes. These were everyday girls, not Olympic stars. They provide role models for aspirational young women.

The song made its debut on Mumbai's top radio station, Radio One. The station accepted an eight-week Nike challenge to inspire youth. Social media turned the song into a hit. The International Indian Film Academy launched the video featuring movie star Deepika Padukone. Deepika comes from a family of athletes. She delivered an emotional speech at India's Academy awards ceremony proclaiming how sports had shaped her life.

Nike monitored social media to test reactions from target audiences. An app allowed users to learn more about the everyday athletes who appeared in the video. The app provided a channel for purchasing gear. It let people sign up for Nike Running and Training sessions in Mumbai (Bombay). The campaign made Nike India's number one sportswear. Over 1,300 new runners joined the Nike Run Club. The song was streamed online two million times. It generated news articles. The campaign roused women to express themselves with confidence through sport.

---

[164] Michael Jordan, "Winners don't quit:" https://www.youtube.com/watch?v=llU8svpRIsQ
[165] Graeme Newell: "Nike Marketing Strategy; How Nike Branding Flatters Athlete Egos:"
[166] Nike: "Da Da Ding:" https://www.youtube.com/watch?v=2YDrgoRpic8

Keerthana Ramakrishnan, Nike's head of marketing in India, says the campaign empowered women "to be the change that they wish to see through the lens of sports."[167] Nike has used different slogans aligned with its message. *Da Da Ding*'s was "get moving at Nike.com."

"Don't Quit" epitomizes another Nike approach. Many Nike ads showcase elaborate production values. *Da Da Ding* has costly production values. This one you can produce for a song. It is simple and direct. Latvian female weightlifter Rebeka Koha narrates the ad over images of weightlifting:

> "Could I do what I want? Could I do something else? Could I give up my dreams and do something else and lead a regular life? People ask me: what is a little girl like you doing in heavy weightlifting? Is this the right fit for me? And I reply to them… I'm comfortable with the gym. It feels like home. It is the place I want to be. I want to use my chance… do what it takes… no shortcuts. To do it, I have to believe. Could I do something else? Yes. But I will do what I want."[168]

Videos featuring Russian dancer Olga Kuraeva, "To believe" and "Made On," dramatize a Russian girl's dreams for empowerment and self-realization.[169] In "Never Stop Winning,"[170] we see dramatic black and white still photographs of female soccer players resolved to achieve triumph. Beneath the montage, world champion soccer star Megan Rapinoe exhorts women to strive and succeed. The crowd roars approval and repeats "I believe" after her. She proclaims:

> "I… I believe. I believe that we will be four-time champions and keep winning until we become not only the best female soccer team but the best soccer team in the world. And that a whole generation of boys and girls will go out and play

---

[167] Id.
[168] Nike: "Just Don't Quit – Rebeka Koha:" https://www.youtube.com/watch?v=VTgWoPsxIZg
[169] https://www.youtube.com/watch?v=-OgP9JKeM8s and https://www.youtube.com/watch?v=U2y6tJsBEkY
[170] Nike: "Never Stop Winning:" https://www.youtube.com/watch?v=S29GZOR-k9U.

and say things like 'I want to be like Megan Rapinoe when I grow up... and that they'll be inspired to talk and win... and stand up for themselves... and I believe that we will make our voices heard... TV shows will be talking about us every day and not just once every four years... and that women will conquer more than just a soccer field... and blast through every glass ceiling... and there will be fighting not just to make history... there will be fighting to change it... forever!"

The crowd chants: "I believe that we will win. I believe that we will win."

Rapinoe's urgency, echoed by the chants of thousands, intensifies her emotional resonance. While undoubtedly Nike spent a lot of money producing Rapinoe's ad – including her fees – you can create the same type of spot with as much impact on an affordable budget.

Daisy's Explosive Impact

Nike owns no monopoly on emotional resonance. We'll look at other corporate examples. But politics offers the classic ad that motivates behavior. Nearly seven decades later, "Daisy" stands out as "arguably the most influential political spot in history."[171] The legendary Tony Schwartz produced it for President Lyndon Johnson's 1964 re-election campaign. He simplified ad agency Doyle Dane Bernbach's more complex and expensive commercial approach. Interestingly, the Schwartz **ad cost little to produce**, an achievement he never failed to point out. Indeed, most political ads are inexpensively produced. Even Ronald Reagan's classic 1984 re-election campaign ads were done on a budget by using archival footage.

The LBJ ad opens on a little girl standing in a field plucking petals from a flower – the frame freezes. The camera zooms into a close-up of her eyeball and freezes. An "Operations Control" voice calls out a countdown. Her eye dissolves into a nuclear explosion. President Johnson's voice intones: "These are the stakes. To make a world in which all of God's children can live. Or to go into the dark. We

---

[171] Lyndon Johnson for President, "Daisy:" https://www.youtube.com/watch?v=dDTBnsqxZ3k

must either love each other, or we must die." The ad dissolves to a title: "Vote for President Johnson on November 3rd."

The ad played exactly one time, on an NBC Movie of the Week. Johnson's campaign had read voter emotions perfectly. Voters worried that GOP nominee Barry Goldwater would have an itchy finger on the nuclear trigger if elected President. The ad crystallized these doubts. Schwartz believed that the Goldwater campaign fumbled its response. Goldwater's team ran from it. They could have done an ad that argued that Goldwater's leadership would protect us better. It should have ended with "Vote for Barry Goldwater on November 3." They blew a golden opportunity. Instead, Schwartz destroyed the Arizona Senator's already slim chances.[172]

Nike and "Daisy" illustrate the power of electronic media. Broadcast or streaming images give direct access to the mind. They provide context. Changing fixed beliefs is challenging. Moving images can uniquely provide stimuli that evoke feelings that an audience possesses and enables their expression.[173] They render conscious what the mind senses unconsciously.[174] Daisy made no effort to change minds. It merely tapped into deeply felt emotions buried within voters and channeled them in an implicit message that one could not trust Goldwater's fingers on the nuclear trigger.

Corporate Home Runs

Commercial advertising offers powerful examples of emotional resonance.

- In Apple's recent ad, "Commander," a young girl dreams of being an astronaut and commanding a space vessel. She consults Siri – an interactive Q&A feature of Apple – and asks what it takes. The answers ignite her imagination.[175]

---

[172] https://www.youtube.com/watch?v=dDTBnsqxZ3k; see also: Tony Schwartz, The Responsive Chord, (New York: Anchor Press, 1973), and James P. Farwell, Persuasion & Power (Washington: Georgetown University Press, 2012).

[173] Tony Schwartz, The Responsive Chord, supra, p. 93; and James P. Farwell, Persuasion & Power, supra, p. 184

[174] Tony Schwartz, The Responsive Chord, supra, p. 97.

[175] https://www.youtube.com/watch?v=8L41jtVWSLU

- United Overseas Bank did a touching series defining its values through a story about the life of a Chinese family and its upward aspirations nourished by the importance of hard work and persistence.[176]
- Standard Bank's ad "Never Stop Moving," conveying the energy of its culture, stands out for its vibrancy, optimism, and identification with the will to achieve.[177]
- The Democratic Alliance in South Africa outdid itself in "One South Africa for All," embracing faith and the power of unity, and through a biographical video about its leader, Mmusi Maimane.[178]
- Citibank touted feminine independence in the story of a fiancé as she climbs a mountain. We get the idea that he wants to propose, offering a diamond engagement ring. In the final shot, taken from a helicopter swirling around her, she stands astride the summit and proclaims: "I took him to the rock I wanted."[179] I'm not sure the ad won the bank customers, but it gets your attention and associates Citibank with the values it advocates.

Vital Precepts

The military and national security experts I have quoted convey a good sense of what the military looks for. Let's focus on how their worldviews play out in commercial marketing.

1.   When entering a different cultural environment, set aside national preconceptions.

We've seen how this precept has become a mantra for the military. Each culture has idiosyncrasies. IKEA developed a strategy inspired by the Guggenheim Museum in New York. Designed by Frank Lloyd Wright, the Guggenheim is a

---

[176] United Overseas Bank, "Our values define us:" https://www.youtube.com/watch?v=4tA8wtLaui4; and "UOB Private Bank Vase 90s:" https://www.youtube.com/watch?v=XqBKVztCBE4

[177] Standard Bank: "The Man Who Couldn't Stop Moving Forward:" https://www.youtube.com/watch?v=9COO-PR9hy0

[178] Democratic Alliance, "One South Africa for All:" https://www.youtube.com/watch?v=VQXFhFbf0ys and https://www.youtube.com/watch?v=pdRSCo7Q6rI. One notes that U.S. political consultants handle many international campaigns. An American firm may have done these.

[179] Citibank, "Into the Wild:" https://www.youtube.com/watch?v=CIjGaDUp6FY

spiral. You start at the top and wind your way to the bottom. As you descend, your journey brings you face to face with the art hanging on the walls at each level. Ikea's founder, Ingvar Kamprad, detected an excellent idea for selling affordable, modern architectural furniture. He set up U.S. retail stores so that customers had to follow a designated path. The tactic ensured they saw every item for sale and grew profits.

IKEA's marketing uses sophisticated customer and market research. IKEA sends design experts into people's homes to listen to their concerns and provide feedback," Kamprad says. "This allows IKEA evangelists to make marketing decisions based on people's real-life experiences rather than just surveys or data." IKEA offers a reasonable price point and value. It integrates print and media advertising, sales promotions, events, public relations, and direct marketing as many multi-media ways to communicate.[180]

Many of its customers are working-class people seeking value for their hard-earned money.[181] IKEA switched from a product-based company to a value-based proposition and tailored its marketing. The Swiss are picky about furnishings. They want to present an elite feeling in their homes. They worried that IKEA is not expensive. IKEA showed that its designs could create an elegant look. It advised Brits to "chuck out your chintz." Chintz is a staple of British furnishings, but it's dowdy. In China, living spaces are crowded. It sells furniture in small-scale parcels. It established pop-up stores to sell smaller items targeted at youth and urban dwellers. IKEA's strategic communication touted lower delivery fees. Ikea epitomizes the ability to adjust communication to different cultures and societies.

2. **Provide a unique shopping experience.**

Online competition is forcing brick-and-mortar retailers to think innovatively. Beyond setting up interesting display rooms and showing people how they can arrange their furniture at IKEA, you can also get lunch featuring their famous Swedish meatballs, and daycare for your children.[182]

In Britain, Harrods and Fortum & Mason inspire customers to feel like aristocrats. They sell exceptional products. Assistants wearing Morning Suits

---

[180] John Dudovskiy, "IKEA Marketing Strategy: a brief overview," *Research Metholody.net*, November 17, 2019: https://research-methodology.net/ikea-marketing-strategy/
[181] Hitesh Bhasin, "Marketing Strategy of IKEA," *Marketing91.com*, September 8, 2018: https://www.marketing91.com/marketing-strategy-ikea/
[182] Kevin J. Duncan, "7 Lessons You Can Learn from IKEA's Killer Marketing," *Optinmonster.com*, April 21, 2019: https://optinmonster.com/lessons-you-can-learn-from-ikeas-killer-marketing/

look and act like they just arrived from Ascot to wait upon the customer. Both stores offer gourmet food you cannot find elsewhere. Harrod's grand Food Hall is a destination in itself. Still, both aggressively pursue online retailing.

J. Press's clothes have a preppy look. If you like that that look – I do – you can outfit yourself for a sophisticated townhouse or your country home. I wear their clothes all the time at home to impress my two Labrador Retrievers.

3. **Customers respond to solid brand identity.**

IKEA and big-name brands like Coca-Cola, Nike, Mercedes, Apple, IBM, and others have global visibility. You may lack the resources to match their reach, but that is not the only requirement for success. Your target audience may consist of just a select group of individuals.[183]

Jack Daniels touts itself as a "working man's dream whiskey." Its distinctive flavor comes from four single grains, fifty single-malts, and fingerprint malts from Glenburnie and Milton Duff.[184] The whiskey appeals to nostalgia. Marketing plays up the company's rich heritage. Print and social media often feature a photograph of its Lynchburg, Tennessee distillery. The message underscores that the brand has remained unchanged since 1866. The image harkens to the past, bringing it to life. It targets audiences who like craft cocktails. Photos and videos describe the "charcoal mellowing" distilling process. This strategy has drawn younger customers while sustaining its relationship with older ones.[185]

4. **Provide marketing materials with content that engages the customer.**

Customers want to know precisely what they will be purchasing. You want to capitalize on every relevant channel of communication.

- Ikea uses videos to place customers in real-life situations to understand what the purchases may look like in a home.[186]
- Jaguar's videos guide customers through the features of their cars. This approach makes car buyers comfortable with a product some may find

---

[183] Kevin J. Duncan, "7 Lessons You Can Learn from IKEA's Killer Marketing,"
[184] Hitesh Bhasin, "Marketing Mix of Jack Daniels," *Marketing91*, February 8, 2019: https://www.marketing91.com/marketing-mix-jack-daniels/
[185] Tanya Dua, "Telling, not selling: A peek inside Jack Daniel's social media playbook," *digiday.com*, July 1, 2016: https://digiday.com/marketing/telling-not-selling-peek-inside-jack-daniels-social-media-playbook/
[186] "Bridging the imagination gap with IKEA Place:" https://www.youtube.com/watch?v=vMBTlypMgz8

exotic. The video also reinforces the idea that having a Jaguar shows sophistication and provides luxury, which will make you feel special.[187]
- The real estate and hospitality industries discovered long ago that virtual tours draw customer focus and convey a sense of what they're offering purchasers.
- Online eyeglass companies like Warby Parker, Lingo, GlassesUSA, and others enable you to try on frames online.

These are smart approaches.

---

[187] Jaguar XJ V8 Series Customer introduction video: https://www.youtube.com/watch?v=W9yafT5ggCQ

Discussion Questions

1. What are you doing to understand what shapes opinions and motivates behavior among your target audiences? What techniques are you employing?

2. What are you doing to understand the cultural values and norms of your target audiences? Are you setting aside national preconceptions?

3. What are you doing to *inspire* your target audience? Think Megan Rapinoe and her ads for NIKE or the Daisey TV ad for Lyndon Johnson.

4. Are you forging a solid brand identity that customers respond to? Think about Coca-Cola Classic, Jack Daniels Tennessee whiskey, or Jaguar, which have strong identities.

5. Where does your target audience obtain information about a service or product that you want to sell?

6. Who does your target audience trust? Who in their minds is a credible source of information?

7. Who are the key influencers for your target audience? Who serves as a "gatekeeper" to whom your target audience looks to for "permission" or encouragement to purchase your service or product?

8. How are you achieving emotional resonance? Think about ads for Apple, United Overseas Bank, Standard Bank, the Democratic Alliance in South Africa and Citibank, and, always, NIKE.

9. Are you offering a new product, or like IBM, are you in a situation in which you are engineering a course change or rebranding? How are you going to achieve your goals?

CHAPTER FIVE

ELEMENTS OF STRATEGY

What are the elements of strategy? The notion of strategy has proven notoriously difficult to define.[188] A ton of books cover the topic. Different nations invoke different descriptions. The US military has a consistent, broad concept of it. Let's examine these elements.

"Today's U.S. military," as Information Operations and strategy expert Jack Guy observes, "think of strategy this way: strategy = ends + ways + means."[189] Strategy, he says, "is about *how* (way or concept) leadership will use the *power* (means or resources) available to the state to exercise control over sets of circumstances and geographic locations to achieve *objectives* (ends) that support state interests. The strategy provides direction for the coercive or persuasive use of this power to achieve specified objectives."

Guy points out that the means include the essential elements of power such as (again) DIME (Diplomacy, Information, Military, and Economic), "but the key is the objective or the ends."[190] Military historian B.H. Liddell Hart, among the

---

[188] William Murray and Mark Grimsley, "Introduction: On Strategy," in The Making of Strategy: Rulers, States and War, William Murray and Alvin Bernstein (London: Cambridge University Press, 1994).
[189] Interview with Jack Guy, April 2021.
[190] Id.

most influential voices on the topic, famously defined it as "the art of distributing and applying military means to fulfill the ends of policy."[191]

In the military, strategy exists at the grand, operational, and tactical levels. Few generals are adept at grand strategy, and the U.S. has been clumsy in formulating one to deal with a competitive world.

Grand Strategy

Liddell Hart is credited with coining the term "grand" strategy, although its substance has long been part of strategic thinking. Not easily defined, it is generally a national policy that guides all aspects of activity towards achieving war aims. Thomas Christensen explains it as "the full package of domestic and international policies designed to increase power and national security" in peacetime as well as wartime. Andrew Monaghan defines it as the art of "using all of the nation's resources to promote the state's interests, including securing it against enemies perceived and actual.[192]

R.D. Hooker, Jr. describes grand strategy as "the use of power to secure the state."[193] I think that's too broad. He agrees that actions tell the real story.[194] Edward Luttwak said it better. He declared: "national strategies, grand or not so grand, must *always* be inferred from what is done or not done, and are *never*

---

[191] B.H. Liddell Hart, Strategy, supra, p. 335.

[192] See: Alasdair Roberts, "Grand Strategy Isn't Grand Enough," *Foreign Policy,* February 20, 2018: https://foreignpolicy.com/2018/02/20/grand-strategy-isnt-grand-enough/#:~:text=Liddell%20Hart%20defined%20grand%20strategy,society%20in%20which%20war%20occurs.%E2%80%9D.

[193] R.D. Hooker, "American Grand Strategy," Strategic Monograph, National Defense University, October 1, 2014: https://ndupress.ndu.edu/Media/News/Article/718184/the-grand-strategy-of-the-united-states/. Citing various academics, he acknowledges that "defining *grand strategy*" is admittedly onerous.

[194] "What the state *does* is more important than what the state *says*," id., p. 8. While I personally happen to share many of Hooker's views on what the U.S. strategy should embrace, his description of U.S. vital interests was not necessarily shared by Presidents Donald Trump or Barack Obama. Trump believed the U.S. was over-extended. Whatever one may think of Trump or how he has addressed the topic, he was the first American President to recognize the steep challenge that China posed. A moralist, Obama believed that the U.S. had no moral standing to exert the kind of forward leadership that Presidents Ronald Reagan, G.W.H. Bush. or G.W. Bush believed in. Biden and Trump appear to hold different views on dealing with Russia and NATO. A detailed comparison of the national security views of Presidents from Reagan through Biden lies beyond the purview of this book. They differed considerably.

described in documents – or not, at any rate, in documents that might see the light of day."[195]

The U.S. pursued a grand strategy of containment during the Cold War. President G.H.W. Bush forged a smart strategy in Desert Storm by carefully defining and limiting Coalition goals to ousting Saddam Hussein from Kuwait, while consciously avoiding the overthrow of Saddam. That was a tactical strategy, focused on one aspect of the nation's larger security challenges.

Mostly one sees strategy at the tactical level, where our senior officers, whose remarkable talents might astonish those who haven't witnessed them in action, excel. The two battles of Fallujah in 2004 illustrate tactical warfare, just as the blowback nationally despite winning the second one demonstrates the absence of a grand strategy that might have enabled coalition forces to capitalize better on their success.

Hooker argues that the U.S. has one set on firm foundations such as economic strength, nuclear deterrence, alliances and partnerships, and full-spectrum dominance in all warfighting domains.[196] Every major nation feels that way about itself, and in including so much, it's too broad.

China does employ a sophisticated notion of strategy that it has purported to put in writing, but the document is disingenuous in propounding a propaganda narrative about China's desire for partnership and mutual dependence that isn't true. You can look at its actions, commentaries by military leaders, and the speeches of President Xi Jinping for a more accurate sense.

A detailed analysis of China's notion of grand strategy lies beyond the scope of this book. I'd argue that China sees strategy as aggressive, a different perspective than Western nations employ. Set that aside. Broadly, Chinese doctrine embraces three strategic elements: objectives, or *what to do;* guidance, or *how to do it;* and means, or *what to use doing it.*[197] That formulation echoes the one invoked by

---

[195] Edward N. Luttwak, The Grand Strategy of the Roman Empire, (Baltimore: Johns Hopkins University Press, 2016), p. xi.
[196] R.D. Hooker, "American Grand Strategy," supra.
[197] China's Science of Military Strategy, *China Aerospace Studies Institute* (2013), p. 7: https://www.airuniversity.af.edu/Portals/10/CASI/documents/Translations/2021-02-08%20Chinese%20Military%20Thoughts-%20In%20their%20own%20words%20Science%20of%20Military%20Strategy%202013.pdf?ver=NxAWg4BPw_NyIEjxaha8Aw%3d%3d. This 372-page doctrine moves from describing strategy to analyzing the structure of strategy, the system of strategy, the characteristics of strategy including its overarching nature, confrontational nature, realism and foresight, stability and response to change, factors that affect strategy and many other considerations.

Admiral Stavridis related to me in a spring, 2021 conversation. "Strategy is three things," he says. "Ends, ways, and means are about where you want to go, how you'll get there, and the resources that provide the means. That's true whether you're leading a three-person team at Google or three million men and women under arms."[198]

Stavridis agrees with the Chinese view that "you may adopt confrontation as an element of strategy. Still, you need to do that smartly and selectively. For instance, in dealing with China, we need to confront China on intractable issues like human rights and its spurious claim that it owns the South China Sea, and its bullying neighborhoods. But we should cooperate where possible. That includes humanitarian operations and pandemics."[199]

Stavridis respects the classic Chinese strategist, Sun Tzu, who argued that victory should be achieved without armed conflict.[200] "You have to know where your existential challenge is," he points out. "At that point, confrontation may be mandatory. But the object of smart strategy is to avoid war and reduce confrontation. Sun Tzu was right. I follow his tenets."[201]

Russian commentators concur with modern American political consultants' insistence that one must look beyond science in analyzing strategy. "They view strategy as a work of art," advised my colleague at King's College, University of London, Dr. Ofer Fridman, in one of our frequent conversations. "The Russian Imperial School believed that great commanders artfully combined moral, geographic, tactical, administrative, political, and ethical elements, as well as the essence of chance, to meet the requirements of a given situation."

What do you as an executive need to know about the notion of strategy? It starts with asking: *what do you want strategic communication to accomplish?* Here, the military and companies have the same task. Stavridis applies Sun Tzu to corporate challenges. "While companies aim to earn profits for shareholders, increasingly, environmental concerns and social justice play a key role in attracting and sustaining a customer base. The bottom line for commanders and CEOs is the same. Where do I want to go? How do I get there? Where resources do I have that get me to that place?"[202]

---

[198] Interview with Admiral (Ret) James G. Stavridis, June 2, 2021.
[199] Id.
[200] Sun Tzu, <u>The Art of War</u> (R.D. Sawyer, Trans. By Ralph D. Sawyer) (LITTL, 1994; Kindle).
[201] Interview with Admiral (Ret) James G. Stavridis, June 2, 2021.
[202] Id.

Executives may not invoke the same language, but they need to apply the same analytical framework in forging their strategies. Another colleague, Lt. Colonel (Ret) Mike Williams, is an influence operations expert. Today he is involved in five businesses. He advises:

> "[A] good strategist needs a healthy dose of humility. You have to be open to all ideas. You need to understand what motivates the people you work with and target audiences. That goes for the military and business. You need to align strategy with the culture that out of which it grows. You need a clear strategy, but understanding motive and culture helps to ensure it can be executed successfully."[203]

Executives who tout corporate citizenship or caring for the environment are conducting the equivalent of diplomatic engagement. Performance marketing – consider ads for pain relievers like Tylenol and Aleve that depict a problem which these products solve (e.g., pain) – is about providing information. Marketing that touts the impact of their product or service on creating opportunities and careers is a form of *economic,* strategic communication.

Colonel Thomas X. Hammes places the debate over strategic purpose in the context of Fourth-Generation Warfare (4GW). In his view, 4GW unfolds over a period that exceeds a single event's duration and requires a deep understanding of the strategic situation. 4GW's aim shifts away from the destruction of enemy forces to influencing political decisions. Hammes describes the goal of 4GW as:

> "[t]o convince the enemy's political decision-makers that their strategic goals are either unachievable or too costly for the perceived benefit. It is an evolved form of insurgency. Still rooted in the fundamental precept that superior political will, when properly employed, can defeat greater economic and military power, 4GW makes use of society's networks to carry on its fight. Unlike previous generations, it does not attempt to win by defeating the enemy's military forces. Instead… it directly attacks the minds of enemy

---

[203] Interview with Lt. Col. (Ret) Mike Williams, May 19, 2021.

decision-makers to destroy the enemy's political will."[204]

An Israeli View

Retired Israeli Defense Forces Brig. Gen. (Ret) Shimon Naveh views strategic campaigns as a "complex of operations and actions to accomplish a strategic goal. The campaign, like the theatre, is related to a comprehensive aim and a defined framework of time, space, and force."[205] The strategy allocates resources and provides a framework for articulating operations and tactics that achieve defined strategic aims. Naveh's sophisticated approach applies to corporate strategy.

While Naveh goes beyond precepts that interest executives, his viewpoint is worth knowing. He argues against the destruction of an enemy in favor of inflicting "operational shock" that defeats an enemy's ability to achieve its aims and knocks out its operational equilibrium. Successful operations attack the enemy's center of gravity by identifying exact points of enemy strength and weakness, creating operational vulnerabilities, and exploiting those through maneuvering strikes.[206]

Strategy and Industry

Bob Giesler, well-respected in the Pentagon for his finely tuned strategic mind, points out that sound strategy provides a clear road map to an endpoint. Absent a good one, especially in the corporate world, "all you're doing is transactions." He believes that executives often do a better job of forging strategy than military leaders:

---

[204] Col. Thomas X. Hammes, USMC, The Sling and the Stone (St. Paul: Zenith, 2004), p. 208.
[205] Shimon Naveh, In Pursuit of Military Excellence: The Evolution of Operational Theory, supra, pp. 12-13; and discussions with General Naveh at US SOCOM.
[206] Id., pp. 18-19.

> "I've done strategy with the military and industry," he reminded me. "Industry forces you to quantify details. What are your numbers today? What are they going to be next week? Wall Street rewards you not for how well you are doing but for how well it predicts you'll do. The military tends to be more ambiguous, perhaps because the military's challenges are often more ambiguous. But neither military nor corporate leaders get far without thinking through, writing down, and executing clear strategy."[207]

General (Ret) Sir Richard Shirreff is today the Managing Partner of a significant firm that advises internationally on understanding risk and linking risk and strategy. In his view, "all too often in business, people talk about strategy when they mean plans." He stresses the need to articulate a vision, think through objectives, and achieve them through what the military terms of operation and companies think of as activities or, simply, operations.[208]

Colonel (Ret) Mark Neate served in the British Army as an operational planner. He served as part of David Petraeus's broad team during the 2007 surge in Iraq and today works with Sellafield Ltd. on environmental and safety matters. Like former Acting Assistant Secretary for Special Operations – Low-Intensity Conflict, Mark Mitchell, he stresses that "strategies have to be agile and clear in their assumptions. From a business perspective, one looks at risk and opportunity and measures them against the ambitions for a strategy. These need to be integrated into a vision of success, calibrated against a defined timeframe, and rooted in values that resonate with target audiences."[209]

General Joseph Votel looks beyond communicating the big idea – the key narrative, themes, and messages that define a rationale for a strategy – to execution and to the importance of thinking about how you'll execute a strategy as you forge one. He stresses the need for "centralized planning, decentralized execution. You want people to handle things at the lowest competent level. That's where providing the right guidance and the right structure is

---

[207] Interview with Bob Giesler, supra.
[208] Interview with General (Ret) Sir Richard Shirreff, May 5, 2021.
[209] Interview with Colonel (Ret) Mark Neate, April 15, 2021.

indispensable. People will make mistakes. You can recover from those if you properly orchestrate decentralized execution on a centralized plan."[210]

Mark Neate notes that the military focuses on particular operations. But in business, he advised me, one focuses on being quick and agile in

> "recognizing what's out there, grasping it, investing in it, accepting that some things may fail but that one can change strategy rapidly to exploit an opportunity." He stresses that "executives need to recognize that windows of opportunity open and shut. An opportunity may work for a time, but market shifts may mandate major strategic adjustments to meet market demands and a shifting customer base."[211]

Strategy is integral to national security thinking, but our military often limits strategy to the tactical level and fails to forge a coherent grand strategy. Let's return to the second battle of Fallujah in November 2004. Brilliantly planned and executed, as kinetic and information warfare, Coalition forces soundly defeated the insurgents at the tactical level. Yet, that victory set off widespread anger among Iraqis. Many reacted harshly to images of western – in their vocabulary, "infidel" – soldiers slaughtering Muslim fighters, however distasteful they found the insurgents. In warfare, emotion often trumps reason. Indeed, 2005 was the worst year of the 2003 War for Coalition forces.

Industry advertisers often jazz up the notion of strategy with jargon without understanding what the term connotes. Strategy comes from the Greek word *strategos*, meaning *general*. In Athens, generals got elected for one-year terms. Some of its greatest generals, including Cimon and Pericles, started as political leaders.

Strategy is fluid.[212] It requires an appreciation of all ends, ways, and means. Whether you're selling a service or a product or achieving a political or military objective, set no strategy in stone. Pepsi's John D. Sculley said it well: innovatively adjust and adapt flexibly. US Special Operations employs a similar mandate: be agile, adaptable, and flexible.

---

[210] Interview with General Joseph L. Votel, May 5, 2021.
[211] Interview with Colonel (Ret) Mark Neate, April 15, 2021.
[212] This section draws upon my chapter on strategy in Persuasion and Power, (Washington: Georgetown University Press, 2012), Chapter 13, p. 153.

You should translate strategy into actionable tactics. The French have a saying: Strategy must work not only in practice but in theory. I'm not sure about that one, but I don't advise their military. Americans are pragmatic. The strategy that opens a campaign may differ from the one that closes it. Battlefield success may settle nothing. Indeed, in military theatres of war, an enemy is not defeated until it recognizes that it has been. Success creates new challenges – another competitor, a different product, shifting consumer tastes, a revitalized adversary, revolutions in technology, emerging ambitions of actors. Success today must set the stage for success tomorrow. One must sustain success.

The lessons military and national security leaders have drawn find excellent parallels in industry. We discussed four critical examples in Nike, Apple, IBM, and Starbucks. They rely almost entirely on positive messaging.

What about *comparative* messaging? We began this discussion by noting that federal law imposes restraints on it in the commercial world. That differs from what occurs in national security communications. In national security, we define the stakes and explain why target audiences should support our views and actions.

Industry is thin-skinned about comparison marketing. When Pepsi launched its Pepsi Challenge, Coke went off the deep end. A good comparative competition in recent times has pitted Apple against PC. It's light-hearted stuff. Ads featured actors, each playing the role of their respective brands. The Apple ads are witty and clever. In "Gisele Bundchen,"[213] a dull obese guy plays PC. A handsome, cool guy plays Mac. Both introduce their "home movie." Supermodel and football QB Tom Brady's wife, Gisele Bundchen, enters and introduces herself as Apple's movie. A disheveled guy wearing the same dress enters, introducing himself as PC's home movie. It's hilarious and gets the point across.

PC folks weren't going to let Apple steal their customers. In "Mac v PC – The Revenge,"[214] a performance ad compares capabilities. Images of an iPhone appear next to various PC phones, as a voice itemizes the positive contrast in favor of PCs. The PC ad is well produced. The ad Mac is funnier.

Marketing expert Donald Miller offers an opinion into why Apple's narrative stories worked. It identified what customers wanted: to be seen and heard. It defined the customer challenge: people didn't recognize their hidden genius. It offered a tool they could use to express themselves: computers and

---

[213] Apple, "Gisele Bundchen:" https://www.youtube.com/watch?v=WcDpFLSTZWU.
[214] "Mac v PC – The Revenge:" https://www.youtube.com/watch?v=TDf1TuBrgBI

smartphones.[215] That may be true for some consumers, but I'd argue that the appeal to free spirits, rebellion against convention, ease of use, and using cutting-edge technology that is better than the competition is more powerful. Miller is more on target when he acknowledges that the real key to Apple's success lay in surmounting the intimidation many users felt about computers.[216]

Strategic Positioning

What about strategic positioning? Al Ries and Jack Trout have written an informative book, Positioning: The Battle for Your Mind.[217] I don't always agree with them, but they raise a valid point that getting there first matters. Once you're the market leader, new competitors start behind the eight-ball. Coke had all the resources in the world. Its soft drink Mr. Pibb ran into a brick wall trying to displace the well-established Dr. Pepper. Xerox seized ownership of the photo-duplication industry by getting there first. Kodak and 3M had a tough time trying to compete.

One lesson is that if you make multiple products, give each its own identity. Ries and Trout note that Xerox spotlights a second trap to avoid. Known as a copier, Xerox spent a billion dollars for a computer company and renamed it Xerox Data Systems, on the premise that Xerox was a better-known name. But when people hear Xerox, they think copier, not a computer. The brand name was not easily transferrable. Their account of this misfire is enlightening.[218]

Taking on the market leader fascinates journalist Lawrence Ingrassia in writing about Internet unicorns like the Dollar Shave Club and how they have used new technology and imagination to enter an occupied zone and seize turf.[219] This was also the theme of Malcolm Gladwell's Outliers: The Story of Success.[220] People like Bill Gates, corporate takeover uber-lawyer Joseph Flom, and the Beatles all achieved success by satisfying the "10,000-Hour Rule." It's not about book learning.

---

[215] Donald Miller, Building a Story Brand (New York: HarperCollins, 2017), p.18.
[216] Id., p. 64.
[217] Al Ries and Jack Trout, Positioning: The Battle for Your Mind (New York: McGraw Hill, 2001).
[218] Id., Chapter 14, page 127.
[219] Lawrence Ingrassia, Billion Dollar Brand Club, (New York: Henry Holt and Company, 2020).
[220] Malcolm Gladwell, Outliers: The Story of Success, (New York: Little Brown and Company, 2008).

Gladwell credits the Beatles for performing that many hours *before* they became famous. The price for being the best is putting in the time, even when you don't feel like it. Yes, it's a different expression of Nike's theme. I once asked Michael Bloomberg what makes an individual a success. He replied without hesitation, "hard work and recognizing that you win the tough ones by inches." You need focus, discipline, and you never give in or give up.

Nothing Good Comes Easy

Michael Jordan sums up the truth in a Nike ad that he narrates: "Maybe you think my high life started at the free-throw line and not in the gym," he says over images of a dilapidated gym. As pictures of basketball court diagrams appear, he continues, "[maybe you think] that my game was built on flash, and not fire. Maybe you didn't see that failure gave me strength, and my pain was my motivation." Images flash depicting his childhood home and of Jordan growing up. "Maybe you believed that basketball was a God-given gift and not something I worked for every single day of my life."[221] His message: making excuses is the path to failure. He's like Bloomberg: becoming a legend requires discipline, plans, and hard work.

Malcolm Gladwell extols preparation. His heroes prepared hard and proved capable of jumping in first when the window of opportunity opened. Bill Gates is no rags-to-riches story. His mom was an IBM Board member. Gates had unique access to a computer at a time when they were rare. He got an edge by gaining the opportunity to learn about them early on, but he made the most of his chance. Those who followed in their footsteps may have possessed equal or more extraordinary talent. The folk wisdom, *the early bird gets the worm,* applies to business.

A Presidential Comparison

Barack Obama's 2012 re-election campaign used Facebook to mirror-image potential voters likely to support him and focused its communication on those voters. In 2020, Donald Trump used even more sophisticated techniques to micro-target his supporters.

---

[221] Nike: "Maybe it's my fault:" https://www.youtube.com/watch?v=mgVSw_4rJbc

The Ries/Trout model argues for seizing a market niche occupied by higher-priced products.[222] Mercedes, BMW, and Lexus prove his point. Apple computers are overpriced, and its sunset 3-year customer support term drives some of its users up a wall. But Apple has won its case. It has built a large, hard-core base of loyal customers.

Reason Persuades, Emotion Motivates

Reason persuades. Emotion motivates. Stories are the best way to evoke emotion. This is especially true for information warfare and politics. Americans are aspirational. As the late pollster Dick Wirthlin pointed out, they want leaders who reflect their values and vision for the future that appeals to their hopes and dreams while answering their fears. They want ones who are likable and sincere, have strength and integrity, care about them, and present a track record of success.[223]

Insightful marketing commentators like Seth Godin hold a different view. He focuses heavily on emotions and making consumers feel good about their purchases as the key to selling. That theory may work for selling ice cream. But generally, strategy needs to strike deeper.

Godin argues that good marketers invent a thing worth making that benefits people, makes them care about it, and yields a story that excites consumers. One spreads the word to build confidence in the changes to lifestyle that a product affects. Godin sees marketing as about making change.[224] That strikes me as an overstatement. It *may* be essential to marketing, and creating change *is* one way to draw attention.

But lots of products that effect no real change in anyone's life succeed in the marketplace. His basic view echoes almost exactly what Buzzy Killeen, the late head of Fitzgerald Advertising in New Orleans, told me years ago: when people buy products, they are not purchasing a thing. They acquire toothpaste for clean, brighter teeth. They believe the car makes them feel good about themselves, proud that they got it for the right price.

Jim Stengel rightly says that sound strategy positions a service or product as something that will improve lives. Positioning draws attention, but too much

---

[222] Al Ries and Jack Trout, Positioning: The Battle for Your Mind, supra, p. 56.
[223] See: James P. Farwell, Persuasion & Power, supra, Chapter 10.
[224] Seth Godin, This is Marketing, (New York: Penguin-Random House, 2018), p. 11-12.

information overwhelms consumers. Still, you must answer tough questions. Why should customers be interested in your product or company? Why do you matter? What does your product or service offer? Just getting their attention is a feat.

Statistics on publishing vary. Most sources report that America publishes well over a million books a year, counting self-published books. The American Association of Publishers says 130,000 books a year are published. Newspapers use more than 10 million tons of newsprint. Most supermarkets carry 12,000 products. The Thomas Register identifies 80,000 companies, half a million suppliers, and over a million engineers and decision-makers who decide what is purchased.[225] The landscape for standing out is crowded.

Getting noticed requires appealing to the values, identity, sense of excellence, and relevance of what you offer. Here the military and commercial worlds align. As noted above, military strategy starts with the leader's intent. Companies reflect the purpose in their strategy and project it through what commercial people term "consistent branding." As in politics, the military calls this "message discipline." The most successful strategies position companies well by developing precise target audience analysis. They root their culture, operations, services, or products in solid values that motivate customers to identify with themselves.

Companies have to tell customers what they are going to do for them and do so distinctively. Take Starbucks' mission statement: "To inspire and nurture the human spirit, one person, one cup, and one neighborhood at a time." Starbucks fosters connections among customers, but also between them, the baristas, and their organization.[226]

Starbucks' strategy has been to offer a distinctive premium coffee that was so good customers would pay 25% more than competing brands. Starbucks' cafes maintain a consistent look, and they build visibility and awareness through personal customer service, social media, and selling quality brand merchandise. Starbucks targets upper-middle-class and upper-class economic strata with a fast-moving lifestyle. It stresses "ethical sourcing," paying fair prices to coffee growers, and positions itself as environmentally sensitive. Initially, it relied upon

---

[225] See: https://business.thomasnet.com/about. See also: Al Ries and Jack Trout, Publishing, supra., p. 11, 16.
[226] "Starbucks Marketing: How to Create A Remarkable Brand," *GoSchedule.blog*: https://coschedule.com/blog/starbucks-marketing-strategy/.

word-of-mouth recommendations, social media, and a talented workforce. Today it also does broadcast advertising.

It invests heavily in social media. Starbucks' Twitter account has over 11.8 million followers.[227] It uses Instagram and social media videos. It maintains consistent content across social media channels, maintaining message discipline.

Elsewhere I've described how a changing market forced Starbucks to reboot. It did so with its exuberant "Meet Me at Starbucks"[228] campaign that stressed the cafes as places where you can make happy connections worldwide. That implemented its concept of serving as a "third place" between work and home where customers can connect. Its "Morning Yes"[229] celebrates starting the day with a cup of Starbucks coffee. Consistent branding, epitomized by Norse woodcutting containing a siren, a mermaid-like figure,[230] boosted a great product. That, and personal services, has made Starbucks well-recognized globally.

Although 2020 was its final year of production in shifting to electric cars,[231] Volkswagen's Beetle classically challenged the prevailing wisdom that more prominent was best. When it first hit the market, it made a splash. It looked different, was perceived as a good car, and people liked the product and its idea. Cheeky ads sparked attention.[232] That held for the product's original ads as well as more modern ones.[233] Sadly, production on the vehicle ceased as demand for

---

[227] Abhijeet Pratap, "Marketing Strategy of Starbucks," *Notesmatic*, August 25, 2019: https://notesmatic.com/2017/01/marketing-strategy-of-starbucks/

[228] Starbucks, "Meet Me at Starbucks:" https://www.youtube.com/watch?v=LZVCLVGymmo

[229] Starbucks, "#MorningYes:" https://www.youtube.com/watch?v=y2Ea1-5jj48

[230] "Starbucks Marketing: How to Create A Remarkable Brand," *GoSchedule.blog*: https://coschedule.com/blog/starbucks-marketing-strategy/. The logo has been redesigned several times.

[231] Arunima Banerjee and Joseph White, "Volkswagen to end production of the Beetle next year," *Reuters*, September 13, 2018: https://www.reuters.com/article/us-volkswagen-beetle/volkswagen-to-end-production-of-the-beetle-next-year-idUSKCN1LT315#:~:text=The%20Jetta%2C%20Tiguan%20and%20Beetle,cheating%20on%20diesel%20emissions%20tests.

[232] Volkswagen, three ads: https://www.youtube.com/watch?v=tc-kekzH2dU

[233] Volkswagen 2013 Superbowl Ad, "Happy People:" https://www.youtube.com/watch?v=N4ggToPSsK8

light trucks killed the bug's market.[234] Despite great advertising, price and value were critical.

Today, there's a market for smaller cars, but the nature of the market has changed. Leading the way is the Mini Cooper. It's chic and fashionable while offering cool performance.[235] Critics don't like Fiat's 500, but it's stylish and the market as a whole isn't buying, but it appeals to a particular market segment. Pope Francis is among those chauffeured about in one.[236] Stodgy doesn't resonate so well anymore.

What About Humor?

Humor is effective, but the military doesn't employ it much. That is a weakness in military-strategic communication, especially in dealing with terrorists, because humor strikes a responsive chord with many audiences. Moliere taught us centuries ago that authoritarian figures (and terrorists certainly qualify) are perfect targets for satire.

Lt. Col. (Ret) Mike Williams believes that humor is a great way to reach audiences, "especially where you see the humor in everyday life. But it works only if the humor is culturally relevant. Something Americans find funny may not be funny to foreign audiences. Where it's properly attuned to their humor, it's an excellent device. I think it's far too underplayed in planning."[237]

The Middle East illustrates William's point. Many people think Middle East populations are dour. Actually, humor is a staple of Middle East politics in print and broadcast. Arabs employ it for entertainment and politics. Iraq has used television to mock ISIS. The state-run Al Iraqi TV had a show, *State of Superstition,* which made fun of former ISIS leader Abu Bakr Baghdadi. Calling him The Beheader portrayed him as unbelievable, with a long, tangled fake

---

[234] Al Root, "Why Did Volkswagen Kill the Beetle? Blame SUVs," *Barron's*, July 11, 2019: https://www.barrons.com/articles/why-did-volkswagen-stop-making-the-beetle-blame-light-trucks-51562845905

[235] MiniCooper: https://www.youtube.com/watch?v=PUxlWrQYmj4 and https://www.youtube.com/watch?v=Nh-sEeIHPNI

[236] Larry Prinz, "The least popular car in America is practical and affordable. So why isn't it selling?" *Detroit News*, December 11, 2019: https://www.detroitnews.com/story/business/autos/chrysler/2019/12/11/fiat-least-popular-car-america/40802115/

[237] Interview with Lt. Col. (Ret) Mike Williams, May 19, 20201.

beard, and positioned him as a buffoon.[238] On state-run Iraqiya TV, a reality show, *In the Grip of the Law*, brought convicted terrorists face-to-face with victims in surreal encounters. There are dozens of Middle East programs, cartoons, and musical public service announcements to counter ISIS.[239]

In Afghanistan, until the Taliban took over, Afghans did a chaotic quiz and satirical comedy called *The Riddle Show.*[240] It combined music, comedy, and irreverence. *The Ministry* targeted a fictional Minister of Garbage, satirizing corruption, drug trafficking, and nepotism.[241] *Danger Bell* used mockery, hoping to shame the government into cleaning up its act. In one example, a militant is put on trial for killing people with explosives he placed on a couple of donkeys. The prosecutors present an airtight case, but the Judge buys the defense that the *donkeys* are to blame. He frees the militant and issues an arrest warrant for the owner of the animals. The courtroom erupts in chaos. The point was to indict Afghanistan's corrupt criminal justice system.[242] The actors attracted death threats but courageously persisted.

Commercial marketing loves humor. As noted above, the Volkswagen ads for the Beetle, Pepsi's challenge to Coca-Cola, and Apple's challenge to PCs used humor well. Pepsi knocked the socks off people with a Brittany Spears ad that ran on the Super Bowl. She steamed up every male viewer with a noisy music video that featured Senator Bob Dole. What made the ad especially funny was that the good-natured Dole had filmed a widely-viewed ad for Viagra. Dole was a great American – the real deal. During World War II, he distinguished himself for heroism under fire. Badly wounded, he became the first successful recipient of penicillin. In politics, he stood apart for his funny, self-deprecating humor.

---

[238] David Zucchino, "Great Read: Iraqi TV comics make fun of Islamic State at huge risk," *Los Angeles Times*, October 29, 2014: https://www.latimes.com/world/la-fg-c1-iraq-isis-tv-comedy-20141029-story.html; See also: Ahmed Al-Rawi, "Anti-ISIS Humor: Cultural Resistance of Radical Ideology," *Journal of Politics, Religion & Ideology*, Vol. 17, No 1 (2016).
[239] "Terrorists forced to face victims on Iraqi reality TV," *CBS News*, December 22, 2014: https://www.cbsnews.com/news/terrorists-forced-to-face-victims-on-iraqi-reality-tv/
[240] Rory McCarthy, "Heard the one about the Afghan comedy show?", *Guardian*, January 2, 2003: https://www.theguardian.com/culture/2003/jan/02/artsfeatures.television
[241] Michelle Nichols, "Afghan TV series pokes fun at government with 'The Ministry," *Reuters*, August 5, 2011: https://www.reuters.com/article/afghanistan-television-ministry-idUSL3E7J21C020110805
[242] Sean Carberry, "Despite Many Threats, Afghan TV satire mocks the powerful," July 23, 2013: https://www.wmot.org/post/despite-many-threats-afghan-tv-satire-mocks-powerful#stream/0

The Spears ad is advertising at its finest.[243] Pepsi has always maintained a light touch. "The Way of Kung Fu"[244] satirizes martial arts movies as martial artists crush a Pepsi can. "Football Warriors" depicts medieval marauders sacking a hapless town until soccer star David Beckham employs ingenuity to crush the bad guys with a cascade of Pepsi cans.[245]

Not every Pepsi ad is funny – or works. In its controversial "Jump In"[246] video, Kendall Jenner abandons a photoshoot to join in a march. She meets a police officer and hands him a cold Pepsi. The message suggests Pepsi can bring about a better future, as Ian Bogost wrote in an admiring *Atlantic* commentary by putting "the consumer in a more important role than the citizen anyway. And to position Pepsi as a facilitator in the utopian dream of pure, color-blind consumerism that might someday replace politics entirely."[247]

Coke has clear messaging related to its theme of creating fun and connections, but skeptics argue that Coke's famous "Hilltop" ad,[248] using the slogan "The Real Thing," was an artistic success but didn't sell much Coca-Cola. Creativity does not, per se, equal effectiveness.

Quirky Works

Godin points out that some successful strategies focus on a small audience and direct all energy towards them. The Grateful Dead had only one top 40 Billboard hit, but while Jerry Garcia was alive, the band grossed $350 million and spawned generations of avid "Dead Heads." Garcia had the guts to be quirky.[249] Godin's description is worth reading. The strategy was to rely on a small but loyal group of fans to spread the word. Garcia's music found enough fans to make the band members very rich.

---

[243] Pepsi: "Britney Spears Pepsi Commercial with Bob Dole:" https://www.youtube.com/watch?v=yu5dIRv9Czc
[244] Pepsi, "The Way of the Kung Fu:" https://www.youtube.com/watch?v=DFkPZ8GRImo
[245] Pepsi Football Warriors: https://www.youtube.com/watch?v=JdxH5-E7gfk
[246] https://www.youtube.com/watch?v=dA5Yq1DLSmQ
[247] Ian Bogost, "Pepsi Ad Is a Total Success," *Atlantic*, April 5, 2017: https://www.theatlantic.com/technology/archive/2017/04/pepsi-ad-success/522021/
[248] The original aired in 1971 and was updated for the Superbowl in 1991: https://www.youtube.com/watch?v=Wqd5K5goilo. Here is the original: https://www.youtube.com/watch?v=1VM2eLhvsSM
[249] Seth Godin, This Is Marketing, supra, p. 79-80.

The French frozen food producer Picard has used an eccentric campaign that combines true love with foodie love. Every Valentine's day it produces a podcast entitled "Love Begins in the Kitchen." Each podcast brings couples together to make a Valentine's dinner from starter to dessert with four hands, using Picard's original recipes. It's a clever idea that teaches us that small ideas can achieve big impact in raising awareness and elevating our spirits.[250]

The French train company OUIGO devised a simple, imaginative campaign built on the narrative that taking the train avoids getting stuck in traffic jams. The campaign kicked off with print advertising on tarpaulins placed on the backs of large trucks. It continued with witty ads that captured the frustration of getting stuck in traffic.[251] The images are funny and stark: a car packed uncomfortably with passengers and luggage as a teenager sucks loudly on a Slurpee; a dad stuck behind the wheel as his 8-year old daughter screeches; an elderly lady reaches over to place her hand in front of her sleeping husband's face to make sure he's still breathing. The punchline is why put up with this grief when you can take the train? The TV ads energized OUIGO's campaign, but simple ads emblazed on low-cost tarpaulins were extremely effective.

France's Starwax won acclaim for a poster campaign touting its disinfectants that "only kills 99.9% of bacteria."[252] Starwax teaches three lessons. Clever gains attention. Functionality matters; you don't need to spend a lot of money if you satisfy the first two requirements.

The Italian company Barilla's Mulino Bianco brand makes popular chocolate cookies. This team took Jim Stengel's notion of improving the lives of people to its logical end. Instead of selling the product's specific merits, it positioned itself as an advocate for fair pricing to cocoa growers.[253] Its customers know the cookies. But the idea that patronizing Mulino Bianco was a noble act elicits emotional resilience. Starbucks has capitalized on the same message.

---

[250] "Ten of the most creative advertisements in France 2020," *Adintime.com*, December 29, 2020: https://adintime.com/en/blog/top-10-of-the-most-creative-advertisements-in-2020-in-france-n82#

[251] https://www.youtube.com/watch?v=zlir4owqVfo

[252] Id.

[253] "Pan di Stelle: Focusing on sustainability and responsibility," *italianbusinesstips.com*: October 9, 2018: https://www.italianbusinesstips.com/inspiring-italian-commercials-2018/.

1984: Go with Your Gut Instinct

The Apple 1984 ad merits further comment, given its emotional power and the lesson it reveals about the value of having the guts to stand up for a controversial strategy in which you believe. Apple needed to loosen Microsoft's grip on the personal computer market. It appealed to young, innovative minds – free spirits who didn't go along with the crowd and valued both freedom and cutting-edge technology. Apple's much-commented-on 1984 masterpiece targeted a narrow audience of talking heads and nerds. As Godin suggests, "the lesson: Apple's ad team only needed a million people to care. And so they sent a signal to them and ignored everyone else."[254] I agree with Godin.

More curiously, the merits of the "1984" ad strategy eluded the "experts." Apple hired ASI Market Research, the leading market research company of the day, to test it. They predicted it would bomb. Jobs loved the ad, but Apple's Board greeted it with stony silence. Jobs aired it anyway. It's among the most famous TV ads in history. The impact echoed our military's "shock and awe" strategy against Saddam Hussein in 1991 and 2003.

The lesson is that once you devise a strategy, you need to stand by it confidently unless evidence shows the results mandate a course correction. After the ad aired, consumers flooded electronic stores, purchasing $155 million worth of Macintoshes within three months. The ad established Apple as an innovator and drew a sharp contrast with Microsoft.[255] Chiat/Day's Lee Grow, who helped conceive the ad, says it earned $150 million worth of free airtime as new shows repeatedly rebroadcast it.[256] Fortune favors the bold. Military bureaucracy disdains that precept, but strong commanders embrace it. That's what leadership is about. Apple has proven that smart and daring works.

---

[254] Seth Godin, This Is Marketing, supra, p. 151.
[255] Aaron Taube, "How The Greatest Super Bowl Ad Ever – Apple's '1984' – Almost Didn't Make It to Air," *Business Insider,* January 22, 2014: https://www.businessinsider.com/apple-super-bowl-retrospective-2014-1
[256] Id. In 2008, supporters of President Barack Obama modified the ad on a laptop for perhaps a couple of hundred dollars. The million spent on the original was a fortune in 1984. Very few ads are produced today with that kind of budget, much less a budget adjusted for inflation.

Perceptions of Status Motivate

Seth Godin's books are fun, and they illuminate. Yet I'd argue that his shrewdest insight was to embrace an idea advanced by theatre director, actor, and writer Keith Johnstone.[257] In assessing character motivation, Johnstone, a pioneer of improvisational theatre, argues that the notion of *status* motivates and drives behavior. Johnstone asks how characters perceive their status. Status, Godin says, is about our position in the social hierarchy and how we perceive that position. It protects us, gives us leverage to make changes, provides a place to hide, creates a narrative that can change our perceived options, alters our choice, and undermines or supports our future. Status addresses the desire to change our status or protect us. Godin's conclusion: "Every big decision is made based on our perceptions of status."[258] I view advertising differently than Godin, but his comments on status make sense and apply equally to the military, politics, and the business world.

Information warfare in the Middle East on all sides revolves partly around the status of stakeholders. Al-Qaeda and ISIS argue that supporting them makes an individual a "good" Muslim. Arab states that Al-Qaeda and ISIS both denounce as friendly to the West are branded apostates. The former Government of Afghanistan condemned the Taliban as murderers. The Taliban, a Pashtun-based movement in a multi-ethnic nation, used ethnicity and religion and exploited anger over central government arrogance and corruption and its inability to make families secure.

Franklin Roosevelt used Nazi atrocities in Lidice to demonize Hitler and the Nazis. George Bush demonized Saddam Hussein in 1991 as a tyrant. He treated the broad international coalition that his diplomacy assembled as parallel to the allies in World War II. The strategy made coalition members feel a part of an operation to the right an injustice larger than themselves.

In the commercial world, Harley Davidson tapped into a market for motorcyclists who see themselves as champions of rugged individualism, excitement, and bad boy rebellion. Its targeted strategy revived a dying brand.[259]

---

[257] Keith Johnstone, Impro: Improvisation and the Theatre, (Theatre Arts Books, 1985); Seth Godin cites him in This is Marketing at 125. Johnstone's original discussion is worth studying. He is an original thinker with a well-merited reputation for creative thinking.
[258] Seth Godin, This Is Marketing, supra
[259] Glenn Rifkin, "How Harley Davidson Revs Its Brand," *Strategy + Business*, October 1, 1997: https://www.strategy-business.com/article/12878?gko=dcfc8

Its sexy ads feel like a biopic for rebel actor James Dean.[260] The stories its ads tell, featuring ruggedly handsome actors, express that message. Take a look at the enormously moving, German-produced spec ad, "Inner Child," footnoted below. Director Andreas Bruns won the Young Director Award at Cannes for his breathtaking story about a child's hardy, rebellious spirit expressed in an adult male character.[261]

Levis are Hip

Like Harley Davidson, Levi Strauss & Co. recognized that it needed to be hip to appeal to younger audiences. The company owns many sub-brands – Levi's, Dockers, Denizens, and Signature. Founded in 1853 to sell wholesale dry goods, tailor Jacob Davis used copper rivets to reinforce the points of strain on pants. For over a century, it dominated the market. Then it lagged. What could it do about that? James Lee, James Moon, and Michael Lin conducted an astute case study that defined Levi's strategy and success.[262] One problem lay in challenges from new competitors that ate into its market share. Its jeans had survived the Great Depression when Levi had shown cowboys wearing them. During World War II, the Defense industry issued them to workers. Veterans wore them on campus, rendering jeans hip, as people viewed veterans as heroes. Culturally, jeans evolved into a symbol of youth and rebellion.

Then jeans became fashion icons. Calvin Klein, Gap, Wrangler, L.L. Bean, and Tommy Hilfiger chipped away by targeting segments. Wranglers were made for low-end consumers, while Calvin Klein aimed at fashion buffs, labeling its denim "designer" jeans. Using Brooke Shields to endorse the product added élan. Then premium jeans arrived, led by Seven for All Mankind, True Religion, and Rock & Republic. Before 2007 Levi's had lost sales nine out of ten years.

---

[260] Harley-Davidson, "Life is a Highway:" https://www.youtube.com/watch?v=f8mNK_R-_Ok; and "Motorcycle Lifestyle:" https://www.youtube.com/watch?v=js66YLVTWIY. These are longer videos but fully capture the rebellious spirit of Dean that Harley-Davidson wanted to express.
[261] Harley Davidson, "Inner Child:" https://www.youtube.com/watch?v=X1NYIYd54JQ. See also: "Epic Harley-Davidson Film Tells You to Unleash Your Inner Child," *Creative News/Cheat*: https://www.lbbonline.com/news/epic-harley-davidson-film-tells-you-to-unleash-your-inner-child.
[262] J. Lee, J. Moon, and M. Lin, "Levi Strauss & Co: An Analysis:" https://are.berkeley.edu/~sberto/Levis.pdf. This analysis draws on theirs.

New CEO Chip Bergh devised a simple mantra: "Grow more profitable core, expand for more."[263] Men comprised 72% of its business through Levi's and Docker's men's bottoms. Like an excellent military commander, he identified his strengths and capitalized on them. His big cash generators came in five mature markets – the US, France, Germany, Mexico, UK, and ten wholesale customers. He solidified these.

Then, like a hilltop commander, he moved out, developing new markets, especially for tops and women's clothing. Its logo t-shirts and Commuter denim jacket were hits. Bergh led an incursion into China, India, and Russia. Levi revitalized its strategy, narrative, themes, and messages to reach targeted audiences. Its strategy stressed brand loyalty, using the word "original" to define its identity. Its 501 product targeted youth. Its message appealed to those wanting to be hip.

Check out the footnotes that link to ads. An ad for Levi's Men's 501 CT jeans shows a handsome guy getting out of bed on waking and putting on his jeans. Lying amid the sheets, his drop-dead gorgeous woman watches him leave. He then goes to a café and flirts with a waitress. Finally, his girlfriend impatiently dresses and is about to leave, then opens the door. He's standing there with a smile, holding coffee and coffee cake. *Cool*.[264]

A young Brad Pitt sizzled in a Levi's ad that pictured him as a released convict wearing the jeans. A hot girlfriend collects him in a convertible, and they haul off together.[265] Status is about identity. Those ads appeal to self-identity. Today Levi's sells in stores ranging from supermarkets to company-owned and franchised outlets. A partnership for Wranglers with Walmart broadened its impact in the low-end market, where you can buy a pair of jeans for about $14. I grabbed one. They're not as nice as my "fancier" jeans, but they're comfortable. You might not wear them with a blue blazer and tie, the way couture stores do in Milan, but so what? They're a great value.

Levi's has also shown corporate responsibility. It was among the first companies to extend healthcare to employee spouses. It educated people about AIDS. Corporate responsibility especially appeals to youth. In 2018, Levi's recorded the

---

[263] Marc Bain, "The simple mantra that helped Levi's turn its business around," *qz.com*, May 1, 2018: https://qz.com/work/1265943/levis-turned-around-its-business-by-following-a-simple-mantra/

[264] Levi's Men's 501 CT "Beautiful Morning:" https://www.youtube.com/watch?v=SvUv6qQhUMk

[265] Levi's Brad Pitt Commercial: https://www.youtube.com/watch?v=gqpX4EZ64Dg

highest sales growth in a decade.²⁶⁶ That gives it status and appeals to those whose perception of their station in life motivates them to favor environmentally friendly companies, demonstrate ethical behavior to suppliers, and prove socially responsible. It's the commercial echo of what the military does in "winning hearts and minds."

Chip Bergh had advantages denied military commanders. Executives generally have more time to let a strategy unfold and register, even in a turnaround. Military brass has to move within minutes or hours, especially at the tactical level. Examples from both worlds do not lend themselves to formulas. The ads I've linked to bear study. They excite the imagination and provoke thinking.

Tailor Your Strategy to the Culture

What works for a U.S. audience may misfire in other cultures. British ads often invoke snob appeal. French ads use edgy wit and eccentricity. An extensive analysis of Japanese advertising lies beyond the scope of this book, but the ads are worth looking at. Jim Kersey has written thoughtfully about Japanese consumer tastes. This draws on his observations.²⁶⁷ Trust me, you won't find such ads in Boise and probably not even in Manhattan.

Much of Japanese advertising appeals to what is cute or to beauty in nature. The Japanese eat up ads that express the innocence of childhood. Seasonal campaigns associating products with spring or cherry blossoms appeal to Japanese sentiment. The nation responds to jingles that rhyme, baby animals, adorable animations, and pastel colors.

Strategically, Kersey points to a confluence of core factors marketing and strategic communication:

- Japan is homogenous, with little ethnic diversity.

- Japan is nationalistic. Those folks buy Japanese.

- Japanese consumers are suspicious. You need to build and sustain credibility to sell a product.

---

[266] Marc Bain, "The simple mantra that helped Levi's turn its business around," *qz.com*, May 1, 2018: https://qz.com/work/1265943/levis-turned-around-its-business-by-following-a-simple-mantra/

[267] Jim Kersey, "Five Timeless Japanese Advertising Style Tips for the Uninitiated," *Humble Bunny:* https://www.humblebunny.com/5-japanese-advertising-style-tips/

- Japanese are selective buyers and want information about products.

- An aging population means older consumers have the greatest purchasing power. Ads need to appeal to that group, not just Gen Z.

- Japanese appreciate ancient and modern aesthetics.

- Japanese are image-conscious, and brands play a significant role in personal identity.

That might make you think Japanese ads are stodgy. Japanese advertising can be *weird*. You have to *see* them to appreciate that. The weirdness is expressed in the Japanese notion of *Kawaii*. Japan's largest ad firm, Dentsu Inc., created a video promoting Miso soup for Marukome. It defies description. Here's the YouTube link: https://www.youtube.com/watch?v=VvUzDn5usVw&t=4s.

Average Americans will swear the video was created by ad guys who mixed LSD and Cocaine with Jack Daniels. This video is expensive and complex, but you could create one that is simple and interesting on a laptop and disseminate it on social media and through posters. The lesson is that, as the song goes, there are different strokes for different folks. All this goes back to what we discussed above. Strategic communication and marketing need to key into specific cultural values and tastes.

Discussion Questions

1. Do you agree that "ends, ways, and means" is an adequate description of the notion of strategy? If not, how would you adapt or reformulate the notion?

2. How do you distinguish "grand strategy" from other forms of strategy?

3. What differences do you discern between China's approach to strategy and that of Western nations? The Chinese view strategy as a confrontational notion. Do you agree or disagree, and why?

4. What are you doing to prepare yourself to capitalize on opportunities that open up, as Bill Gates and Steve Jobs did with computers, so that when the window of opportunity opens, they can be the first to move aggressively to capitalize on opportunity?

5. Seth Godin argues that making consumers feel good about their purchases is pivotal. Others say Godin is too narrow in his focus. What is your view?

6. Do you agree with Jim Stengel that successful companies stand for improving lives? What are you doing to ensure that your organization or company improves lives?

7. Do you agree or disagree that perceptions of status motivate? How does this notion fit into your idea for marketing or strategic communication?

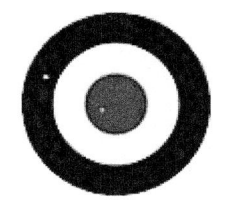

CHAPTER SIX

CRITICAL ELEMENTS OF A STRATEGIC COMMUNICATION PLAN

In the preceding chapter, we took a look at the notion of strategy. Now let's identify elements of a strategic communication plan. These apply to any size project, campaign, or company.

1. **Write it down.**

The celebrated Prussian military strategist and military leader Helmuth von Moltke, who led Prussia's army in the 19th century, stated that no battle plan ever survives contact with the enemy.[268] Dwight Eisenhower put it more practically: "In preparing for battle, I have always found that plans are useless, but planning is indispensable."[269] Warfare is unpredictable. In his epic treatise, On War,

---

[268] One wag quipped that "No business plan survives first contact with the customer." See: Sean Newman Maroni, "No battle plan survives contact with the enemy," *blog.seannewmanmaroni.com*, January 10, 2015: https://blog.seannewmanmaroni.com/no-battle-plan-survives-first-contact-with-the-enemy-966df69b24b9

[269] Moltke's comment comes from his essay, "Ueber Strategie," or "On Strategy," written in 1871 as part of *Militarische Werke (Military Works)*. See also: Moltke on the Art of War (New York: Ballantine Books)(downloaded online)(ed. Daniel J. Hughes; trans. By D.J. Hugh and Harry Bell).

Count Carl von Clausewitz declared that warfare entails random and unpredictable events within a conflict that create frictions.[270]

Lt. Gen. (Ret) Frank Kearney had a distinguished career that included serving as the Deputy Combatant Commander for the U.S. SPECIAL OPERATIONS COMMAND and planning the opening campaigns of OPERATION IRAQI FREEDOM in Iraq and OPERATION ENDURING FREEDOM in Afghanistan. Today he advises large corporations. Kearney argues that both military leaders and executives need to put a strategic plan in writing and deal with frictions that arise in both their worlds. He told me one of the most important things about strategic planning:

> "If it's just in your head, it's not a strategic plan. You have to write down the strategic plan, and you need a process for developing one. The military thinks in terms of ends, ways, and means, but ends are always moving. In my experience, a problem companies confront is that too many of them don't prepare to compete in the marketplace. They chase shiny objects. Writing down a strategic plan provides a roadmap for moving into the future."

As Dwight Eisenhower wisely stated, 'what counts is planning, not the plan.'"[271]

I first met Lt. Gen. (Ret) Dell Dailey at USSOCOM, which I advised and where he held the critical position in dealing with counterterrorism. Dell also served as Director for the Center of Special Operations for the US SPECIAL OPERATIONS COMMAND. Later, he would become an Ambassador and serve as the State Department's lead on counterterrorism. He's been a great source of wisdom to me over the years.

Dailey reflects Kearney's views on the need to write down a strategic plan. "You need a clear path to success. You don't want to lock it in concrete. But there are times when you step off to the side and analyze what you've accomplished. You ask if it's consistent with your plan, and does the plan give you the end-state you wanted? The military does this routinely. I advise fourteen companies, and we impose the same discipline, to examine whether we've met our monthly,

---

[270] Carl von Clausewitz, <u>On War</u>. (Kindle Edition; trans. By Col. J.J. Graham) Kindle Loc. 1285/4381.
[271] Interview with Lt. Gen. (Ret) Frank Kearney, April 13, 2021.

quarterly, and yearly financial and sales goals. A written plan lets you look at the far end of what you want to do. It's a little easier in the corporate world, where goals tend to focus a lot on financials. Still, the ability to make adjustments is the difference between success and failure in both the military and corporate worlds."[272]

Kearney cites a defense company – it'll go unnamed here – to illustrate the point.

> "They had no strategic plan. They were increasing revenues but losing money because the CEO thought revenues were the right measure of success. He was dead wrong. Companies are in business to earn profits, and profits define the bottom line. The company recruited a new CEO. He instituted a planning process that defined a vision and corporate identity. Planning identified core strengths, set priorities based on an alternative futures analysis, focused on the right market niches for profitable growth. The company invested in infrastructure and talent to achieve a solid strategic end-state. A clear, five-year strategic plan paved the road ahead. Without that, the company would flop around like a fish, sucking for air, until it died. That leadership turned the company around, and its prospects today are brighter – and more profitable – than ever."[273]

He adds: "Plans should orient themselves on goals and objectives. What do you want to achieve? The plan ought to articulate those and do so in measurable terms to determine whether you're achieving them. That goes for whether the goals are financial, developing a workforce, or changing the corporate culture. We do that in the military, and it's a strength of military planning."[274]

Kearney cites a national security example to illustrate what a clear vision can produce. President Ronald Reagan's success in helping to bring down the Soviet Union was a "cost imposition strategy. He devoted considerable funds to build up the military, with an outcome to put them out of business by bankrupting

---

[272] Zoom Interview with Lt. Gen (Ret) Dell Dailey, April 1, 2021.
[273] Id.
[274] Id.

them. Star Wars struck critics as fanciful, but it had a good strategic goal: drive home to President Mikhail Gorbachev that the Soviets' rigid socialist system could never keep pace with our free enterprise's ability to leap ahead technologically. Gorbachev came to grips with the grim reality of that, and it shaped his strategic thinking and helped lead to the downfall of the Soviet state."[275]

The commercial world uses creative briefs to express strategic communication plans.

Generally, these describe the company and its mission. They define a project and its objectives, target audiences and ethnographic research, the competition, the brand image, strategy, plans and operations, story, narrative, themes, and messages geared to target audiences, deliverables, the timeline, and a budget. It lists vital stakeholders. Here's an example of one for Proctor & Gamble's detergent company, Tide: https://ccfyock.files.wordpress.com/2015/05/tide-creative-brief.pdf

Companies seem to adhere to creative briefs more closely than the military does to its planning. That's no surprise. Battles often feature rapid shifts in ground realities. The military employs detailed written communication plans. But instead of expressing creative messaging, they focus on strategy, operations, and tactics.

Being agile, flexible, and adaptable applies to commercial and military worlds. Markets change. Competition creates new dynamics as products or services compete in shifting marketplaces. While Nike had established itself as the market leader in the U.S., in Europe, the traditional leader for sneakers was Adidas. Today, Nike has passed Adidas and now ranks behind the leader, Christian Dior/LVMH,[276] for global sales.

Nike's challenge forced Adidas to rethink its positioning strategy. Led by resourceful management, Adidas' marketing strategy[277] is innovative and targeted.[278] It collaborates with sports stars like Pharrell Williams. It has made a bold appeal to younger people for whom environmental issues are essential. By

---

[275] Id.
[276] D. Tighe, "Adidas, Nike & Puma Revenue comparison 2006-2020," July 26, 2021: https://www.statista.com/statistics/269599/net-sales-of-adidas-and-puma-worldwide/
[277] "Marketing Strategy of Adidas," *heartofcodes.com*, July 28, 2019: http://heartofcodes.com/marketing-strategy-of-adidas-adidas-target-market/
[278] Seb Joseph, "Adidas unveils new global brand strategy," *Marketingweek.com*, February 11, 2013: https://www.marketingweek.com/adidas-unveils-new-global-brand-strategy/

2024 it will use only recycled plastics in all its shoes and clothing to fulfill a vision to get rid of virgin polyester overall by then. Adidas believes that will impact the fashion industry. It limits the availability of two flagship sneakers, the "Stan Smith" and "Superstar" sneakers. It uploads thousands of promotional videos onto social media channels like Facebook and YouTube. Twitter connects it to fans and followers.[279]

Unable to devote as significant a share as Nike of its smaller revenues to communication, Adidas CEO Kasper Rorsted forged an unconventional targeting strategy. One strategic decision you face with fewer resources is whether to spread resources everywhere or focus them on smaller audiences. Rorsted focused Adidas on younger people, aged 20-29, and geographically, on six major cities: Shanghai, New York, London, Paris, Tokyo, and Los Angeles.[280] It broke ground in striking a deal with Stonewall FC, a British non-league team in the Middlesex County Football League Premier Division. This is the league's 11th tier. A distinctive point that reveals a powerful message about the company's vision and values, Stonewall FC consists of members of the LGBTQI+ community. Stonewall players may not be celebrities, but the record its talented players have amassed speaks for itself. The team has garnered 20 international trophies.

Journalist Matt Barker praises the collaboration. It capitalizes on the team's strong identity and vibrant social presence. It provides a robust platform as the team "looks to combat homophobia and drive real change within the game from the grassroots up."[281] Equally, he observes that Adidas shows off its commitment to LGBTQ issues and gains narrative opportunities from the playing staff to the supporters.

I like its ads for "Change is a Team Sport." You can see some of the ads that define this campaign through links in the footnotes.[282] They appeal adroitly to their target demographic. I don't find them as inspirational as Nike's, which cut

---

[279] Id.
[280] "Sporting Goods Manufacturer Adidas Focuses its Marketing on Six Major Cities," *ISPO.com*, August 17, 2017: https://www.ispo.com/en/companies/id_79710992/new-marketing-strategy-adidas-is-focusing-on-chosen-cities.html
[281] Matt Barker, "Adidas's partnership with Stonewall FC could be a game changer," supra.
[282] https://www.youtube.com/watch?v=DpR50O1nGNs;
https://www.youtube.com/watch?v=qW5rYf-BHYc;
https://www.youtube.com/watch?v=lIPb46ARQhQ; and
https://www.youtube.com/watch?v=MRflp74uUOw

to the heart of personal identity more urgently, but the Adidas strategy has proven successful.

Never mind that Nike and Adidas are global brands. The precepts of having a written strategic communication plan apply to every company.

2.   Oriented towards winning and inspiring.

General George S. Patton reputedly declared:

> "America loves a winner and will not tolerate a loser."[283]

NFL Green Bay Packer's coach Vince Lombardi put it this way:

> "Winning is not a sometime thing; it's an all-time thing. You don't win once in a while, and you don't do things right once in a while; you do them all the time. Winning is a habit. Unfortunately, so is losing."[284]

Patton's view was not new in military history. Again, the military thinks in terms of strategy, plans, operations, tactics, and metrics. The interplay between these notions gives rise to Operational Art.

I worked closely for years with Colonel Al Bynum (USAF-RET). He served in the Pentagon as a Special Adviser to the Director of the Joint Staff for Plans & Policy and advised the Commander of the US STRATEGIC COMMAND there. He feels Patton got it right. In his view, plans "should be oriented towards winning – and by that, I mean achieving defined goals and objectives. It's vital to understand what that means in the context of each strategic situation."[285]

Julius Caesar and Scipio Africanus stand out in the ancient world.[286] Relatively unknown outside of historians and military professionals, Scipio was the one

---

[283] "Quotes," GeneralPatton.com, accessed 5 May 2018, II-3:
https://www.jcs.mil/Portals/36/Documents/Doctrine/pubs/jp3_0ch1.pdf?ver=2018-11-27-160457-910
JP 3-0 is the keystone document in the joint operations series and is a companion to joint doctrine's capstone, JP 1, *Doctrine for the Armed Forces of the United States.*
[284] https://www.brainyquote.com/quotes/vince_lombardi_125237.
[285] Zoom interview with Colonel Alvin Bynum, March 29, 2021.
[286] See: James P. Farwell, Persuasion and Power, supra; Simon Elliott, Julius Caesar: Rome's Greatest Warlord (Casemate Publishers, 2019)(Kindle Ed.) and B.H. Liddell Hart, Scipio Africanus: Greater than Napoleon, (London: BNpublishing, 2018).

Roman general who met Hannibal on a level playing field and defeated him. Arguably he was Rome's most gifted general.

In the American Revolutionary War, only one general, George, Earl of Cornwallis, merits praise as both a strategist and tactician. His story is worth recounting. Because he capitulated at Yorktown in the face of overwhelming American and French forces, Americans often grow up thinking he was a second-string player. Although historian John Ferling argues that Cornwallis could have broken out of the cordon he found himself in,[287] and his superior, General Sir Henry Clinton criticized him, Cornwallis was an outstanding commander. His Virginia campaign near the end of the war was a masterpiece. Like Steve Jobs and Michael Dublin, imaginative strategy marked Cornwallis. He had a firm grasp of what was actionable.

Cornwall commanded a mobile army, kept on the move, and threw the Colonials off balance. He destroyed sanctuaries where rebels could rally or stockpile arms. His hardened, well-trained professionals were equally adept at traditional European tactics and open-order woodland skirmishing that rebel irregulars favored. He told civilian "loyalists," who had a habit of getting in the way, to stand down. Important to his thinking, about 40% of Virginia's population were slaves.

He came up with the inspired idea of offering liberty to slaves who joined his forces. Significant numbers accepted the offer. Indeed, of the 500,000 Blacks in the thirteen colonies, 20% of them joined the King's troops in a bid for freedom. The gambit proved chaotic. But had Cornwallis superior, Clinton, permitted him to forge the slaves into a cohesive offensive force, Cornwallis might have tipped the balance in Virginia and perhaps the entire war in Britain's favor. Happily for America, Clinton was jealous of his subordinate. In mid-1781, he ordered Cornwallis to retreat to the coast, leading to the Yorktown surrender.[288]

Cornwallis's experience offers lessons. He grasped the strategic realities on the ground. He saw opportunities to leverage action. He articulated a compelling message. He knew that disruptive tactics would establish credibility and how to execute them. He was brave and bold. He seized control of the narrative and combined action, symbols, and words.

---

[287] See: John Ferling, Winning Independence, (London: Bloomsbury, 2021).
[288] Gregory J.W. Urwin, "When Freedom Wore a Red Coat: How Cornwallis' 1781 Virginia Campaign Threatened the Revolution in Virginia," in The U.S. Army and Irregular Warfare, 1775-2007: Selected Papers from the 2007 Conference of Army Historians (Ed. Richard G. Davis), (Washington: Center of Military History, United States Army 2008).

During the U.S. Civil War, President Abraham Lincoln showed himself to be a wily strategist. Only Lincoln, Ulysses Grant, and William Sherman proved great grand strategists and tacticians. Luminaries like Robert E. Lee, Philip Sheridan, Nathan Bedford Forrest, and Stonewall Jackson[289] were ferocious tacticians but not great strategists. During World War II, Generals George Patton, Bernard Montgomery, Heinz Guderian and Erwin Rommel achieved great fame. These were all tactical generals, although of course they forged strategy at the tactical level.

Relevant is that their *actions* constituted strategic communication. Guderian got lucky in ignoring orders from his higher-ups in pressing forward in beleaguered France in 1940, but he had the guts to push over any obstacle. His *blitzkrieg* tactics intimidated the French into suing for an armistice even though France's formidable navy and three-quarters of its armed forces, much of it based outside of Europe, remained intact. A winning attitude inspires everyone. The lesson these leaders teach is, play to win or don't play.

Executives, take note. Sales projections and goals, strategic positioning, and winning support from internal and external stakeholders can bolster a company's brand. And, strengthening culture can define winning.

Lee Iacocca turned Chrysler around through forceful leadership and a clear vision. He possessed strong leadership traits:[290] curiosity, creativity, thinking outside the box, an ability to communicate, the character to know the difference between right and wrong, and the courage to do the right thing.

Leaders display passion for getting things done. Leaders need charisma: a magical quality that inspires people to follow you. Leaders must be competent – a person who gets results. Leaders have common sense. Iacocca declared: "If you don't know the difference between a dip of horsesh**t and a dip of vanilla ice cream, you're never going to make it. That's just common sense. Some people call it savvy."

---

[289] The Confederate generals have today come under fire for opposing the U.S. and fighting to save slavery. That's a different discussion and does not affect assessments of them as military strategists or tacticians, any more than it affects purely military assessments of Rommel and other German commanders in World War II.

[290] Lee Iacocca, "Where have all the leaders gone?" November 27, 2007: https://www.youtube.com/watch?v=0JrpewVQMi0

Maj. Gen. (Ret) John Davis offers insight into distinguishing leadership from management:

> "Leadership is about inspiring, helping, and guiding people. It can be direct or indirect. It deals directly with people, not issues. The ability to combine true leadership with intelligent, effective management is a rare skill. It's not about technology. Leadership demands human interaction. That's how you inspire extra effort, devotion, and purpose. This applies equally to the military and corporate worlds. The best leaders are more like gardeners than kings. You till the soil, plant the seeds, provide the water and fertilizer, get rid of the weeds, and allow the process to happen. You don't smother it with micromanagement."[291]

Davis credits General (Ret) Stanley McChrystal with influencing his thinking. Davis says that management is about managing issues: "While leadership is art, there's a more scientific approach in management. In both cases,

> "you have to have a strong sense of values, of vision, and you have to lead. You need an intense personal will. Secretary of Defense Bob Gates told me that a good leader could distinguish between antelopes and chipmunks. You don't want to waste energy chasing down chipmunks. You go for what's important, and you need to distinguish between the two."[292]

Davis' views on values-based leadership reinforce Jim Stengel. As noted above, Stengel is renowned for assembling his list of the "Top-50" companies in America. This is a study of 50,000 brands from which the best-performing companies were grouped into a "Top 50" cluster. He focuses on winning and success. Partly that's about strategic communication. But Stengel stresses a company's values. He argues that growth companies aren't in it for the money –

---

[291] Zoom Interview with Maj. Gen. (Ret) John Davis, March 18, 2021.
[292] Id.

they're trying to change the world. **Improving the lives of people and places defines their way forward**.

His book, Grow: How Ideals Power Growth and Profit at the World's Greatest Companies[293] merits a close read. He argues that successful companies espouse a brand ideal rooted in a strong culture, from which all else in communication flows. Stengel defines strong company culture as essential for a business. Success requires telling a story that explains the higher-order benefit that a company brings to the world.

He argues that the ideal core beliefs of executives and employees must connect with the fundamental values of clients and customers[294] I agree with much of what Stengel says but disagree with some of it. He's right about having a brand ideal, and I like his examples.

While its founder, Jeff Bezos attracts enormous controversy, Amazon.com would claim that it exists to enable freedom of choice, exploration, and discovery. FedEx exists to deliver peace of mind to everyday transactions. Red Bull exists to energize the world. IBM exists to help build a smarter planet.

Stengel's view of leaders aligns with Iacocca's. The top ones make no bones about making a positive difference. I question his view that only five traits reflecting fundamental values define high-growth, but they provide valuable milestones. The five include eliciting joy, enabling connections, inspiring exploration, evoking pride, and impacting society. He argues that strategic communication arises from discovering a brand ideal that flows from those values and resonates with customers. Good strategic communication articulates the ideal honestly. Communication flows from culture and organization that aligns with ideals and that regularly tests whether companies measure up to the ideals.

His analysis of Pizza Hut and Jack Daniels is enlightening. Pizza Hut reinvigorated itself partly by showing off the morale and pride of its workforce. Proud of its heritage, Jack Daniels brings employees to Camp Jack in Lynchburg to immerse themselves in the company culture. Stengel feels that the unified appreciation of the whiskey maker's history reinforces the "authenticity" of the brand. I challenge his notion of authenticity; it's a loose term whose meaning is elusive. The definition of *authenticity* means "not false or imitation;" "true to

---

[293] Jim Stengel, "Grow: How Ideals Power Growth and Profit at the World's Greatest Companies," (New York: Crown Business, 2011).
[294] Id., 7-8.

one's own personal spirit or character;"[295] "the quality of being real or true."[296] Every company feels (or should feel) that way about itself.

Take Jack Daniels, a Tennessee whiskey and the top-selling American whiskey globally, which I started drinking in college. Stengel's view that it succeeds because it is "true to itself" is facile. Its loyal customers *may* feel that drinking it says something about their *status*: how people perceive who they are. Jack Daniels has a cachet. I drink it because I like it. Friends who are avid bourbon fans favor their own hierarchy of brands. Jack Daniels meets that taste for its patrons. Ascribing its success to a nebulous term like authenticity seems a stretch. For decades, Jack Daniels marketed one label. Today it markets 27. That renders making the case that its product has some special authenticity even more tenuous.

For those who like bourbon, the top executive in the industry is New Orleans native and wildly successful entrepreneur Bill Goldring. He advises that many different factors determine the characteristics of each bourbon. The top spirits writers in the world regularly rate his bourbons among the top five. With a smile on his face, he suggests that Buffalo Trace is arguably the best and that some bourbon aficionados believe Pappy van Winkles is the best. Goldring's company makes both of those[297].

The military thinks about this in assessing *credibility*. Credibility is about being believable, plausible, and convincing. Winning requires credible ideas, narratives, themes, and messages, from people, groups, organizations, movements, or nations that are credible.

In politics and military theaters of operation, one thinks about winning or desired end-states. Companies exist to earn a profit. The military acts to advance national security interests. Successful communication defines the choices that confront target audiences and drive a message that defines the stakes. Our military communication narratives are rooted in the idea that what we do benefits those affected.

Stengel calls on leaders to be clear about company ideals and to align people to them. He embraces collaboration, standards, innovations, getting the team right, training, and other factors. All admirable traits. What he neglects is the reality of the executive ego. Many executives talk big about collaboration and receiving honest input. In my experience, most of them hate being challenged. That people

---

[295] Merriam-Webster: https://www.merriam-webster.com/dictionary/authentic
[296] Cambridge Dictionary: https://dictionary.cambridge.org/us/dictionary/english/authenticity
[297] Author's interview with Bill Goldring, April 4, 2020.

avoid rocking the boat or taking risks, except in a highly structured program established for gathering input, compounds the challenge.

Effective leadership means standing up and speaking out. The military may be less adept than executives in encouraging risk-taking. General Stanley McChrystal and other top commanders welcome new ideas. They like being challenged. McChrystal's "team of teams" concept fosters horizontal networks that promote sharing ideas and information. The idea was not original – Ronald Reagan's team used it – but McChrystal elevated it to a new level. Today he leads a successful company that applies his concepts to the corporate world and government.[298]

During the Vietnam war, General Creighton Abrams earned a stellar reputation. Abrams articulated a "one war" strategy whose end-state was to help the Vietnamese achieve security.[299] Sadly, Abrams in Vietnam and McCrystal, when he assumed command in Afghanistan, lacked the political clout to persuade the civilian political leadership to buy into their ideas. But their fortitude and imagination stand out and offer a lesson for great leadership.

Stengel's criteria offer an idealized construct that, he argues, yields high growth. But consider his core mantra. These companies dedicate themselves to improving the lives of others. The more significant point is orienting yourself towards winning. Stengel's criteria make sense, but it's less clear to what extent in practice his Top 50 measure up to them or whether fulfilling them is really needed to achieve high growth.

3. Engage with stakeholders about the plan.

The military is strong on process. Once a plan is written down and distributed, commanders visit with operators to ensure their team understands "commander's intent," answer questions, and entertain suggestions. One reason General Wesley Clarke proved effective in Bosnia lay in his insistence on gathering input from lower-ranking members of his staff. He accepted suggestions from lower-ranking officers that contradicted the views of their superiors.[300]

Lt. Gen. (Ret) Frank Kearney advises:

---

[298] General Stanley McChrystal, Team of Teams, (New York: Portfolio, 2015).
[299] See: Maj. Thom Duffy Frohnhoefer, "General Creighton Abrams and the Operational Approach of Attrition in the Vietnam War," *School of Advanced Military Studies, United States Army Command and General Staff College*, 2013:
https://apps.dtic.mil/dtic/tr/fulltext/u2/a583871.pdf
[300] This comment is based on conversations that the author had with the late U.S. Army Colonel (Ret) Dan Devlin, who served in Bosnia with General Clarke.

> "Bring them in early, bring them in fast, get their opinions. People are afraid of change. They fear power centers that do planning and leave them out of the loop. The decision-making process is critical. Like flag officers, executives need to lay out the task and explain why a company is carrying it out. People need to understand the *why*. Bringing in stakeholders early lets them see how a plan advances their best interests. They'll fight you or support you, depending on how they believe your intended consequences affect them."[301]

Colonel Al Bynum agrees:

> "You have to consider their inputs seriously," he says. "You do not have to agree with them. But listening shows respect and lets you work your way through disagreements on the front end. I prefer face-to-face meetings at the outset because you have a better chance to establish rapport and personalize engagement and connections. You get a better feel for where folks are. Later, video conferences or phone calls can work well. That's the lesson I learned in the military that I took to industry. Generals can issue orders. Executives work in a more collaborative environment. You want people to do something not because you ask. You want them to use initiative to achieve even more than they are asked."[302]

Petraeus' approach applies to companies. Executives need to foster a culture that achieves a clear understanding of their strategic situation, the obstacles they confront, and a clear vision that defines objectives. They need leadership that motivates people to support it.

---

[301] Interview with Lt. Gen. (Ret) Frank Kearney, April 13, 2021.
[302] Zoom interview with Colonel Al Bynum, supra.

IBM illustrates the lesson. Founded in 1911 as Computer Tabulating Recording, IBM grew from a producer of meat slicers and census tabulators to a $100 billion business whose "product is nearly impossible to articulate."[303] In 1924 it became IBM, with five business units: Financing, Systems and Technology, Technology Services, Business Services, and Software. It has considerably evolved through the years. As vice president for corporate marketing John Kennedy stated:

> "The enduring idea that is the essence of IBM has meant different things at different points in our history. At one point, that meant automating the office. At another point, it meant helping put a man on the moon in the Apollo space program. Today it means all the systems that keep the world working in health care, transportation, the power grid, the infrastructures within industries. We have to talk with many audiences about these things, and what 'building a smarter planet' does is it enables us to engage all these audiences at the level of deeply held beliefs about the world. The conversations we have with our customers, for example, start with a shared way of looking at the world, a common belief in how technology can improve the world."[304]

Though far-sighted, IBM is not perfect. It failed to adapt to the PC revolution. In the 1990's IBM – known as "Big Blue" – faced $5 billion in losses and a lack of focus or direction. CEO Louis Gerstner decided IBM needed to reimagine its product. His leadership focused on IT and consulting and shifted IBM to a "cognitive solutions and cloud platform company." Its revival offers a model of excellence. Gerstner ensured persistent, granular engagement between executives and employees. IBM launched an online forum for employees to update company values. As military leaders like Petraeus and McChrystal did, IBM made sure employees understood the company's mission, vision, and values.[305]

---

[303] Eric Tsytslyin, "Brand IBM: Strategy, Rediscovery, and Growth," *brandingstrategyinsider.com*, June 20, 2012: https://www.brandingstrategyinsider.com/brand-ibm-strategy-rediscovery-and-growth/#.XhefRRdKhBw

[304] Id.

[305] Ryan Rieches, "IBM: How employees bring 'smarter planet' positioning to real-world engagement," *Branding Business,* February 20, 2014:

About 350,000 IBM employees collaborated on an internal platform to update Human Relations. IBM logged in wish lists and shared everything with employees, who voted on what should change. Employees got feedback, leadership behavior changed, managers were held accountable. Every year, 98% of employees visit the learning platform. Learning is central to IBM's culture.[306] IBM's strategy defined stakeholders broadly. Michele Grieshaber, Vice President of Demand Programs at IBM North America, has stated that "we serve forward-thinking clients, employees, investors, and communities, and invest in all of those stakeholders to create the experience we want to deliver for our brand."[307]

Dave Patterson points to Don Kozlowski, the C-17 cargo aircraft program manager at McDonnell Douglas for a similar lesson. Kozlowski's skill lay

> "...in his ability to use strategic communication to reach out across the company and to make certain that everybody who laid hands on an airplane in production, or any aspect of the manufacturing, understood that they were important to key decisions, starting with safety. Everybody could identify with safety. Everybody said immediately, oh, yeah – right! He got everybody on board with him from the first, then moved on to other items. His approach set up the C-17 program as a model for the Department of Defense."[308]

---

https://www.brandingbusiness.com/insights/ibm-how-employees-bring-smarter-planet-positioning-to-real-world-engagement/

[306] Riia O'Donnell, "From buzzkill to benefit: How IBM rebranded its HR department," *hrdrive.com,* April 1, 2019:

https://www.hrdive.com/news/from-buzzkill-to-benefit-how-ibm-rebranded-its-hr-department/551162/

[307] Ryan Rieches, "IBM: How employees bring 'smarter planet' positioning to real-world engagement," supra.

[308] Interview with J. David Patterson, April 7, 2021.

Virgil Scudder, one of the nation's top corporate communication counselors whose client base consists of Fortune 100 CEOs also agrees. Scudder declares:

> "When the people in charge, especially the CEO, but also key project executives, engage face-to-face, or otherwise connect individually with employees, it makes an impact. It motivates people to do their best. It inspires new ideas. A key part of this is *listening* and *hearing*. Executives who spend more time listening and hearing, and less time talking will inspire their employees, many of whom at most companies feel abused, underpaid, and neglected. Calling them *associates* or *teammates* is useless unless management backs that up with explicit appreciation."[309]

Maj. Gen. (Ret) James "Spider" Marks believes that

> "if you're an effective, serious listener, you are encouraging others to participate. You want a broad range of opinions. If I was the only voice being heard, I'd guarantee one outcome, and that can produce failure. Eliciting other views, especially contrarian views that tell me where I may be wrong, acknowledging vulnerabilities, and discerning what others will contribute to a solution, always produces a better result."[310]

Spider's warm, outgoing personality complements a strong intellect. It's not surprising his peers hold him in such high esteem.

Retired United Kingdom Colonel Stephen Padgett's experience – sharpened as commander of British forces in Afghanistan – affirms the importance of personal contact with an executive's team members. Stephen and I were paired together for several years at the US STRATEGIC COMMAND, and his analysis of problems always merits a close hearing.

---

[309] Interview with Virgil Scudder, May 3, 2021.
[310] Interview with Maj. Gen. (Ret) James Marks, May 7, 2021.

> "You overcome obstacles by connecting with people you think are going to help you find a solution. You need their insights, experiences, and perspectives that differ from yours. That helps you to encourage the most talented ones to stretch themselves beyond their comfort zone. It inspires top performance up and down the line. I depend on face-to-face engagements, but I also send notes, emails and meet regularly with my team. We talk about things as a collective to ensure people feel they've had the opportunity to express their views. Clients pay money for services that satisfy their requirements, and they expect you to deliver at a high level."[311]

The lesson the military leaders and executives teach is to keep an open mind, gather all the information you can as early as possible, and inspire people to follow rather than securing compliance by pulling rank. Before you sell customers on your ideas, sell your own people.

General David Petraeus teaches a related lesson. He earned praise for his ability to devise and execute strategies, operations, and tactics by engaging with a broad swathe of his forces. People understood his intent as a Commander, and he had a clear view as to what he expected. Petraeus teaches the lesson that developing a clear vision, then making certain your team understands it and helps to fulfill it is key.

President John F. Kennedy famously bypassed principals and engaged directly with desk officers to solicit their opinions and recommendations. It annoyed higher-ups, but JFK understood that getting the facts from people on the front lines cut through red tape and got him the most accurate information possible. The lesson JFK's experience teaches is that higher-ups may or may not have all the facts. Their views color what they pass on from subordinates. If you want to get informed, talk to people up and down the ladder.

As Speaker of the United States House of Representatives, Newt Gingrich consciously solicited opinions from everyday people. Everywhere Newt went, from company offices, a café, to a manufacturing plant, he sought grassroots feedback. The information he gathered shaped his perspectives, and that helped

---

[311] Interview with Col. (Ret) Stephen Padgett, March 22, 2021.

enable him to strike historic deals with President Bill Clinton to reform welfare and balance the budget. The lesson that Newt espouses is that you can get good ideas from outsiders, not just experts or internal staff. Newt has always depended on making himself widely informed.

Okay, outside views matter. Let's talk about the inside team. Lt. Gen. (Ret) Dell Dailey recommends assembling a close team of perhaps three to seven company leaders who cover intelligence/information, personnel, logistics and finances, cyber, and communication to review plans. He advises: "You do a desktop rehearsal to see how things work in. Then as needed, you broaden the group. They need to be individuals with impeccable moral, legal, and ethical standards who are open to ideas. Get everybody on the same page, sharing the same vision and goals, and you move the organization forward. That applies to flag officers and executives."[312] Dailey teaches that you need a team to get things done – but keep it small enough to be cohesive and trust the judgment and integrity of its members.

Taking those action steps paves the way for collaboration.

As former Defense Under Secretary for Policy and today CEO of Momentus John Rood puts it:

> "You aim to achieve collaboration. Whether in the military or the boardroom, you want to hear ideas from everyone involved in a project or operation. You receive that feedback better through the give-and-take of personal discussion when you're sitting across from other people. Video-conferencing gives focus, but discussion is sequential and doesn't produce the same level of collaboration. The goal is getting the best results by inspiring teamwork, and that's about leadership."[313]

---

[312] Zoom Interview with Dell Daily, supra.
[313] Interview with Former Under Secretary of Defense (Policy) John Rood, April 15, 2021.

Vogue editor Ana Wintour adds nuance to the notion of collaboration. She says:

> "You need someone who can push you, not somebody's who pulling you back," she declares in her video Master Class on learning to be a boss.[314] "You need to empower those around you... you need to surround yourself with a team whose opinions you can trust, who are not in any way frightened of disagreeing with you, and you have to listen."[315]

Her buy-ins are about developing a creative vision, recognizing talent, investing in your team, making tough decisions, and using that to evolve a brand and find your voice.

Here is another nuance: how do you secure buy-in from your stakeholders? The average business decision includes 5-6 internal stakeholders.[316] Different company project teams may think differently. Find out what works. Bonuses or performance benchmarks? Work-life balance? Opportunities for career growth? Even the smallest company needs to link the project to company goals, along with stakeholder values and motivations. Transparency inspires team members to be honest with one another. Give credit where it's due. Be consistent in reaffirming goals and communicating progress as a project is executed. Provide positive feedback after the project ends.[317]

What about community projects? Companies need to engage community stakeholders affected by decisions early and intensively. Twin Metals Minnesota wanted to develop a large underground copper mine near a popular outdoor

---

[314] Ana Wintour, "MasterClass: Learn How to be a Boss:" https://www.masterclass.com/classes/anna-wintour-teaches-creativity-and-leadership?utm_source=Paid&utm_medium=AdWords&utm_campaign=AWi&utm_content=Brand-{keyword}-US_EM&utm_term=Aq-Prospecting&gclid=Cj0KCQjwmdzzBRC7ARIsANdqRRk_Xexiz98UCObxN_Ltv0BasX7yhGfQrvOWptwvQDto2XO-UJZKC-IaAjI_EALw_wcB

[315] Id.

[316] Freddie Ossberg, "How to Guarantee Internal Buy-In for Your Big Content Projects," *Content Marketing Institute*, July 13, 2015: https://contentmarketinginstitute.com/2015/07/buyin-content-projects/.

[317] Moira Alexander, "How to increase buy-in from project stakeholders," *Techrepublic.com*, April 12, 2018: https://www.techrepublic.com/article/6-ways-to-increase-buy-in-from-project-stakeholders/

recreation area. Its challenge: assure the public that it could mine in a socially and environmentally responsible way. Moving early, supported by global nonprofit organization BSR, Twin Metals Minnesota conducted extensive interviews with local, state, and federal officials, community leaders, and NGOs. It incorporated the input and recommendations into their planning. The process revealed innovative opportunities for partnerships and training for technical mining jobs and locally sourcing materials.[318]

4.   Be Realistic.

Be realistic. Assess the strategic situation objectively. Lack of a cohesive strategy that aligned with the strategic realities on the ground plagued our efforts in Afghanistan.[319] Afghans have historically favored decentralized government. Power has emanated from tribes, clans, villages, and ethnic groups. Neither the U.S. nor its coalition partners developed a realistic grasp of Afghan political dynamics, or strategic vision and plan.

The Coalition was never going to succeed while placing its bet on a corrupt federal system that lacked legitimacy and proved unable to provide security at the local level. No wonder the Taliban prevailed. Complicating matters, the Biden administration lacked a smart, realistic plan to evacuate both U.S. citizens and 250,000 Afghans who had worked with the U.S. or its allies. People can debate the merits of getting out. But the August 2021 withdrawal was a debacle.

Lack of a realistic plan that defined success doomed the 2011 NATO intervention in Libya. NATO intervened, invoking the doctrine of the Responsibility to Protect civilians in eastern Libya. Confusion followed. Hillary Clinton persuaded Russia to refrain from vetoing a United Nations Security Council Resolution by promising that the intervention would not topple the Libyan dictator. Vladimir Putin believes that she lied, a view that appears to have strongly motivated his meddling in the 2016 Presidential elections to secure payback. After rebels murdered Gaddafi, she proclaimed, "we came, we saw, he died." Today Libya is entangled in civil war. That is what happens when armed conflict is instigated without a realistic plan to bring that conflict to a peaceful close.

---

[318] "Twin Metals Minnesota: Using Early Stakeholder Engagement to Improve Strategy," *BSR.org*, October 22, 2012: https://www.bsr.org/en/our-insights/case-study-view/twin-metals-minnesota-using-early-stakeholder-engagement

[319] See Craig Whitlock, The Afghanistan Papers: A Secret History of the War, (New York: Simon & Schuster, 2021); the reports of the Special Inspect General for Afghanistan Reconstruction, accessible on Google; and my interactions with numerous military who served in the Afghanistan war.

How does the military try to ensure realism in planning? One approach is wargaming. Some companies call the process red teaming. Frank Kearney again:

> "We game against the desired end-state. You play off against alternative outcomes and make contingency plans. You ask – and this applies to the corporate world – what changes are needed to succeed or stay competitive. Always remember: campaign plans are a series of decision points. The successful plans define a series of orderly decisions that move you from one phase to the next. These examine how one decision affects other parts of the plan, resources, priorities, and understanding what information is required to make prudent decisions along the way. The process enables, and requires, you to dig deep."[320]

U.S. Marines Colonel (Ret) Paul Huxhold led engagement for the J5 Strategy, Plans & Policy Directorate at the U.S. SPECIAL OPERATIONS COMMAND. Upon retirement, he became COO of a defense contractor. He also praises wargaming. Ideally, he says,

> "it pays to assemble a dedicated group of individuals who have the knowledge and experience to understand an adversary or a business competitor. These folks can think like the opposition and provide crucial insights into what to expect and how they will react to your initiatives. In the military, you draw on academics, military, intelligence, and diplomatic experts. In the corporate world, you make a judgment as to who is likely to understand the marketplace, the relevance of your marketing ideas, and the resilience of the competition. The process keeps your planning informed and realistic."[321]

For executives, gaming outcomes require measuring plans against possible alternative outcomes in the market. Stephen Padgett feels that the key to keeping

---

[320] Id.
[321] Interview with Colonel (Ret) Paul Huxhold, April 7, 2021.

plans realistic and achievable lies in understanding the environment in which a plan is forged and properly assessing the talent that executes the plan.

> "You have to know who you're dealing with, where you're going, and the dynamics that drive a situation. Whether in industry or the military, you need to do careful target audience analysis. You need to make certain you deliver on every promise made, or you lack credibility and won't attain influence. It's vital not to let short-term effects force action. You have to place things in perspective and think in both the short and longer-term."[322]

General (Ret) Sir Richard Shirreff's strategic consulting firm uses the term "business gaming," but the idea is the same as red-teaming.

> "They enable you to build a scenario derived from risks, and individuals play stakeholders, competitors, regulators, any party that may try to block or oppose a plan. You run through that business game, move by move, in sequence. The process enables you to identify your strengths and weaknesses, identify risks and opportunities and adjust strategic thinking to produce desired outcomes."[323]

Gaming lets you examine your narrative's strengths and weaknesses and measure how they stack up against competitors. From there, you can devise or affirm that you have a realistic, actionable plan. Plans that are confusing, unclear, too complicated, untimely, or impossible to carry out are self-defeating.

Startups won't necessarily know what is realistic. Lawrence Ingrassia's engaging book, <u>The Billion Dollar Brand Club</u>,[324] describes how thinly capitalized startups just put their heads down and charged ahead. They employed pluck, imagination, and innovative leadership to grow into billion-dollar brands – nicknamed "unicorns." His lead example focuses on Michael Dublin, the founder of Dollar Shave Club. Dublin understood that technology could level the playing field

---

[322] Interview with Colonel (Ret) Stephen Padgett, March 22, 2021.
[323] Interview with General (Ret) Sir Richard Shirreff, May 5, 2021.
[324] Lawrence Ingrassia, <u>Billion Dollar Brand Club</u> (New York: Henry Holt & Co., 2020), p. 4, 15-19.

because the Internet reduced or eliminated a company's need to carry a massive supply of goods.

Ingrassia's point is that Dollar Shave Club had an innovative *idea*, not an innovative product. I discussed Harry's Razors previously because I started using their blades when they first appeared. Ingrassia sets forth Dublin's similar but distinct strategy. Dollar Shave may not have had the best razor, but customers found it good enough. Ingrassia's analysis of direct marketing to consumers offers a playbook for entrepreneurs. Successes he cites include Quip electric toothbrushes, Glossier cosmetics, Allbirds and Rothy's shoes; Prose shampoo; and Madison Reed hair colors.

Dollar Shave teaches that even if you don't have the resources to conduct gaming or other forms of research that help ensure realistic plans, sometimes you have to trust your idea and the people you surround yourself with and take the plunge. That may not be ideal, but a lot of unicorn successes have done precisely that. They had a good idea, imagination, and they didn't take no for an answer. That's a great lesson!

Discussion Questions

1. Is your strategic plan specifically oriented towards winning? If so, in what ways?

2. Does your plan take a grand strategic view or are the plans and operations merely tactical?

3. In devising and presenting plans, are you providing leadership that inspires people to make the plan work because they have provided input into it, and *want* to make it work, or are they taking action merely because you issued orders? In other words, are you inspiring the team or pulling rank?

4. Is the plan rooted in your core values? Does your plan enable you to seize the moral high ground? Does success improve the lives of your customers or clients?

5. Does your strategy aim to elicit joy, impact society, evoke pride, enable connections, or inspire exploration?

6. Is your plan credible to customers and clients? What steps does it incorporate to ensure that you establish and sustain credibility?

7. Who are the stakeholders that your strategy or plan seeks to affect? What steps are you taking to engage with stakeholders and to secure their buy-in? Are you doing face-to-face engagements or other forms of engagement with them? How are you motivating them?

8. What steps are you taking to ensure that everyone on your team has a clear understanding of the challenges your strategy or plan seeks to overcome?

9. What steps are you taking to manage the expectations of your team and other stakeholders?

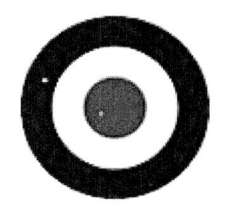

CHAPTER SEVEN

DEVELOPING YOUR STORY AND NARRATIVE

Integrated narrative, story, themes, and messages form the bedrock of strategic communication and information warfare. Humans make sense of the world through the stories they tell. Joseph Campbell, author of *The Hero's Journey: The Power of Myth,* summed it up when he said, "Man is a storytelling animal."

In his book, *Human Communication as Narration*, Walter R. Fisher has described how stories play out in our decisions. He makes four key assertions: 1) people are essentially storytellers; 2) we make decisions based on reasons that seem good to us and which vary depending on the situation, media, and genre; 3) history, biography, culture, and character determine what we consider good reasons; and 4) life is a set of stories from which we choose and constantly re-create our lives.[325]

Narrative, the telling of a story, has two components: *what* is told and *how* it is told. These components shape our understanding of the world, whether it's a scene in a movie, a passage in a novel, or news of current events.[326] Edward Branigan has defined it more academically as a "perceptual activity that

---

[325] Walter R. Fisher, Human Communication as Narration: Toward a Philosophy of Reason, Value and Action, (Columbia: University of South Carolina Press, 1983), Kindle Loc. 61/2523 – 68/2523.
[326] D.L. Bernardi, P.H. Cheong, C. Lundry, S. Ruston, Narrative Landmines (New Brunswick: Rutgers University Press, 2012), Kindle Loc. 332/2523.

organizes data into a special pattern which represents and explains experience."[327] And, as the authors of *Narrative Landmines* say, "It organizes events into a chain with a beginning, middle, and end. It provides a context for action. The stories that flow from narrative involve character, time, space, events and objectives placed in settings and recounted for rhetorical purposes."[328]

I find it amazing that so few people charged with forging a strategic communication plan think through what goes into one. Winning information strategy integrates narrative, story, themes, and message. Mostly, people think in terms of message. You need to think in four dimensions.

Story defines the context for action. People make sense of the world through story by describing events, action, setting, and characters. They talk about conflict resulting from character actions or event circumstances.[329] The allies invaded Normandy in 1944 to secure a foothold in France in order to defeat the Nazis. The preparations for this risky venture were extreme, but strong leadership from General Dwight Eisenhower and other leaders, good fortune, combined with excellent execution of a strategic plan, produced success. That's a story. Narrative makes sense of the information. It provides coherent meaning to what people have understood and explains the reason why actors take action. Events cause characters to react and produce conflict.

The Al Qaeda story in Iraq was that many centuries ago, Western infidels wanted to repress Islam and Muslims, conquer their land, and steal their treasure. So they mounted crusades to achieve that goal, and that led to many years of fighting in which Muslims managed to prevail.

Narrative explains why action is taken. It consists of interlocking stories that share story elements, cultural references, and a rhetorical desire to resolve a conflict by structuring audience expectations and interpretations. Narrative provides a framework for story.[330] We invaded Normandy to liberate France and Europe from Nazi repression. In Al Qaeda's narrative, infidels invaded Muslim land centuries ago to repress and pillage and now they're back, met by brave Muslims who are fighting back.

---

[327] Edward Branignan, Narrative Comprehension and Film (New York: Routledge, 1992), p. 3.
[328] D.L. Bernardi, P.H. Cheong, C. Lundry, S. Ruston, Narrative Landmines, supra, Kindle Loc. 332/2523.
[329] Id., Kindle Loc 219/2523. I'm drawing on this book because its four well-versed authors understand these concepts and write about them clearly.
[330] Id., Kindle Loc. 223, 229/2523.

Themes are not narratives. They define the cause or rationale for which action is taken. We invaded Normandy to defeat the evil Nazis. For Al Qaeda, their fight is about protecting Islam and Muslims from evil infidels.

Message is the exhortation to a cause that flows from the above three. The message to the French and Europe was: the Nazis are evil and must be defeated. Al Qaeda invoked a similar message: the infidels are evil and it is the duty of every good Muslim to defeat them.

Story and narrative can give rise to different themes and messages. Around the world, the story of COVID has given rise to competing themes and messages about vaccination. Whether or not you like Donald Trump, in 2016, his mantra of "Make America Great Again" was a coherent, resonant theme – as to their horror, Hillary Clinton's advisers belatedly recognized as they set about preparing her for the debates.[331] Even more horrifying to them, they realized that despite her disparaging Trump, she lacked a theme or message.

In 2020, Democrats had a simple theme and message: Trump is evil. Let's Throw the Rascal Out. It papered over mutually exclusive agendas from the diverse coalition that supported Biden. I thought Trump ran a disjointed campaign until the final ten days. Biden's admission in the final debate opposing the energy industry enabled Trump to attack Biden as a tool of socialists. The message struck a responsive chord. Trump still believes he won. Had the campaign gone on for another ten days, he might have been able to assert that without exciting much debate. He had Biden's number.

Emotional Intelligence

Military strategic communication is rooted in the view that story, narrative, theme, and message work best in appealing to the *emotional intelligence* of a target audience. There is no single formula for ensuring a compelling narrative. Still, one element, my close colleague U.S. Marine Colonel (Ret) Paul Huxhold argues, is maintaining the "integrity and consistency of who you are, what you're trying to accomplish. In the commercial world, it's about making brand identity believable and relatable."[332]

---

[331] Jonathan Allen and Amie Parnes, Inside Hillary Clinton's Doomed Campaign, (New York: Crown, 2017).
[332] Zoom Interview with Colonel Paul Huxhold, April 7, 2021.

Russia's intervention in the Syrian civil war offers a superb illustration of how Putin's regime articulated a believable story about its 2015 military intervention in Syria in support of Bashar Assad's regime. Putin turned a smoke-and-mirrors strategy into a narrative designed to create shock and awe. Ofer Fridman's take on the Russian intervention in Syria is worth hearing. Fridman explains,

> "Putin was clever and smart. He started with a call to arms in speaking to the UN General Assembly days before deploying Russian forces to Syria. Six months later, he declared 'mission accomplished.' It was less a military intervention than a well-staged theatrical production on a grand scale, staged with silver rockets, shiny hardware, brave soldiers and fast achievements aimed at influencing the behavior of target audiences. Putin carefully limited the airpower and boots-on-the-ground and used proxies from the mercenary Wagner Group to handle much of the combat."[333]

Putin felt that Russians would not tolerate a repeat of that nation's 1979 intervention in Afghanistan, which cost lives and squandered Russian credibility. He treated the intervention as a classic exercise in information warfare, "starring the Russian military as Assad's savior. There were two audiences: domestic and international. He assured Russians that action in Syria would prevent the civil war from coming to Russia, a narrative the Russians wanted to hear. Internationally, he built prestige and influence in the new, multi-polar world order. The strategy was well-conceived, executed, and proven successful."[334]

Let's revisit Seth Godin, the compelling advocate for his school of thought emphasizing the importance of appealing to customer *feelings.* In the corporate world, Godin argues that people buy compelling stories. I believe his notion that they mainly buy products that make them *feel* good is too facile. Perhaps someone who buys Puma Limited Edition sneakers does treat Puma itself rather than the sneakers as the product. He contends that while cheaper brands may be equally good, buying Puma makes a person *feel* better. Puma builds a narrative about being hip, belonging, and fashion.[335]

---

[333] Zoom Interview with Ofer Fridman, March 31, 2021.
[334] One notes that General (Ret) Richard Sheriff was one of only a small handful of four-star generals in the British army.
[335] Seth Godin, All Marketers are Liars (New York: Portfolio, 2009), p. 8-9.

I question his view that there is almost no connection between what is *there* and what we *believe*, from hospital cribs to soup to cars. He believes that Coke's message is rooted in themes of fun and happiness. Here again, that's too narrow. Coke is about shared experience and identity. Those traits are about the company's values and what it stands for. Godin argues that people shop at Whole Foods because it makes them feel good.[336] That's nonsense. People shop there because they like the quality of the food and the service. I suppose that makes them feel good, at least until they get to the cash register, an experience that can make you wish you had won the lottery.

He embraces the ideas of Bernadette Jiwa[337] who, like Tony Schwartz long ago, recognizes the importance of emotional resonance in successful narratives. Jiwa's criteria for good stories are those that connect purpose and vision to career and business, reinforce core values, make value-based decisions, attract customers who reflect their values, and keep people motivated. These apply to the military and politics. They appear less often in commercial marketing. That's not surprising. Companies sell products or services to earn profits.

The military confronts more complicated challenges. It treats narratives as a tool for subverting or defeating an adversary's will or their command and control while winning support from affected audiences or ensuring their neutrality. In that view, narrative is used to define the stakes. Strategic communication used to discredit and delegitimize Al Qaeda and ISIS and drives the narrative that we stand for freedom of speech, security, religious tolerance, democracy, prosperity, and hope, while terrorists offer repression, violence, fear, and poverty.

Seizing the Moral High Ground

Both the military and executives face similar challenges in seizing the moral high ground. In military operations, a strong narrative persuades an enemy that the cost of opposition exceeds the benefit of fighting, in order to weaken or destroy their will to fight. Seizing the moral high ground helps win support from foreign audiences or neutralizes hostility. The U.S. Army/Marine Corps Counterinsurgency Field Manual cautions that "Commanders must recognize and continually address that [taking the view that] 'the American way is best' bias is unhelpful." You must gear narrative to culture history, mores, values, priorities, structure, and dynamics.

---

[336] Id., p. 115.
[337] Bernadette Jiwa, Story Driven, (Perceptive Press, 2018).

When the U.S. Navy deployed its hospital ship, *Mercy*, to Indonesia to provide humanitarian aid in the wake of the tsunami, the U.S. carefully set the stage through press conferences with local and national media outlets, one-on-one interviews between host nation press and U.S. Navy medical professionals, along with events that established an "interlocking system of stories around the *Mercy* visit, emphasizing cooperation and inter-operability, goodwill, and cross-cultural exchange." These ensured that Indonesians and Indonesia's government and military understood and supported the Pacific Partnership mission.[338]

Jim Stengel addresses the notion of moral high ground in talking about companies, but his interpretation is about his view of what companies need to stand for and how they best organize and function. Levi's, Patagonia, and Starbucks seize the moral high ground in standing for ethical behavior and environmentally sound practices and manufacturing. Patagonia's campaign "Facing Extinction" offers an example of an inexpensively produced ad that communicates an emotionally resonant message.[339]

Deeds Matter as Much as Words

How does the moral high ground help you as an executive? It can motivate your customers or clients to buy your product or service. Method manufactures environmentally friendly cleaners. Its narrative, theme, and message appeal to reason and the heart, arguing that it is a great product, is safe, and helps the environment. In Britain, Innocent has shown honest commitment to a safe environment in marketing fruit smoothies.

You can't quarrel with its success: it owns 71% of its market. Its narrative is about inviting customers to share a fun-loving, carefree approach to life. Its clever packaging enhances that appeal. It uses recycled plastic containers and Rainforest Alliance-certified bananas. It has its own charitable foundation that funds "building sustainable futures for the world's poorest people.[340] These

---

[338] D.L. Bernardi, P.H. Cheong, C. Lundry, S. Ruston, <u>Narrative Landmines</u>, supra, Kindle Loc. 1592/2523. Their detailed discussion of this case study offers a model for public affairs operations.
[339] Patagonia: "Facing Extinction:" https://www.youtube.com/watch?v=h1l_hFwzOYA
[340] Adam Vaughan, "You ask, they answer: Innocent drinks," *Guardian*, December 14, 2009: https://www.theguardian.com/environment/blog/2009/dec/14/innocent-you-ask; and "Market leader of UK in Fruit Smoothies," *UK Essays*: https://www.ukessays.com/essays/marketing/market-leader-of-uk-in-fruit-smoothies-market-marketing-essay.php;

companies delivered products that customers wanted. The most incredible ads in the world wouldn't have mattered otherwise.

One lesson is that tremendous market opportunities exist if you show a persistent, plausible commitment to improving the environment. It matters to a lot of people, and they will prefer your products over products from a competitor that fails to show similar commitment.

Whose Narratives and Stories Are Emotionally Resonant?

How does the military appeal to emotional intelligence? Former Under Secretary of Defense (Policy), John Rood explains that the Pentagon aims to understand

> "the belief structure of audiences. You need to understand what they care about that deepens the emotions in their hearts. You have to frame topics in ways they relate to, recognizing that using the right language is critical. Words that mean one thing to us may mean something different to them. Forging messages they recognize as sincere that touch their hearts in a culturally appropriate way rooted in historical norms is essential to strike a resonant chord. It's something the Marines have done well historically. It's a focus of Special Operations in carrying out their indirect mission of building partnerships. We're getting better at it as a whole, but there's room for improvement."[341]

Commercially, many examples stand out. Coke's best ads achieve emotional resonance. It stands tall with familiar examples cited above: Nike, Apple, Levi's 501 jeans. It is vital to Dodge's branding ads such as those featuring Clint Eastwood,[342] Paul Harvey,[343] Kentucky farmer Grayce Emmick,[344] and

---

[341] Interview with John Rood, April 15, 2021.
[342] Dodge Ram Trucks: Clint Eastwood, "It's Half Time America:"
https://www.youtube.com/watch?v=8iXdsvgpwc8

Wyoming farmer/rancher Arnold Pennoyer.[345] Not every ad requires expensive production values. Google did a simple ad you could produce on a laptop that tells a Paris love story[346] to show that Google can answer questions.

Let's consider Paul Harvey's ad for Dodge. Using black and white images, it told the story of a farmer's son who tells his dad that he, too, has decided to become a farmer. The ad invoked powerful images that amplified the eloquence of his distinctive voice. Harvey infused his language with a sense of gravity. The ad shows how the sound and feel of communication make a difference. One is reminded of the late critic Pauline Kael's observation about Greer Garson, who remarked that the actress could make reading names from a phone book sound like an incomparable cant.

I'm not clear who narrated the original Volkswagen Beetle ads; it sounds to me like Richard Basehart. Whoever, the quality of the voice and the cadence enhanced the impact. The ads work at every level. They were amusing and told a great story.[347]

Stories connect us. They humanize events and make them relatable. They involve a character, an objective, and the action that unites them as the protagonist overcomes a challenge to resolve the tension and story. Clint Eastwood's Super Bowl ad for Dodge, "Half Time in America," is even better than Paul Harvey's. Eastwood is iconic, and his message was about identity and who we are. It associated Dodge's resilience with that core value, integral in American culture. IBM, Coke, and Dove share a common thread in their narratives. They exist, as Ogilvy Executive Chairman Miles Young observes, to help people achieve their human potential. As noted above, Nike is about self-realization. All of them have designed narratives that evoke emotional resonance.

Each campaign noted below featured ads that evoke powerful emotions. You have to watch them in order to appreciate this. The footnotes provide YouTube links. Some were costly to produce, others relatively inexpensive. It's the

---

[343] Dodge Ram Trucks: Paul Harvey, "Farmer," https://www.youtube.com/watch?v=AMpZ0TGjbWE; See also: Dodge Ram Trucks, Grayce Emmick, "Farmer in All of Us:" https://www.youtube.com/watch?v=-J40DSdV6jE.

[344] Dodge Ram Trucks, Grayce Emmick, "Farmer in All of Us:" https://www.youtube.com/watch?v=-J40DSdV6jE

[345] https://www.youtube.com/watch?v=IKT7eJQHePg

[346] Google, "Parisian Love," 2009: https://www.youtube.com/watch?v=nnsSUqgkDwU

[347] https://www.youtube.com/watch?v=ZY-D-GPosPM; and https://www.youtube.com/watch?v=tc-kekzH2dU&t=159s

creativity, vivid stories and images, and the *thinking* that went into the ads that make them great.

Procter & Gamble's "Thank You Mom – Strong" for the 2016 Olympic Games captures the emotion of young boys and girls who dream of achieving greatness, and through the strength of their relationship with their moms, do so. The message is that it "takes someone strong to make someone strong. Thank you, Mom."[348]

Gillette offered two fantastic videos. "Handle with Care" tells the touching story of a son taking loving care of a disabled father. "It's an honor to do that for your father, because he did it for me as a kid," the son tells us, as he prepares his dad for a shave and provides one.[349]

Airbnb's "Let's keep traveling" asks that we imagine a world without travel, with images of cars moving backward, passengers boarding a plane stepping down backward, joggers running backward. A clip of Albert Einstein stepping backward appears beneath the caption "There would be no immigrants." A covered wagon in the west moves backward, under the caption "There would definitely be no United States of America." The message: to limit travel is to turn back progress.[350] Airbnb did even better with "Never a Stranger," which praises Airbnb for creating connections, as one woman who travels around the world advises that staying at an Airbnb makes you always feel at home.[351] Airbnb's ads consistently maintain a high standard in their strategic communication.

Lysol's "Protect like a Mother"[352] powerfully tugs at the heartstrings. The ad opens on a blackboard across which is written, "Mom, you are the best!" We dissolve to a young schoolgirl escorted across a crosswalk by a grizzly bear. A car races up, stops just in time. The grizzly roars up on its hind legs. A bald eagle uses its wings to shield a little boy from the rain. A young boy sitting beside a pool eyes two attractive girls. A monkey sits on his shoulder, stroking his hair. An elephant protects children in a field. A lion sitting atop a couch watches protectively over a little girl nuzzled against her, as the girl sleeps. *Talk about an attention-getter.*

---

[348] "Thank You, Mom – Strong Rio 2016 Olympic Games:" https://www.youtube.com/watch?v=x-rh5NKXjkQ

[349] Gillette, "Hand with Care – Gillette's New Assisted Shaving Razor:" https://www.youtube.com/watch?v=0Yvbhincl40

[350] Airbnb, "Let's keep traveling forward:" https://www.youtube.com/watch?v=wuF2nI1Ugcc

[351] Airbnb, "Never a Stranger:" https://www.youtube.com/watch?v=s4WVhcXogGk

[352] Lysol, "Protect Like a Mother:" https://www.youtube.com/watch?v=mQLj9KQyVNA

Lean Cuisine's "#Weighthis"[353] campaign dramatizes the trauma of losing weight, a challenge for which Lean Cuisine offers a solution. It opens in a well-lit grand ballroom. Positioned amid it is a weight scale. Different women gingerly approach. They react nervously when asked to step on it (who among us doesn't?). Relatable, true to life, women speak candidly about their challenges and weight loss accomplishments. The message is: If you're going to weigh something, weigh what matters." As the ad concludes, we're all ready to overcome our fears.

Nike's "Believe in Something" opens with a kid on a skateboard recklessly performing a stunt as he careens down the handrailing of steps. A voice urges: "If people say your dreams are crazy… if they laugh at what you say you can do…good…stay that way." A quadriplegic child performs wondrously on a gym mat. Dissolve to faces of people around the world. The narrator states: "There was a time when we cared for each other, when people would lend a helping hand." Images appear of a surfer challenging the highest, meanest wave in history, so high you have to be crazy to surf it. Narrator: "What happened? What happened is you can be whoever you want to be."

Now we see images of a female boxer, an African marathon runner. Narrator: "Instead, we judge by what we can see. We should always respect other people's opinions." Now come images of a footrace and a high school football game. Narrator: "Just because the opinions are not yours, doesn't make them unequal."[354]

The ad makes an appeal for respect and unity. Images of Tiger Woods, Serena Williams, and other athletes appear. "So, believe in something, even if it means sacrificing everything." We hear Dr. Martin Luther, Jr.'s classic invocation "To judge a person not by the color of their skin, but the content of their character. I have a dream." Narrator: "So don't ask if your dreams are crazy. Ask if they are crazy enough. Just do it." Maybe I'm biased, but I think Nike's message speaks the truth to who we are and what we should aspire to. I love it.

Procter & Gamble's deeply moving ad, "The Talk," is built around a mother's alternating conversations with her daughter and son. The ad summons us to overcome racial prejudice and systematic racism and to forge a just society.[355] The ad opens with a Black mom combing her young daughter's hair. She shares

---

[353] Lean Cuisine, "#WeighthisCampaign:" https://www.youtube.com/watch?v=h1I_hFwzOYA.
[354] Nike, "Believe in Something:" https://www.youtube.com/watch?v=SpwBlGmZcjE
[355] Proctor & Gamble: "The Talk:" https://www.youtube.com/watch?v=ovY6yjTe1LE&t=34s

truths about racial bias that their children will experience. "Who said that?" Mom asks, concerned. The daughter looks at us, exuding the innocence of childhood. "The lady at the store," the daughter replies. Now we see an image of mother and daughter reflected in a mirror. Mom says: "That is not a compliment." Dissolve to a closer shot of someone running hard. We see only the legs. A different angle reveals a young Black boy rushing home, pursued by whites. His mother warns him: "It's an ugly, nasty word. You are gonna hear it." They sit on a porch. She says: "Nothing I can do about that. But you are never going to let it hurt you. Do you hear me?"

Now we see her son wearing a baseball uniform, behind home plate. We hear his mother say: "There are some people who believe you don't deserve the same privileges just because of what you look like…. It's not fair. It's not." Now we dissolve to later in her daughter's life. She is older, seated by the wheel of a car. Her mother sits next to her. Mother says: "Remember you can do anything they can. The difference is you have to work twice as hard and be twice as smart." The daughter takes that in. Mother continues: "Now, when you get pulled over." The daughter pushes back: "Mom, I'm a good driver. Ok? Don't worry." Mom brushes that off, declaring: "This is not about you getting a ticket. This is about your coming home." The ad presents an uplifting story about courage and persistence. It closes with a written exhortation across the screen: "Let's all talk about The Talk. So we can end the need to have it."

Great advertising can stir the heart. We love a good story. But the best stories flow from credibility, whether you're commanding a Marine Stryker Force or steering a company in the marketplace. The trap to avoid is allowing a gap to emerge between the image you present, the story you tell, and the reality. People see through gaps. Gaps turn a narrative into a fraud and people reject it. Understanding that is a key lesson.

Dove's Self-Esteem Project

The Self-Esteem Project for Unilever's Dove brand shows what you can achieve with a splendidly conceived and executed strategy. It's worth taking the time to analyze this project. It shows what smart thinking and imagination can accomplish. Unilever had a lot of money to spend, but when you break down the campaigns into their constituent tactical elements, you'll see that, like Special Operations, your tactics can create a big strategic impact without spending a lot of time or money.

The advertising firm of Ogilvy & Mather played a central role. Disruptive, gutsy, controversial, the campaign's objective was ambitious: blow up the beauty and skin-care industry's mantra that beauty = youth. Dove understood that many women do not realize how beautiful they are.[356]

The project emanated from Dove's mission statement and vision. There is a difference between the two. Vision, notes Lt. Gen. (Ret) Frank Kearney, focuses on "the future operating concept or organizational structures. Vision statements build a strategic, operational or tactical strategy and plans to achieve the goals."[357] Mission statements are task-focused. UK Colonel (Ret) Mark Neate echoes Kearney, stating: "Mission statements will be aligned to operating plans, ideally looking forward three to five years, and focused on different stakeholders."[358]

Dove's Self-Esteem Project respected those precepts. Dove's vision states:

> "We believe beauty should be a source of confidence and not anxiety. That's why we are here to help women everywhere develop a positive relationship with the way they look, helping them to raise their self-esteem and realize their full potential."[359]

Dove's research revealed that few women consider themselves beautiful. Anxiety about appearance begins at an early age. Six out of ten girls are so concerned with how they look that they opt out of participating fully in daily life – from swimming and soccer to visiting the doctor, going to school, or just offering their opinions on a topic.[360] Brand research in 2016 found that 77% of women think all images they see in media are distorted and that pressure to look like women they see in media makes 69% feel anxious.[361]

---

[356] Miles Young, <u>Ogilvy on Advertising in the Digital Age,</u> (London: Bloomsbury, 2018), p. 125.
[357] Interview with Lt. Gen. (Ret) Frank Kearney, supra.
[358] Interview with Colonel (Ret) Mark Neate, April 15, 2021.
[359] Dove vision: https://www.dove.com/us/en/stories/about-dove/our-vision.html. The description of the Self-Esteem Project draws upon information that Dove provides online.
[360] Id.
[361] Molly Fleming, "Dove: We will make mistakes but we aren't going to lose the diversity game," *Marketing Week.com*, August 2, 2018: https://www.marketingweek.com/dove-real-women-strategy/

Dove's mission statement – its promise or commitment about what one will do or stand for no matter what – states:[362]

> "We want women and girls of all ages to see beauty as a source of confidence, not anxiety. Because when women and girls choose not to participate fully in life, society as a whole misses out. So we're on a mission [*emph. Added*] to help the next generation of women develop a positive relationship with the way they look – helping them raise their self-esteem and realize their full potential."[363]

The Dove Self-Esteem Project was founded in 2004 to help women grow up feeling confident about their appearance. It launched the Dove Campaign for Real Beauty "as an agent of change to educate and inspire girls on a wider definition of beauty and to make them feel more confident about themselves."[364] While drawing initial criticism for lack of diversity – which P&G has striven to correct – the campaign proved a sensation.

The Project delivers self-esteem education to young people (primarily girls) aged 8-17 through lessons in schools, workshops for youth groups, and online resources for parents. The Project initially reached 20 million young people with self-esteem education. Dove committed to doubling that number by 2020. The complex, sophisticated project targeted parents and mentors, teachers and educators, and youth leaders.

Dove sought to awaken women and girls to the pitfalls of the celebrity culture and how media influences body image. The campaign blasted the $200 billion beauty industry for defining the traits of beauty as young, tall, slim, flawless skin, frequently blonde. Research that Dove conducted with Harvard and the London School of Economics revealed startling results. Only two percent of women think they are beautiful. Half think female beauty is too narrowly defined. Two-thirds believe the media sets unrealistic standards for beauty. Dove

---

[362] See: Kirsten Daley: "Let's talk business culture and aligning your mission:" https://www.youtube.com/watch?v=21QDGfd22jQ

[363] Dove vision: https://www.dove.com/us/en/stories/about-dove/our-vision.html. The description of the Self-Esteem Project draws upon information that Dove provides online.

[364] http://web.archive.org/web/20070816112659/http://www.campaignforrealbeauty.ca/supports.asp?url=supports.asp&section=campaign&id=1560

challenged the stereotypes. It viewed its Campaign for Real Beauty as a rebellion. Its narrative was that real beauty comes in different shapes, sizes, and ages. The heart of the campaign was to inspire more women to feel beautiful every day.[365]

The campaign kicked off with billboards that showcased photographs of everyday women rather than professional models. It engaged with ordinary people on the street about them. Passers-by were invited to vote on whether the woman depicted was "Fat or Fab," had "Ugly Spots or Beauty Spots," or were "Wrinkled or Wonderful." Dove updated results and displayed them on the billboard. An integrated campaign included broadcast ads, TV sponsorship, press, SMS voting, outdoor advertising, web communication, charitable support, events, retail, and public relations.[366] A website created a central point for debate and thought leadership. It commissioned over 70 women photographers to photograph women.

Dove also launched a social media "ad makeover" campaign. It created short films featuring women drawn by FBI-trained forensic artist Gil Zamora. Videos explored the gap between how others perceive us and how we perceive ourselves. Each woman is the subject of two portraits. One is based on her own description, and the other uses a stranger's observation. The results are inspirational.[367] The original video drew almost *10 million* views.

The social media video "Dove Evolution"[368] is a classic. Produced off the cuff by an Ogilvy creative artist, a volunteer crew, and a support staff, the ad featured the artist's girlfriend. The video's duration is a minute. His girlfriend is attractive but no *Vogue* magazine model. Cut frame by frame, the ad morphs her into a *Vogue*-level beauty. Following photoshop touchups and styling, her image appears on a billboard. She's a knock-out. The video exposes an urgent truth: *fashion beauty is hype.* The video ends with the pronouncement: "No wonder our perception of beauty is distorted." If you're a guy and you wondered where the Vogue beauties are hiding, the answer is that with *very* few exceptions, they are myths.

---

[365] "Campaign for Real Beauty," Dove film by Ogilvy: https://www.youtube.com/watch?v=R5Ynz3eje9s

[366] Id.

[367] Dove Real Beauty Sketches: You're More Beautiful Thank You Think:" https://www.youtube.com/watch?v=litXW91UauE

[368] "Dove Evolution:" https://www.youtube.com/watch?v=iYhCn0jf46U

Taking things a step further, Dove stopped retouching its photos. Images of "real women" became more credible after a title beneath them stated "No Digital Distortion." Dove touched up photos to eliminate stray hairs, rashes, or food particles in teeth but listed 12 things it would not do. These included whitening teeth, misrepresenting hair color, and removing natural wrinkles. That built credibility. Brand research in 2016 found that 77% of women think all images they see in media are distorted and that pressure to look like women they see in media makes 69% feel anxious.[369]

One measures the impact of a social media video partly by its penetration. Dove Evolution has drawn *20 million* views. Its ingenuity, smarts, and execution qualify it as art. It says something relevant and vital. The Campaign for Real Beauty was what marketing people term transcendent, inviting people to participate in a larger movement.

Journalist Izzy Liyana Harris notes that Dove's interactive ad makeover campaign showed ads of women that were obese or had other flaws that preyed on female insecurities. It invited viewers to make them over. A Facebook-based venture could replace depressing ads about weight loss and cosmetic surgery with eight feel-good messages that Dove designed. Dove identified negative terms: *plastic surgery, I hate my body, holiday, bikini, diet,* and *gym*. All expressed negative vibes.

In place of these, Dove encouraged women to create their own uplifting language: *Hello, beautiful. The perfect bum is the one you're sitting on. Your birthday suit suits you. Beauty is an all-ages show.*[370] SMS, in-store media, interactive, and sponsorship elevated campaign visibility. Public relations got people talking. Coverage took off. News media generated $12 million worth of exposure *without* television advertising. Walmart put its workers in the spotlight for a multi-media campaign to get people talking. Grassroots initiatives enhanced the campaign's credibility.

The statistics attest to the campaign's success: 5.5 million women saw 171 million banners with negative messages. Over 50% of the women who visited Dove Ad Makeover created a message. And 82% of the ads were seen by friends

---

[369] Molly Fleming, "Dove: We will make mistakes but we aren't going to lose the diversity game," *Marketing Week.com*, August 2, 2018: https://www.marketingweek.com/dove-real-women-strategy/

[370] Izzy Liyana Harris, "How Dove Empowered Real Women and Achieved Success in 80+ countries," *ReferralCandy Blog*, November 25, 2015: https://www.referralcandy.com/blog/dove-marketing-strategy/

of the viewer. And then the pay-off: 71% of the women polled said they felt more beautiful.[371]

Dove has collaborated with the Girl Scouts of the USA to promote self-esteem and leadership among tween and teenage girls with programs such as *UniquelyME!* and *It's Your Story – Tell It!* Dove started an annual Self-Esteem Weekend to inspire moms and mentors. It blasted the beauty and skincare companies that summon women to "fix their flaws." It empowered women through empathetic branding. Dove scored big on all counts.

Unilever could devote immense resources to make its campaign work. It probably paid Ogilvy a lot of money for its work. But you could do a lot of the most effective elements that Dove used for little money, even "Dove Evolution." It bears stressing: imagination, well-targeted communication, and smart thinking are not necessarily expensive. But they can help change the world.

---

[371] Id.

Discussion Questions

1. What story are you telling? What is the beginning, middle, and end? What is your story trying to accomplish?

2. In what context does your story arise?

3. What narrative drives the story? What theme and message grow out of your story and narrative? How do character, time, space, events, and objectives integrate into your narrative? Are all of the above integrated cohesively and persuasively?

4. Do your story and narrative humanize events and make them relatable?

5. Will the decisions your story, narrative, theme, and message (SNTM) ask audiences to make feel that choosing your product or service is good for them?

6. Do story, narrative, theme, and message align with the target audience's culture and values?

7. What limitations frame your SNTM? Example: President G.H.W. Bush promised to end the war once Kuwait was "liberated," and to refrain from going to Baghdad and attempting to overthrow Saddam. He assembled his coalition to achieve only the former and not the latter Had he attempted the latter his coalition would have fallen apart or even turned on him.

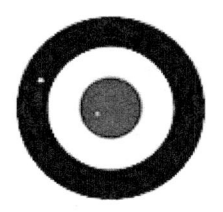

CHAPTER EIGHT

OVERCOMING OBSTACLES TO YOUR SUCCESS

Chapter Three defined obstacles to success. How do you surmount them? Here are essential questions:

1.   Who presents obstacles, and what is their significance to you?

Never presume to consider the answers obvious. Failure to understand has led to many debacles.

General Bernard Montgomery bull-headedly insisted on launching Operation Market Garden in the Netherlands to create a salient into Germany with a bridgehead over the Rhine. Ike's overall strategy was to encircle the Ruhr in a pincer movement and circumvent the northern end of the Siegfried Line. Montgomery argued that he could establish the north end of the pincer and enable the Allies to bulldoze their way into Germany. Montgomery's reckoning lacked adequate military intelligence, sense of geography, or grasp of German strength. The Germans handed him his head.

General William Westmoreland, President Lyndon Johnson, Secretary of Defense Robert McNamara, Henry Cabot Lodge, and other American leaders like JFK[372] who got us into Vietnam acted without knowing what they were

---

[372] In fairness, I question whether JFK would have jumped into Vietnam with both feet, the way LBJ did. JFK was a curious individual. He had an unusual ability to divide his life into

facing, starting with Vietnamese nationalism and the out-of-touch incompetence of the Ngo Dinh Diem regime. Westmoreland combined political incomprehension with a misguided military strategy that emphasized killing the enemy instead of providing security to the population. After assuming command of American forces, Creighton Abrams tried to implement a "clear and hold" strategy to provide security at the village level. He had a good idea but both Republican and Democratic leaders in Washington undercut him.

Secretary of Defense Donald Rumsfeld and George W. Bush proved no smarter than Westmoreland. Both assumed that the 2003 Iraq War would "drain the swamp" in the Middle East and produce stability and democracy. The U.S. spent trillions of dollars on these wars to help a largely ungrateful population and spent a treasure in the blood of our men and women in uniform. The lesson is, never assume that well-intentioned leaders will do the smart thing or that evil leaders will do the stupid one.

Executives commit their own blunders. Some examples: The flawed testing of Real Coke. The Edsel. Firearms manufacturer Smith & Wesson's ill-judged decision to enter the market for bicycles. Understanding what obstacles you need to overcome and that you can overcome, is step one in overcoming the ones that frustrate success.

2.   Define how each action step in the plan connects to and helps surmount your identified obstacles, considers your targets of opportunity, and makes provision to address unanticipated or new obstacles.

Message discipline is vital. Events, distractions, and unanticipated problems can distort operations. Communication strategy may look easy on paper but bear in mind execution can be a sensitive process. Most influence activities provide no easy or quick solutions. They require time, tweaking, and constant evaluation.

The CIA and Special Forces helped eject Usama Bin Laden from Afghanistan. But then the U.S. commander, General Tommy Franks, ignored prudent counsel from the Joint Chiefs to insert a blocking force between the Taliban and their

---

compartments. His womanizing was a disgrace, and arguably by the time of his death, poor medical treatment for his back may have turned him into a drug addict. But in politics, he was objective and cold-blooded. Most historians think he would have fought because he was a "cold warrior;" I disagree. Kennedy knew a loser when he saw one, and he was a very rapid learner who was getting better and better. He was a far more capable President at his death than when he was inaugurated. I think he would have declined to go all-in on that war.

opponents as the latter drove the Taliban southwest towards Kandahar. Lack of a coherent strategy, understanding of Afghanistan's culture, coordinated planning and execution are among the flaws that the Special Inspector General for Afghanistan Reconstruction (SIGAR) identified as impairing success. A consensus supporting SIGAR's view has emerged as the US exited the country.

Historian Stephen E. Ambrose has written cogently about Dwight Eisenhower. On national security matters, he was extraordinary. Ike had the presence of mind to reject his national security team's urging to employ nuclear weapons in Korea and Vietnam. He attracted top talent and it's been said that no one he asked to join his administration turned him down. Ambrose – a fellow resident of New Orleans until his untimely death – once told me that Ike had such strong charisma that people just wanted to be physically in the same room with him as if hoping that some of Ike's charisma would rub off on them. It's a rare gift. Ike was a born political executive.[373] He kept his eye on the ball. He had a clear goal: defeat Communism. He pursued it ruthlessly. Read historian Fred L. Greenstein for the best account of how Ike operated.[374]

Ike displayed a fuddy-duddy, grandfatherly public face. Spending time with Ike opened the eyes of major figures like Henry Kissinger. Kissinger admitted that, to his surprise, he found the President enormously thoughtful and well-informed. Ike understood power and organizations and how to bend them to his will. He used the Operations Coordinating Board and the National Security Council, whose meetings he actively chaired, and a small coterie of advisers, to push diplomatic and psychological warfare to fight Communism.

Ike took decision-making away from the Departments of State and Defense. Ike didn't trust bureaucrats. His private papers reveal a razor-sharp mind and an excellent strategic sense. Eisenhower's handling of Operation Overlord and the Presidency are master classes in executive leadership. Every executive can learn from how he did things.[375]

Apple's Steve Jobs seems to have been a challenging personality. Yet his achievements reveal a passionate genius who stood his ground and stared down severe opposition to his idea. In his excellent biography of Jobs, Walter Isaacson

---

[373] Stephen E. Ambrose, Eisenhower: Soldier and President, (Political Biography Press, 2007).
[374] Fred L. Greenstein, The Hidden Hand Presidency: Eisenhower as Leader, (New York: Basic Books, 1982).
See also: Susan Eisenhower, How Ike Led, (New York: Thomas Dunne Books, 2020).
[375] Id.

details Jobs' laser-like focus, ability to cut to the core of things, insistence on excellence, and strategic excellence.[376]

3. Define the key players.

Imagine a diagram with concentric circles. The circle contains four separate questions, positioned here as A to D, that leaders need to pose in defining a successful communication strategy:

> A) **Who is indispensable to success**? Without these players, you will fail. You need to decide who is indispensable to your organization's success. Abraham Lincoln and Franklin Roosevelt were indispensable to our nation's survival. Had Stephen Douglas won in 1860, the nation would have split, as Douglas supported state choice on slavery under the banner of "popular sovereignty." Had George McClellan defeated Lincoln in 1864, the Union might have settled for an armistice.
>
> Lincoln fired incompetent generals and kept searching until he found Ulysses S. Grant and William Sherman. He deftly goaded the Confederacy, led by the arrogant, tone-deaf former soldier Jefferson Davis – who thought himself a military mastermind – into firing the first shot at Ft. Sumter. As Lincoln anticipated, Davis blundered, enabling the Union to enter the war united.
>
> Franklin Roosevelt understood that Adolph Hitler posed an existential global threat, compared to Japan, whose ambitions were regional. None of his talented advisers saw things as clearly. Secretary of Defense George Marshall and commanders including Eisenhower put defeating Japan as the priority.
>
> FDR was politically savvy, and he had superb military judgment. He skillfully navigated an isolationist America into World War II with a united front through a strategy that waited until Japan fired the first shot. Showing how close a call the war's outcome was, it took Hitler's ill-advised decision to unilaterally declare war on the United States on December 11 to enable FDR to unite the country against the Nazis. We would not likely have initiated hostilities, in which case beleaguered Britain might well have collapsed.
>
> What FDR accomplished is amazing. His physical condition was frail. He lacked the staff support of a modern President. FDR had flaws. But he rightly ranks among our nation's greatest Presidents.

---

[376] Walter Isaacson, <u>Steve Jobs: A Biography</u>, (New York: Simon & Schuster, 2011).

B)   Who is important to success? Napoleon's greatest victories came at Austerlitz and Friedland. At his best, Napoleon was a great tactical commander, but his able Marshals made a difference. General Louis DeSaix arguably saved Bonaparte's bacon at Marengo. Marshal Louis-Nicolas Davout, perhaps Napoleon's finest corps commander, probably saved Bonaparte at Jena. Marshal Louis-Gabriel Suchet and Marshal Louis-Alexandre Berthier were critical to his triumphs. But he was erratic in his selection of commanders. He tolerated the far less gifted Marshal Jean-de-Dieu Soult, Marshal Michel Ney, and General Emmanuel de Grouchy.[377]

Waterloo reshaped European history. Most military historians believe Napoleon should have won the battle.[378] Noted historian Andrew Roberts has written a concise account of the battle. He presents a case study for executives on what to avoid when the chips are down. For example, a myth has cropped up that Bonaparte had a second-rate army. While there was no equaling his elite force that fought at Austerlitz, Napoleon's forces at Waterloo were both capable and better than Wellington's army.

Not everyone agrees that Napoleon turned in a sub-par performance at Waterloo. But the better view seems to be that poor command, strategy and tactics, and catastrophic leadership, including his decision to go into battle with mediocrities like Grouchy, produced a fiasco.

Who is *important* to you varies by company or by situation. For Nike, its choice of ad companies like Chiat/Day worked superbly. But there's lots of ad talent. Nike uses many great agencies. They are all gifted. No single agency is indispensable. A skilled, coordinated, informed workforce is important to any company, although individuals can be changed out.

C)   Who is merely helpful?

Knowing who fits into this category helps to ensure the best allocation of time and resources. The answer varies according to the situation.

---

[377] See: Douglas Allan, "Waterloo – Bias, Assumptions and Perspectives: Why the French lost – The Reality," *Napoleon Historical Society*, June 2015:
https://napoleonichistoricalsociety.org/waterloo-perspectives/?gclid=CjwKCAjwjqT5BRAPEiwAJlBuBdUVODKRtPbPXzMOd5Z-9Zn1L0t3080INim8uWZzTAsXQXW1Xp68SBoC9BkQAvD_BwE#reality

[378] Frank McLynn, Napoleon: A Biography, (New York: Arcade Publishing, 2011) Kindle Loc. 102027/15527, 13051/15527. McLynn's view of Ney is the opposite of Allen, who attributes Napoleon's victory at Borodino to Ney's leadership.

D) Who could help but doesn't matter?

Knowing this also avoids wasting time and resources so that you can focus on who and what counts.

4. Divide responsibility with clear assignments.

Information strategies involve moving pieces. As noted above, the battles in Fallujah, Iraq in April and November 2004 provide vital lessons. We lost the first battle because insurgents seized control of the narrative. Coalition forces lacked an information campaign to mitigate false media reports that Americans had caused terrible Iraqi civilian casualties.

The insurgents won over the international media. Television screens and news reports broadcast phony images of children's toys lying on the ground, damaged hospitals, and untrue reports about massive civilian casualties. The public relations blow-back caused President George W. Bush to heed the recommendation of Provisional Coalition leader Paul Bremer and the Coalition Forces ground commander, Lt. Gen. Ricardo Sanchez, to halt the attacks.

In a lesson that executives should remember, neither Bremer nor Sanchez reported the recommendation of the ground commanders to continue the battle, or their view that victory would be achieved militarily within 72 hours. The lesson is that you must ask the hard questions essential for decision-making and show zero toleration for subordinates who fail to adequately inform higher-ups of relevant information.[379]

---

[379] Carter Malkasian of the Center for Naval Analyses has written incisively about the first battle. See Carter Malkasian, "Signaling Resolve, Democratization, and the First Battle of Fallujah," Journal of Strategic Studies 29, no. 3 (June 2006): 423–52, https://doi.org/10.1080/01402390600765843. Gen Stanley McChrystal has offered key insights on the challenge that the strategic situation there presented. See Gen Stanley McChrystal, My Share of the Task: A Memoir (New York: Portfolio/Penguin, 2013). A team led by Dr. William Knarr of the Joint Special Operations University and by Maj Robert Castro conducted an intensive analysis for the Institute of Defense Analyses that examined both battles. See William Knarr et al., Seizing the Peninsula, a Vignette from The Battle for Fallujah: An Education and Training Resource Guide (Alexandria, VA: Institute for Defense Analyses, 2011); Dr. William Knarr and Maj Robert Castro, Institute for Defense Analysis Non-Standard Document NS D-3787, Log H09-000669, "The Battle for Fallujah: Al Fajr, the Myth-buster," May 2009, a short version of the following study; Dr. William Knarr and Maj Robert Castro with Dianne Fuller, The Battle for Fallujah: Al Fajr, the Myth-Buster, IDA Paper P-4455 (Alexandria, VA: Institute for Defense Analyses, 2009), the full study report; and transcripts of

In November 2004, the Coalition rejoined the battle, but this time, with careful planning for information warfare and kinetic activities. The attacking force coalesced U.S., NATO, and Iraqi forces. We won that battle. A realistic plan delegated clear lines of responsibility and ensured accountability. Communication was tightly organized. Public affairs and psychological operations teams were unified. Commanders clearly defined operational goals and tasks to achieve them.[380]

Iraqis played a supporting role in sealing off the city to trap insurgents inside it. U.S. Marines led the charge. This time, the U.S. information strategy portrayed the battle on its own terms. Proper delegation of responsibilities helped the Coalition to prevail, at least at the tactical level. Sadly, focus on the battle came at the expense of ignoring the national picture. You might think grateful Iraqis would cheer victory against the insurgents. As no one had made the right effort to explain what the Coalition was doing and how it benefitted all Iraqis, many Iraqis lashed out in anger over images of non-Muslim forces killing Muslims, even though these Muslims were terrorists. The lesson is that you need to think strategically, operationally, *and* tactically.

In competing against Nike, Adidas has its act together. Lisann Costello, the Senior Director of Brand Communication, stresses the need to treat everybody as a leader, giving a team creative freedom while maintaining a cohesive enterprise effort.[381] Returning to CEO Kasper Rorsted, he says collaboration is the heart of its leadership culture. "We collaborate to win and to make decisions." He manages 55,000 employees. "To build a strong team," he says, "first you need to understand what game you are playing and which competencies you need. It's a bit like football. You have eleven players. You've got to get eleven competencies." He emphasizes that each has a role and to make sure people understand and buy into the importance of their role.[382]

---

interviews with key participants in the Fallujah battles by Dr. William Knarr used to inform the aforementioned reports, provided to the author by Dr. Knarr, which are also available on DVD appendices to the printed reports. New York Times journalist Dexter Filkins has written an excellent first-hand account of his time in Iraq and Afghanistan and was present for the second battle. See Dexter Filkins, The Forever War (New York: Alfred A. Knopf, 2008); and West, No True Glory. Comments on these battles and material from which the author extrapolated lessons draw on their superb scholarship.

[380] Id.
[381] Lisann Costello interview on YouTube: https://www.youtube.com/watch?v=j14LhoIuExA
[382] Kasper Rorsted interview on YouTube: https://www.youtube.com/watch?v=DvuDl8b1H_s

Adidas is a large firm. Lawn Butler is a small one. Founded in 1999 by Seth Kehne, the landscape management firm grew gradually. Kehne had never put in place a management system. Everyone reported to him, stretching him thin. He managed instead of delegating. "By failing to delegate," Kehne says, "I'd been holding back my managers. They didn't have the authority they needed to do what they needed to do."[383] Kehne realized he had to fix things. He implemented a new organizational chart that defined managers' duties and responsibilities. He reduced the number of employees who reported to him from 20 to 4. Kehne's stress level went down, and productivity went up. Sales rocketed 50%. Clarity in delegation matters: for the military, for big companies, and small ones.

5. **Measure to ensure progress.**

In armed conflicts, performance metrics – how many missiles are fired, bombs dropped, physical damage or casualties inflicted – are essential statistics. The qualitative considerations are more political. Opinion research helps you assess the impact of armed hostilities or peaceful engagement. But unless you know what you're looking for and what you're doing, you'll waste your money.

The 2012 U.S. Presidential election illustrates the point. Voters responded positively to candidate Mitt Romney's performance in his first debate with President Barack Obama and poorly to Obama. Obama fell victim to over-confidence. He underestimated his opponent. He seemed not presidential. He projected the feeling that the debate was a nuisance. But his team did not let hubris obstruct improvement. He prepared intensively for the second and third debates. He heeded sound advice. He held his own with Romney in those debates.

Obama's team measured success objectively through polling and social media analytics and by monitoring press coverage. The dynamics can change overnight or within hours in military or political campaigns. Executives enjoy a more extended period to measure progress. But you must set up a baseline for judgments and use the right research tools.

Knowing what parts of your plan are working, with whom, when, and why enables you to persevere with the current plan or improve it. Detecting problems enables you to identify and correct deficiencies.[384] Broadly, there are two ways

---

[383] Casey Payton, "Case study: Delegation dilemma," *landscapemanagement.net*, October 22, 2014: https://www.landscapemanagement.net/case-study-delegation-dilemma/

[384] See: For a military viewpoint, Major General Michael T. Flynn, USA, Captain Matt Pottinger, and Paul D. Batchelor, "Fixing Intel: A Blueprint for Making Intelligence Relevant in Afghanistan," (Washington, DC: Center for a New American Security, 2010). Their excellent

to measure the progress of a plan: performance and qualitative. For many executives, performance is more important. Is the plan producing sales and profits? If it isn't, the rest doesn't matter.

Coca-Cola

Let's take another look at Coca-Cola. Coke is the world's most popular soft drink. It sells 1.9 billion servings a day. Producing over 3,000 products, it spends $4 billion annually on advertising. The message is lifestyle-oriented: drinking or sharing a Coke inspires fun, warm feelings, positive emotions. Coke sells an abstract concept of happiness, family, and sharing. Marketing expert Seth Godin summarizes Coke's consistent strategy: run lots of ads, persuade a mass market that Coke is part of the culture that makes them happy and that everybody is drinking it. It maintains a consistent strategic view.[385]

Its "Share a Coke" campaign stands out. The product of extensive global planning and collaboration, one lesson the creators taught was that collaboration requires figuring out who's good at what and assigning tasks accordingly. All executives should write that one down. In my experience, there's a corollary: The important question in judging folks is not whether you can trust them, but with what.

---

report offers sweeping changes to the way the intelligence community thinks about itself from a focus on the enemy to a focus on the population. Focusing too many resources "and brainpower on insurgent groups" has left the intelligence apparatus, they argue, "unable to answer fundamental questions about the environment in which we operate and the people we are trying to persuade." Flynn et al., Fixing Intel, 4. They propose specific initiatives to solve the problem using field analysts to collect information at the grassroots, much like journalists; integrating information collected by all stakeholders (civilian and military); dividing work along geographical instead of functional lines, and providing district assessments covering governance, development, and stability; providing data to teams of information brokers in regional commands as part of stability operations information centers to organize and disseminate information; placing the information centers under and in cooperation with State Department senior civilian representatives administering governance, development, and stability efforts in regional commands; and ensuring that the information centers are staffed by "the most extroverted and hungriest analysts." Flynn et al., Fixing Intel, 4–5.
[385] Seth Godin, This is Marketing (New York: Penguin Publishing Group, 2018), p. 166.

Coke's data-driven campaign focused on millennials and tapped into their behavior of social sharing.[386] The campaign featured ads using Coke cans that can be divided into two, and thus shared with a friend. Coke's ambition was to strengthen the brand's name with young adults and to inspire "shared happiness" in the real and virtual worlds.[387]

Coke's Marketing Director for Coca-Cola South Pacific explained:

> "Our research showed that while teens and young adults loved that Coca-Cola was big and iconic, many felt we were not talking to them at eye level. Australians are extremely egalitarian. There's a phrase called 'tall poppy syndrome.' If anyone gets too big for their boots, they get cut down like a tall poppy. By putting first names on the packs, we were speaking to our fans at eye level."[388]

Launched in Australia, you could select your name from a list of 150 names in a vending machine that prints your name on a can label. Coke made an exhaustive list of banned offensive words and innuendo, then automated the process when customers purchased a Coke. Automation also enabled Coke to track and measure the exact numbers of personalized cans sold.[389] It was a resourceful use of technology to help with sales metrics, a key indicator Coke had set for assessing the success of the campaign.

The campaign scored a hit in Australia. In a nation of 23 million, Coke sold 250 million bottles or cans. Coke expanded the campaign to 70 countries and the list of names you could put on a label was substantially expanded. Inviting someone to share a Coke rather than keeping it fostered connections and fun. Coca-Cola's message is that drinking Coke is fun and creates happiness. Watch the videos, "Happiness Machine" and "Coke Hug Machine." They capture the kinetic spirit that Coke's campaign aims to achieve. Access them on YouTube at

---

[386] Daniel Cotella, "The Winning Coco-Cola Formula for a Successful Campaign," *write.com*, April 6, 2018: https://www.wrike.com/blog/winning-coca-cola-formula-successful-campaign/
[387] Jay Moye, "Share a Coke: How the Groundbreaking Campaign Got Its Start 'Down Under,'" *coco-colacompany.com*, July 7, 2016: https://www.coca-colacompany.com/au/news/share-a-coke-how-the-groundbreaking-campaign-got-its-start-down-under.
[388] Quoted by Daniel Cotella, "The Winning Coco-Cola Formula for a Successful Campaign,"
[389] Daniel Cotella, "The Winning Coco-Cola Formula for a Successful Campaign," *supra*.

https://www.youtube.com/watch?v=lqT_dPApj9U (Happiness) and https://www.youtube.com/watch?v=A45sjUX7mp0 (Hug).

The money spent on its ads shows well on YouTube or a television screen.[390] The ads are slick, expensive, feature good-looking, cheerful people, and maintain tight message discipline. Still, nothing works perfectly. Coke admits that 30% of its ads are less effective than it wants. It partners with Neilsen Consumer Neuroscience to analyze conscious reactions to its ads and to measure whether they resonate emotionally. Research revealed that shorter clips of people sipping coke did better. Clear shots of characters' faces better elicited emotional engagement. Darker shots disrupted emotion and increased critical attention. Coke tailored its ads accordingly.[391]

The campaign was innovative. Then more hidden landmines exploded. Technology can prove treacherous. Some users who tried to personalize a Coke bottle with certain names or phrases discovered the machine could not satisfy the request. Critics faulted a software censor that seems to relate to ethnic or political requests. "Blues Lives Matter" made it onto a label. "Black Lives Matter" did not. "Osama" was not a permitted name. Critics accused Coke of ethnic or racial discrimination.[392]

In response, Coke stated that

> "Names may not be approved if they're potentially offensive to other people, trademarked or celebrity names. We've worked hard to get this list right, but sometimes we mess up. If you think this is an error, please contact our

---

[390] "The Secret Behind Coca-Cola Marketing Strategy," YouTube, October 5, 2017: https://www.youtube.com/watch?v=XhMVWzVXNNk.

[391] Leonie Roderick, "Coca-Cola admits 30% of its ads are not as effective as it wants," *Marketing Week*, March 31, 2017: https://www.marketingweek.com/coca-cola-admits-30-ads-not-meeting-standard/

[392] Krissy Gasbarre, "Coca-Cola Faces Backlash Over This Bottle Feature," *eatthis.com*, June 24, 2021: https://www.eatthis.com/news-coca-cola-backlash-personalized-bottles/; and Mark Fidelmann, "You Won't Believe The Absurdity Of Criticism About Coca-Cola's Brilliant Social Media Campaign," *Forbes*, July 1, 2013: https://www.forbes.com/sites/markfidelman/2013/07/01/you-wont-believe-the-absurdity-of-criticism-about-coca-colas-brilliant-social-campaign/?sh=7af665d057db.

> Customer Care team. Otherwise, please try again,
> keep it fun and in the spirit of sharing!" [393]

Coke's point was that banning Muslim names was not discriminatory and that Muslims would see the use of an Arabic name like Mohammed or other names for commercial purposes as offensive. Coke was proud of its campaign and stands by it.

The lesson is that even the best strategies may contain tripwires, either in design or the technology used to promote them. You need to think about that.

Marketing Toolbox Suite CEO Anni Miteva points to other lessons that Coke's experience offers. First, customize your products. People respond better to products they feel are designed for them. Putting the customer's name on Coke labels did that. Second, leverage social media. Give people something viral to talk about. Users sharing your content will have greater impact than you. Coke designed its campaign to achieve that. Third, keep it simple. This campaign had a simple vision: share a Coke. Fourth, create experiences worth sharing on social media and in real life. People bought Cokes with their names as well as friends' names on them. Starbucks, discussed earlier, has the same aim. Finally, know your target audience. Coke defined its audience clearly and went after it.[394]

The Pepsi Challenge

The "Pepsi Challenge" led to "New Coke," created as a sweeter version of the classic Coca-Cola. In over 200,000 taste tests, people raved about New Coke. But consumers turned thumbs down on the new version. Journalist Tim Murphy reported that Coke CEO Robert Goizueta admitted to employees, sounding like Churchill after Dunkirk, that what happened was a "blunder and a disaster."[395] Murphy declared: "People speak with less clarity about war crimes."[396] Miller's wry account, and Thomas Oliver's book, *The Real Coke, The Real Story*[397] reveal how the consumer backlash linked the change in the soft drink's formula

---

[393] Krissy Gasbarre, "Coca-Cola Faces Backlash Over This Bottle Feature," supra.
[394] Ani Miteva, "Share A Coke Campaign: 5 Valuable Marketing Lessons," *MKtoolboxsuite.com*, April 15, 2020: https://mktoolboxsuite.com/share-a-coke-campaign-marketing/.
[395] Tim Murphy, "New Coke Didn't Fail. It Was Murdered," *Mother Jones*, July 9, 2019: https://www.motherjones.com/food/2019/07/what-if-weve-all-been-wrong-about-what-killed-new-coke/
[396] Id.
[397] Thomas Oliver, <u>The Real Coke, The Real Story</u> (New York: Random House, 1986).

to attacks on the national heritage and a sense of national dispossession. Classic Coke's success had made it more than a soft drink brand. It was a part of customer identity. New Coke failed partly because it confused that identification.

Ironically, tests showed that people *did* like New Coke. The flaw lay in deciding whether to launch the cola by conducting blind taste tests. These neglected to measure the responses when people *knew* which drink they were tasting. Americans like sweeter drinks and consumers liked the taste of the sweeter New Coke. But not knowing they were tasting Coke changed a likely positive to a negative response. Customers rebelled. Over 400,000 angry phone calls later, Coke pulled New Coke from shelves, leaving $30 million in unwanted New Coke concentrate. Coke failed to realize that more than taste preference governs Cola loyalty.

Five lessons emerge. First, you have to ask the right questions. Coke forgot to explore how the brand *name* mattered. Second, in drawing questions, think *unconventionally* to detect hidden resistance.[398] Coke drew its market research too narrowly. Third, understand what motivates a customer. Here that was about identity. Fourth, while pre-testing is critical, post-launch testing is even more so. Fifth, be careful to maintain brand integrity. Changing a product can weaken the core brand.[399]

6. **Sharing with and distributing to relevant parties so everyone is on the same page.**

Relevant stakeholders must receive critical information to assess risks, judge success, and make sound decisions.

EAGLE CLAW

Let's look at EAGLE CLAW, the failed Iranian hostage rescue attempt in 1980. What happened was heart-breaking. This failure is a case study in what happens where you fail to share critical details of a plan with stakeholders, fail to ask the right questions, and fail to ensure that those in the know tell it like it is, no matter the formal decision-making procedures. Bad luck snake-bit this operation. The plan called for six helicopters to fly into Tehran and rescue the hostages.

---

[398] Joe Benjamin, "Market Research Fail: How New Coke Became the Worst Flub of All Time," *business2community.com*, June 22, 2015: https://www.business2community.com/consumer-marketing/market-research-fail-new-coke-became-worst-flub-time-01256904.

[399] "Top Failed Marketing Campaigns," *EZMarketing*: https://blog.ezmarketing.com/top-failed-marketing-campaigns.

Sandstorms turned back some choppers. Rivalries between Marines and the Air Force resulted in the use of Marine choppers when the Air Force's choppers were better suited for the operating environment.

Lt. Gen. (Ret) Charles H. Pitman, then a full colonel, did the final briefing for Joint Chiefs of Staff Chairman General David Jones. Pittman revealed years later that Jones had failed to ask whether the missions could be carried out with only five helicopters. The answer, Pittman said,[400] was that it could, and what's more, had been rehearsed successfully using only five helos.

Pitman failed to volunteer that information, and Jones did not request it. Pittman said that in that era, one answered questions and stayed within the scope of those posed. Jones's failure kept him from communicating this vital fact to the White House. That single missing piece of information governed whether, as chaos engulfed the staging area, Desert One, the White House would give the green light or abort the mission.[401]

I also interviewed former National Security Adviser Zbigniew Brzezinski about what the White House knew about the operational plan. Brzezinski had made clear that he nearly advised Carter – who would have accepted his recommendation – to roll the dice. But not having the full picture, he hesitated and accepted the recommendation of ground commanders to abort the mission.

At the time I interviewed him, he was philosophical. What was done was done. Yet without question, he would have urged the President to greenlight the rescue had he known five choppers were sufficient. The rescue team had five choppers in good operating condition. Carter and Brzezinski just did not know about it.

A mystery is that neither the Delta Force Commander, Colonel Charles Beckwith, nor the Desert One commander, Col. James H. Kyle, seemed aware that the mission could be carried out, in Pitman's view, with just five helicopters. Pitman had worked with the helicopter teams. In interviews with this author, he was adamant that the rescue attempt using only five helicopters had been successfully rehearsed. His account was informally verified by an important

---

[400] Lt. Gen. (Ret) Pitman died in 2020. Because what he said was controversial, when I first reported the incident in my book Persuasion and Power, supra, I had him personally edit the section to ensure I was taking down his recollection accurately.
[401] See: James P. Farwell, Persuasion and Power, supra, p. 124.

member of the Intelligence Community who had served as liaison to the Joint Chiefs for the operation.[402]

The issue is not whether Beckwith made the correct decision. It is the failure to share vital information relevant to how decision-makers viewed their options at a critical point. Perhaps Beckwith made the right call. Intelligence had located the hostages only hours before the operation was to commence. One potential outcome was a successful rescue. Another outcome, as Admiral William H. McRaven emailed me a few years ago,[403] was a mission mishap in the middle of downtown Tehran. A potential third outcome prompted Secretary of State Cyrus Vance's resignation.

Vance argued that the rescue would have ignited huge bloodshed, as angry Iranians flooded the streets to be met by fire from American A-130 aircraft flying overhead. Vance believed any victory would prove pyrrhic as the Iranian government took other Americans hostage. Scores of Americans were present in the city at the time. Looking back, my bet is a favorable outcome seems more likely. As luck had it, U.S. forces knew the exact location of the hostages, and these prisoners were lightly guarded. Absent a helicopter mishap, I suspect the operation would have proven a stunning coup.

Playing out that scenario, success would likely have ensured Carter's re-election. History does not reveal its alternatives. Yet it seems reasonable to suggest that for better or worse, this nation's history would have followed a different course had Carter defeated Ronald Reagan in 1980 and served a second term, while sending Reagan, who proved a strong President, back to Hollywood.

The Challenger Disaster

Was the communication problem that afflicted EAGLE CLAW a one-off? Hardly. On the evening of January 27, 1986, freezing temperatures descended upon Merritt Island, Florida, home to the Kennedy Space Center. NASA and the

---

[402] This affirmation came when another former senior member of the Intelligence Community shared with the author an email addressed to him after the author published a commentary on EAGLE CLAW in *The National Interest.*

[403] At the time, Admiral McRaven was the Commander of the US SPECIAL OPERATIONS COMMAND. He was commenting on my Op-Ed on the topic. See: James P. Farwell, "The Iranian Rescue Operation: A Missed Opportunity?", *Huffington Post*, February 27, 2013: http://www.huffingtonpost.com/james-p-farwell/the-iranian-rescue-operat_b_2773643.html

Morton Thiokol Corporation, which manufactured the solid rocket boosters for the shuttle program, debated whether to scuttle the Challenger launch. The issue centered on whether the rubber O-rings on the booster rockets would fail to seal properly in frigid temperatures. The answer was affirmative. Sadly, on launch day, temperatures did dip below freezing. Despite urgent pleas to delay from five Morton Thiokol engineers, NASA decided to launch.

A failure in the O-ring seals used in the joint in its right solid rocket booster failed at liftoff. That failure allowed pressurized burning gas from within the solid rocket motor to reach the outside and impinge on the adjacent solid rocket booster joint hardware as well as the external fuel tank. A structural failure of the external tank followed. Aerodynamic forces broke up the orbiter, leaving the astronauts trapped in the intact crew compartment, facing their mortal fate. The nightmare the astronauts confronted is unimaginable.

Lawrence Mulloy, the manager of the booster rocket program, claimed that no one had communicated to him the engineers' concerns.[404] That failure to communicate cost the lives of seven valiant Americans: Christa McAuliffe, Dick Scobee, Ronald McNair, Judith Resnik, Ellison Onizuka, Gregory Jarvis, and Michael Smith. The EAGLE CLAW lesson repeats itself. Ensuring that decision-makers receive and understand critical information is about more than success. It can be a matter of life and death.

It Happens to Companies Too

Executives face the same communication challenge. More than seven years before Apple launched the iPhone, Nokia had developed its own model. It also had a tablet with a wireless connection and a touch screen. Sound familiar? "Oh my God," Frank Nuovo, the former chief designer at Nokia Corp exclaimed, "We had it completely nailed."[405] Plus, people judged Nokia's product superior to Apple's. Yet Nokia held back. The window of opportunity slammed shut. Nokia's stock price collapsed. Thousands of employees lost their jobs.

What happened? Internal rivalries and research disconnected from the operations that brought phones to market caused a train-wreck. Two competing

---

[404] Dana Beyerle, "Lawrence Mulloy, a central figure in the decision to launch," *UPI*, May 3, 1986: https://www.upi.com/Archives/1986/05/03/Lawrence-Mulloy-a-central-figure-in-the-decision-to/8857515476800/

[405] Anton Troiannovski and Sven Grundberg, "Nokia's Bad Call on Smartphones," July 18, 2012: https://www.wsj.com/articles/SB10001424052702304388004577531002591315494

development teams clamored for support and attention. Poor organization choked coherent strategy and operations. Chaotic meetings to share information involved 100 engineers and product managers situated from Massachusetts to China. Information sharing was ineffective. Nokia lost a priceless opportunity to get a step up on the iPhone.

The fault for the Deepwater Horizon disaster in the Gulf of Mexico stemmed partly from faulty communication among British Petroleum, Halliburton, and Transocean. As a result, the operators did not fully appreciate their risks.[406]

The cruise liner *Star Princess* failed to stop and rescue two men from a fishing boat. Dehydration took the men's lives after vessel staff ignored shouted warnings from birdwatchers standing on the promenade deck. No one notified the Captain or the officer of the watch.[407] This may seem like a one-off; it's not. Between 2000 and 2018, at least 313 cruise line passengers have fallen overboard.[408]

In the collapse of Enron, unethical and illegal behavior played a role. So did poor strategic communication. Enron leaders failed to communicate the values needed to create a moral climate. They failed to stay informed about organizational operations. They closed their eyes to signs of problems.[409] Enron's behavior was corrupt, but poor internal communication of crucial information helped to enable that corruption

---

[406] Final Report, National Commission on the BP Deepwater Horizon Oil Spill and Offshore Drilling, January 11, 2011: https://cybercemetery.unt.edu/archive/oilspill/20121210200431/http://www.oilspillcommission.gov/final-report

[407] Rob Williams, "Communication failure on luxury cruise liner left adrift fishermen to die," *Independent*, April 20, 2012: https://www.independent.co.uk/news/world/americas/communication-failure-on-luxury-cruise-liner-left-adrift-fishermen-to-die-7665138.html

[408] "14 People Who Fell Off Cruise Ships and Lived to Tell the Tale Gallery," *thedailymeal.com*, August 28, 2018: https://www.thedailymeal.com/travel/cruise-ship-survival-stories-gallery

[409] Matthew W. Seeger, Robert R. Ulmer, "Explaining Enron: Communication and Responsible Leadership," *Management Communication Quarterly*, August 1, 2003: https://journals.sagepub.com/doi/abs/10.1177/0893318903253436

7. **Ensuring unity of command and control.**

A military commander has the authority to direct all forces in pursuit of a unified purpose. It's about "one mission, one boss."[410] Unity of command facilitates communication between superiors and subordinates, clear authority, responsibility, and accountability. It reduces duplication of work, facilitates rapid decision-making, fosters discipline, encourages teamwork, boosts morale, inspires a positive attitude, and produces higher productivity.[411]

Any commander knows that, right? Yet, in Iraq and Afghanistan, command and control proved erratic. In the 2003 Iraq War, the ground commander, Lt. Gen. Ricardo Sanchez, feuded with Coalition Provisional Authority chief Paul Bremer. No one is willing to state precisely who empowered Bremer to do what. That included a disastrous decision to nullify a plan to put the Iraqi army back together.[412] Coalition efforts between military and civilian officials were poorly coordinated.

The Iraq Surge worked well because two able individuals, General David Petraeus and Ambassador Ryan C. Crocker, joined forces, located their offices next door to one another, and coordinated leadership.[413] Their leadership surmounted tough challenges to stabilize Iraq so that its government could be sustainable. It worked until U.S. forces left in 2012, opening up a vacuum into which the genocidal Islamic State stepped.

In Afghanistan, Ambassador Karl Eikenberry, a retired four-star general, clashed with military commanders over strategy. Journalists Mark Mazzetti and Rajiv Chandrasekaran reported substantial differences between White House officials and Afghanistan-Pakistan envoy Richard Holbrooke.[414] USAID pursued competing ideas about civil reconstruction. The U.S. Marines asserted control over their forces, independent of the country ground commander, General

---

[410] MSgt Justin Strain, "Unity of Command Still Important Principle," Joint Base Charleston (website), 16 August 2007.
[411] See, for example, Gaurav Akrani, "Unity of Command Principle—Meaning Example Advantages," Kalyan City Life (blog), 3 February 2012.
[412] See: George Packer, Assassin's Gate (New York: Farrar, Strauss & Giroux, 2005). Bremer also banned members of the Baathist party down to the level of teachers from keeping their jobs.
[413] See Thomas E. Ricks, The Gamble: General David Petraeus and the American Military Adventure in Iraq, 2006–2008 (New York: Penguin Press, 2009).
[414] See: Mark Mazzetti, The Way of the Knife (New York: Penguin Press, 2013) and Rajiv Chandrasekaran, Little America: The War within the War for Afghanistan (New York: Knopf, 2012),

Stanley McChrystal.[415] The United States Special Inspector General for Afghanistan Reconstruction (SIGAR) has blasted the military for its failure to forge and coordinate strategy and operations effectively. The report is a damning case study.[416] Craig Whitlock's book, noted earlier, reaches the same conclusion.

Toyota is a global brand that manufactures automobiles. Coordination is paramount. Toyota's governance connects business decisions with actual operations by integrating front-line operational feedback to policies that reflect management decisions. It uses an International Advisory Board comprised of overseas advisors that offers advice from a global perspective. Conferences and committees reflect and monitor management and corporation action. A "Toyota Code of Conduct" guides employee behavior worldwide. Toyota trains and educates at all levels and in all departments.[417] Toyota's approach to management is a case study on how to do things right. Forget that Toyota is a global entity. The precepts its leaders embrace apply to small companies as well.

8. **Forward-thinking avoids fighting the previous campaign.**

The 21st-century threat environment requires the military to leverage national influence in global competition. Executives face a similar challenge. For one thing, technology has changed the world's operational dynamics. Artificial Intelligence, quantum computing, neuro-technology, and other changes force us to think differently. Both military leaders and executives compete in a global marketplace of ideas characterized by emerging networks and connectivity. Your strategy and planning need to bake that in.

Cyber capabilities, such as those that General McChrystal employed with Task Force 145 in Iraq to track down the terrorist leader Abu Musab al-Zarqawi, have transformed the capacities for intelligence, surveillance, and reconnaissance (ISR). The enemy creates its networks. We establish our own. It takes a network

---

[415] Chandrasekaran, Little America, supra.

[416] See: "At War with the Truth," *Washington Post*, December 9, 2019: https://www.washingtonpost.com/graphics/2019/investigations/afghanistan-papers/afghanistan-war-confidential-documents/. Edited by Craig Whitlock, the six-part series summaries the key findings.

[417] Supadet Promprasit and Nathida Jumreorn, "Business coordination across borders within Toyota," School of Sustainable Development of Society and Technology, *Malardalen University*, May 28, 2009: http://www.diva-portal.org/smash/get/diva2:224180/fulltext01. Although focused on business coordination between Toyota in Japan and Thailand, this comprehensive study offers a clear look into how Toyota manages to be one of the great success stories in global industry.

to beat one. The advent of artificial intelligence will turbocharge such capabilities.

Future networks will mainly be asymmetrical. Gone are set battles on a conventional battlefield such as Napoleon fought at Jena or Austerlitz. They will be, as British General Rupert Smith has astutely written, wars among people.[418] They will occur on land, air, and sea, and in networks, and space, as well as in the mind (cognitive warfare).[419] Fighters and civilians will occupy the same space. Operations will involve non-kinetic engagements, including cyber, high-power microwave pulses, and weaponized neurotechnology rather than forces firing bullets, dropping bombs, or launching missiles. This evolution requires fresh thinking.

Here executives have out-performed the military. Earlier we talked about Lawrence Ingrassia's Billion Dollar Brand Club. He offers a concise treatise in innovative, cutting-edge thinking. Ingrassia's startups outmaneuvered established corporations. When companies like Casper, which sells mattresses, found that people wanted to lie on a mattress before purchasing one, they wasted no money on a big, dull, confusing warehouse floor jammed with mattresses. Instead, they opened boutique stores in places like lower Manhattan and turned them into an *experience*. Saks and IKEA, discussed above, have done similar things.

Target audience analysis is vital. Millennials have their own preferences. They show up and take selfies. Other generations have, or will have, their own. The best entrepreneurial leaders grasp what each market segment wants, move fast, and think ahead. They conceive of retailing as a *holistic experience*. Their customers buy into an *identity*. As Ingrassia puts it: "Brands survive. Products come and go."[420]

Today's entrepreneurs treat the Internet as a bazaar in which they can tailor products and pitches. I purchased a pair of prescription eyeglasses from Eye Buy

---

[418] General Rupert Smith, The Utility of Force: The Art of War in the Modern World, (London: Penguin, 2006).

[419] The Chinese probably offer the most sophisticated analysis of this. See: China's Science of Military Strategy, *China Aerospace Studies Institute* (2013), p. 113-114: https://www.airuniversity.af.edu/Portals/10/CASI/documents/Translations/2021-02-08%20Chinese%20Military%20Thoughts-%20In%20their%20own%20words%20Science%20of%20Military%20Strategy%202013.pdf?ver=NxAWg4BPw_NylEjxaha8Aw%3d%3d

[420] Lawrence Ingrassia, Billion Dollar Brand Club, supra, p. 103, 176, 180. If you want to start a company using cutting-edge techniques for entering the market, read Ingrassia's book. It's one of the three or four best I've seen on commercial marketing and strategic communication.

Direct for $55, for which traditional vision shops would have charged $150-$200. Warby Parker's competitors may argue that they do a better job but give its founders credit. They saw an opportunity, figured out how to make a new business chic, and off they went.

Artificial intelligence (AI), machine learning, and other advanced technologies will make an impact in the commercial world. They're already doing so at Amazon, Costco, Target, and Walmart. AI is helping with product inventory and availability, opening and closing registers, recognizing when bananas are too brown to keep on the shelves, and directly engaging with select target audiences.[421]

9. **Defining team management and how the plan will be implemented.**

Companies like Adidas make this goal a key priority and work hard at making it happen. Toyota, Nike, and Apple do that in their large business. But razor-blade maker Harry's or any well-run small- to medium-sized company also do so.

Assembling the right team requires answering some questions:

- Who is on the team?
- Who leads it?
- Who does the team leader report to? How and when?
- How are team members going to discharge their responsibilities?
- Who will instruct team members?
- Who will supervise team members?
- How will you monitor performance?
- How will you correct or change your strategy?
- How will you facilitate communication to and within the team?

10. **Defining the channels of communication through which the plan is executed.**

Many people think broadcast, especially television and radio, define the best channels of communication. Social media has equaled or supplanted that in

---

[421] Niccolo Mejia, "Machine Learning in Big Box Retail – Walmart, Target and Costco," *emerj.com*, March 11, 2020: https://emerj.com/ai-sector-overviews/machine-learning-big-box-retail/

emerging marketplaces. The military is increasingly using weaponized social media. Which works best for you depends on the strategy, the strategic situation, and your goals. For industry, ad agency Ogilvy & Mather's Executive Chairman, Miles Young, addresses the question in an excellent book, <u>Ogilvy On Advertising In the Digital Age</u>, a follow up to the classic written by the agency's founder, David Ogilvy.[422] It's the most sophisticated and usable book I've seen that explains how companies can use social media effectively to market.

Young refutes the idea that television has seen its day. He offers good reasons as to why TV is vital. First, it provides a way to scale with a net reach that remains otherwise unobtainable. Second, it does not suffer from ad fraud, the way a fake post on social media can. Established agencies have to place a television ad. That imposes control over fake ads. Anyone can post, even though social media companies like Facebook and Twitter have cracked down somewhat on fraudulent ones. Third, you can consume a TV ad on mobile devices. Fourth, television is best for communicating emotion. The adage that a picture is worth a thousand words holds. Print ads and ads in social media can move emotions, but television takes the cake in story-telling. Fifth, statistical evidence, Young advises, shows that reducing television advertising diminishes sales.

The problem with broadcast television and radio is that most small and medium-sized companies lack the resources to exploit it. Creative, effective ads are not necessarily expensive to produce. Take a look at ads featuring Michael Jordan. You can find them at https://www.youtube.com/watch?v=C1Kuz86MLTs. Some are expensive, some are not. Why they stick in your mind is their ingenuity, wit, and solid messaging about earning your success. They're short. Nike positions itself as an *iconic symbol* and as a *thought leader* for sports. These simple stories subtly signal that wearing the Michael Jordan Air sneakers puts you in the same league as a top champion.

We learn from all that several lessons.

First, paid broadcast media is powerful, where you have the resources to use it. But you need to use it strategically. You may find that purchasing ads on Facebook or Amazon is more effective than radio or television and they're a fraction of the cost. But I find there's a tendency among people below age 40 to dismiss the potential impact of paid broadcast media. Miles' argument that it is as relevant as ever is correct.

Second, you can produce effective paid media for little money. You can produce acclaimed Google ads that explain how to use it for practically nothing. "Vote

---

[422] Miles Young, <u>Ogilvy on Advertising in the Digital Age,</u> (London: Bloomsbury, 2018).

Different," a pro-Barack Obama 2008 parody of Apple's "1984" ad, drew nearly 7 million views. It was produced on a laptop and probably cost a couple of hundred dollars. Viewers see through production values. They may appreciate expensive ads. But in my experience as a media consultant, the message, not production values, is what counts.

Third, establishing yourself – or your brand – as a thought leader is an important strategy for services or products. I've spent much of my time over the past twenty years as a consultant to the U.S. Department of Defense or its combatant commands. My research, writing, and participation in conferences have contributed greatly to my ability to secure work. You can't just pose as an expert. You need to demonstrate expertise.

More indirectly, the example of Hush Puppy shoes that Malcolm Gladwell wrote about, noted earlier, illustrates how a product that influences clothing fashion preferences can prove successful without relying on paid advertising.

Indeed, direct-to-consumer (D2C) ads can produce a high return on the cost of broadcasting them.[423] Malcolm Gladwell's account of pitchman Ron Popeil, the first family of the American kitchen, is a case study in these. His television infomercials for kitchen gadgets and chicken broilers are classics.[424] Social media is an ideal channel for D2C. Anheuser-Busch reported a billion dollars in D2C sales while losing $285 million in retail sales from the spread of the pandemic. Shoppers stuck at home purchased more things online.[425]

Fourth, establishing yourself or your brand as an iconic symbol makes sense. Hush Puppy and illustrates this point.

---

[423] See Pricespider's guide to encourage D2C ads: "D2C: An All Channel Approach to Selling Your Brand:"
https://f.hubspotusercontent40.net/hubfs/2427596/Hype%20Free%20Guide/PriceSpider_Hype_Free_Guide_D2C_Ebook.pdf?__hstc=51656758.7d493d94ce3ed232dc55a9ea3ca359ad.1630859601621.1630859601621.1630859601621.1&__hssc=51656758.1.1630859601622&__hsfp=680039800&hsCtaTracking=29693f74-a3c5-41b6-b1a6-2d51b33e0c62%7Ceba0dd75-2724-43ec-8282-f05b09758f8c.
[424] Malcolm Gladwell, What the Dog Saw, (New York: Little, Brown & Co., 2009), p. 3 et al.
[425] Seb Joseph, "Inside Anheuser-Busch's InBev $1b a year DTC business," *digiday.com*, March 2, 2020: https://digiday.com/marketing/inside-anheuser-busch-inbevs-1b-year-dtc-business/.

Social Media

Social media creates nodes and central pathways that enable global connections. Consider Method, maker of environmentally safe cleaning products. It got 1.5 million views on a famous online ad, "Shiny Suds." The ad parodies the household-cleaner genre that supports the Household Product Labeling Act. Smiling, animated soap bubbles from a fictional company, Shiny Suds, prance and dance about a bathtub that is being scrubbed clean. The next morning, a woman takes a shower. Horrified, she discovers that the Shiny Suds are still there. The suds hector her. Shiny Suds turns out to consist of cleaners full of chemicals, to which she is now exposed.[426] It is sexy, funny, and skyrocketed the company's visibility.

There's a lesson here. You need to ask yourself whether an ad could backfire. Some people felt Method's ad touted male aggression and rape. The ad was not about those topics. Still, Method pulled the spot. *Ad Age* rightly criticized the complaints as unfair griping from a grievance culture. But it sided with Method's decision to pull the ad on grounds that advertisers "must consider viewer feelings – not just the target audience but the entire audience."[427]

What about the military? ISIS displays a keen grasp of social media. Sadly, they've proven better at it than us. ISIS uses social media to intimidate its enemies with images of gore, beheadings, and executions,[428] while building support among potential recruits by tweeting the experiences of ISIS fighters and supporters.[429] ISIS employs a dual approach in an "effort to be both loved and feared."[430] Some images depicted fearsome warriors capable of unspeakable

---

[426] Method, "Shiny Suds:" https://www.youtube.com/watch?v=-k9K8V2-ltw

[427] Bob Garfield, "Method did right in pulling the plug on 'shiny:'" https://adage.com/article/ad-review/method-pulling-plug-shiny-suds/140894

[428] Maya Gebeily, "How ISIL is gaming the world's journalists," *Global Post,* June 26, 2014, at http://www.globalpost.com/dispatch/news/regions/middle-east/iraq/140625/ISIL-ISIS-internet-twitter *See also:* Michel Weiss, Hassan Weiss, Inside the Army of Terror (New York: Regan Arts, 2015), Kindle Loc. 105/4871 and Jessica Stern and J.M. Berger: ISIS: The State of Terror (New York: Ecco, 2015), at 3.

[429] Maya Gebeily, "How ISIL is gaming the world's journalists," *Global* Post, June 26, 2014: http://www.globalpost.com/dispatch/news/regions/middle-east/iraq/140625/ISIL-ISIS-internet-twitter; and Abdel Bari Atwan, The Islamic State: The Digital Caliphate (London: Saqi Books, 2015), pp. 15-22. Platforms Atwan identifies include Muslimbook – a closely guarded version of Facebook – KiK, WhatsApp, Nasher.me, and Manbar.me.

[430] Maya Gebeily, supra note 25.

atrocities. Others portrayed a softer, humanistic side through images of its foot soldiers who eat *Snickers* candy bars and nurture kittens.[431]

Facebook aggressively takes down ISIS posts, but that's challenging.[432] *Twitter* finally got going but initially proved frustratingly tolerant.[433] At one point, ISIS social media activity averaged 200,000 uploads per day.[434] ISIS spread a "seductive narrative and employed powerful iconography"[435] and has used it to recruit, radicalize, and raise operational funds.[436]

Foreign Policy Institute expert Clint Watts reports that while ISIS's social media helps provide a window into what is going on in Syria, where poor security renders media coverage sparing, ISIS does not care that they are visible to the enemy.[437] Its members "*want* to communicate back to their families that they are participating."[438] Undeterred, ISIS continues to call for so-called "homegrown" supporters to commit acts of violence within the United States.[439] Epitomizing these calls to action were the July 2015 attack that killed four U.S. Marines in

---

[431] *Id. See also* Vice News, "Beheadings, Snickers and a couple of kittens, GOOGLE +, June 18, 2014: https://plus.google.com/+VICENews/posts/KyawcnRv5Zj.

[432] Lisa Daftari, *Facebook purges pages offering priceless ISIS plunder for sale*, FOX NEWS, (Jun. 11, 2015), at http://www.foxnews.com/world/2015/06/11/facebook-purges-pages-offering-priceless-isis-plunder-for-sale/.

[433] Alanna Petroff, *Hundreds of ISIS social media accounts shut down*, CNN MONEY (Feb. 15, 2015), at http://money.cnn.com/2015/02/10/technology/anonymous-isis-hack-twitter/

[434] *See* John Greenberg, *Does the Islamic State post 90,000 social media messages each day?*, TAMPA BAY TIMES, (Feb. 19, 2015), at http://www.politifact.com/punditfact/statements/2015/feb/19/hillary-mann-leverett/cnn-expert-islamic-state-posts-90000-social-media-/. *See also,* J.M. Berger, *The Evolution of Terrorist Propaganda*: *The Paris Attack and Social Media* BROOKINGS (Jan. 27, 2015), at http://www.brookings.edu/research/testimony/2015/01/27-terrorist-propaganda-social-media-berger.

[435] Gebeily, *supra* note 25.

[436] President Barack Obama, *Interview with ABC News' Chief Anchor George Stephanopoulos*, ABC NEWS, (Nov. 13, 2015), at http://abcnews.go.com/Politics/president-obama-vows-completely-decapitate-isis-operations/story?id=35173579. The President stated: "From the start our goal has been first to contain, and we have contained them." He acknowledged that more needs to be done to "completely decapitate" their operations.

[437] Interview by Scott Simon with Clint Watts, FOREIGN POLICY INSTITUTE (Sep. 6, 2014). *See also,* Scott Simon, *ISIS Runs A Dark Media Campaign On Social Media,* NATIONAL PUBLIC RADIO, (Sep. 6, 2014), at www.npr.org/2014/09/06/346299142/isis-runs-a-dark-media-campaign-on-social-media?utm_medium=RSS&utm_campaign=news

[438] *Id.* (emphasis added).

[439] *Id.*

Tennessee[440] and the 2015 mass shooting at the Inland Regional Center, a non-profit for people with disabilities and their families in San Bernadino, California.

Perhaps ISIS has seen its best days although its civil war against the Taliban in Afghanistan may revive its fortunes. As Yogi Berra said, "It ain't over until it's over."[441] The jihadist group is stocked with cash and is believed to have – no one knows – thousands of dedicated fighters.[442]

The underlying political and social dynamics that gave rise to ISIS and grew its appeal to Muslims by touting its ambition to establish a new caliphate, may produce successor groups. ISIS recruits may make a second-rate field army, but never underestimate its sophistication in the use of technology, its ruthlessness, or its resolve. ISIS currently employs signup menus to gain personal data about new users[443] that mimic some of the most advanced services available, like *Thunderclap*,[444] used by the Barack Obama Campaign in 2012.[445]

The Taliban has always displayed social media savvy. Its use of social media in Afghanistan as part of its information warfare strategy helped spur the Government of Afghanistan's collapse. Now they use it as a tool to threaten, cajole, and control. It has used Twitter effectively. YouTube and Facebook tried to block access. The Taliban gets around that by putting up new accounts. How this will play out remains to be seen. The country that the Taliban took over in the mid-1990s was almost medieval; today 70% of its 38 million population have cell phones, and most of its young population has grown up in a relatively free

---

[440] *Supra* note 26.
[441] "20 Great Yogi Berra Quotes," *Authentic Manhood*, September 24, 2015: https://www.authenticmanhood.com/20-great-yogi-berra-quotes/?gclid=CjwKCAjwvOHzBRBoEiwA48i6ApGktrit0wu34ONvgnj--DYNrWPN10NRSzAPh-yobKbkes8Oislf9RoClbwQAvD_BwE
[442] "IS 'caliphate' defeated but jihadist group remains a threat," *BBC*, March 23, 2019: https://www.bbc.com/news/world-middle-east-45547595
[443] J.M. BERGER, *How ISIS Games Twitter*, Atlantic Monthly, (June 16, 2014), at http://www.theatlantic.com/international/archive/2014/06/isis-iraq-twitter-social-media-strategy/372856/ (last visited, August 14, 2015).
[444] THUNDERCLAP, https://www.thunderclap.it/
[445] Amina Elahi, *How Social Media Strategy Influences Political Campaigns* SPROUTSOCIAL (Sep. 5, 2013), at http://sproutsocial.com/insights/social-political-campaigns/.

society. Repression may work at the outset. It will be interesting to see how well it sticks.[446]

Ukrainians have shown pluck in using Facetime to mobilize their forces against Russia. Anna Sandalova demonstrated the power of this platform to support Ukrainian resistance. She raised over a million dollars along with supplies on Facebook. Anna's experience and that of Israelis and Palestinians illustrate how social media is shifting the balance of power in exerting influence from institutions and governments to individuals and networks of individuals. David Patrikarakos has well described this evolution in War in 140 Characters.[447]

Clausewitz noted that he observed that war is the continuation of politics by other means, but in Ukraine, conflict has been the practice of politics itself.[448] As the Taliban has done in Afghanistan, this conflict has spotlighted the central importance of information warfare. Traditionally, narratives and communication supported armed engagement. In Ukraine, the converse has been true.

Militaries on both sides have tailored their kinetic activities to support the narrative. For Russian President Vladimir Putin, the stalemate that civil war has produced is fine. Putin views the conflict as another "color" Revolution like the Velvet Revolution in Czechoslovakia, the Rose Revolution in Georgia, the Orange Revolution itself in Ukraine, the Tulip Revolution in Kyrgyzstan, and others, as precursors to an effort to overthrow his regime. The stalemate is a poster child for his strategic view and narrative that color revolutions produce violence, hostility, deprivation, anger, misery, and chaos.[449]

These examples teach the power of the Internet to empower you as an individual. Internet access has transformed the way the world works.[450] Many of the successful unicorn startups have built billion-dollar enterprises using the Internet.

---

[446] Paul Mozur and Zia ur-Rehman, "How the Taliban turned social media into a tool for control," *New York Times,* August 20, 2021:
https://www.nytimes.com/2021/08/20/technology/afghanistan-taliban-social-media.html.
[447] David Patrikarakos, War in 140 Characters: How Social Media is Reshaping Conflict in the Twenty-First Century, (New York: Basic Books, 2017).
[448] Id., p.
[449] See: James P. Farwell, "War and Truth," *Defence Strategic Communications*, Vol. 7, Autumn 2019.
[450] See Clay Shirky, Here Comes Everybody: The Power of Organizing without Organizations, (New York: Penguin, 2008). Shirky's book has become a modern classic on the point. See also: Dr. Neville Bolt, The Violent Image: Insurgent Propaganda and the New Revolutionaries, (London: Columbia/Hurst, 2012). Dr. Bolt's brilliant book provides an excellent analysis of how access to the Internet has empowered parties in politics.

Two factors make social media especially valuable to executives. First, it is a relatively inexpensive channel of communication for initiating, building, and sustaining brand awareness. Second, it is an ideal channel for personal engagement with customers or clients, and D2C marketing. You enjoy the same opportunity as the startups.

11. **Integrating information and intelligence.**

Actionable information and intelligence are critical. Not all relevant intelligence affecting communication is classified. Social media intelligence and open source data are often more valuable. So is grasping how the media cover a story.[451] Knowing what flows through the rumor mill matters.[452] But as another colleague and friend, Greg Treverton, former head of the National Intelligence Council – the CIA's elite internal think-tank – points out, "the real challenge of intelligence is assessing intangibles, making sense of them, and relating them to actionable strategies."[453]

You must integrate information about critical players or competitors. Know where they stand on specific issues or as they compete. What are likely to be

---

[451] Bremer and his team did not do this during the First Battle of Fallujah and paid a stiff price for their failure. The team that led the second battle did, and it paid huge dividends.

[452] In Iraq, al-Qaeda spread rumors about vaccinations administered by U.S. veterinarians to cattle. Rumors can create destructive anxiety by making plausible connections between concrete events and real social anxieties. The bovine poisoning rumor had a narrative, story, theme, and message, which was: the Crusades were a Western attempt to pillage and destroy Islam; today, U.S. forces are repeating the pattern. This narrative provided context. The bovine story invoked the crusader narrative to tell a story about "non-Arab/non-Muslim invaders plunder[ing] Arab lands for riches while proclaiming allegiance to a high power and a more righteous religion." This narrative defined the U.S. occupation across Iraq: that U.S. forces were poisoning cattle, using helicopters to stir up dust storms, and using technologies to cause draught as they invaded Iraq to pillage oil fields. The rumor portrayed American forces as an existential threat and the Iraq government as weak and ineffective. The message delivered was: Iraqis must rise and resist the occupation. This example is drawn from Daniel Leonard Bernardi, et al., <u>Narrative Landmines: Rumors, Islamist Extremism, and the Struggle for Strategic Influence</u> (New Brunswick, NJ: Rutgers University Press, 2012), an excellent study of the nature and impact of rumor-mongering. See also: Cass R. Sunstein, <u>On Rumors: Why Falsehoods Spread, Why We Believe Them, What Can Be Done</u> (New York: Farrar, Straus and Giroux, 2009); Patrick B. Mullen, "Modern Legend and Rumor Theory," *Journal of the Folklore Institute* 9, no. 2 (1972): 95–109, https://doi.org/10.2307/3814160; and Nicholas DiFonzo, <u>The Water Cooler Effect: A Psychologist Explores the Extraordinary Power of Rumors</u> (New York: Avery, 2008).

[453] Interview with Greg Treverton, March 29, 2021.

their intended responses to your actions? Branson hasn't leveled a direct accusation, but it's apparent that he felt Coca-Cola exerted undue pressure on retailers to deny Virgin Cola shelf space. What intelligence the U.S. possessed, and which was channeled to decision-makers affected what happened at Pearl Harbor and on 9/11.

When reality dawned on him at the Battle of Little Big Horn, General George Custer probably wished he had been better informed. The Normandy invasion turned partly on the German failure to gather timely intelligence, the Allies' success in keeping it from them, and the Allies' knowing the German Order of Battle. Who possessed what essential information altered the outcomes. We discussed this point as to EAGLE CLAW and the Challenger Disaster. It's worth stressing again.

IBM's experience presents a positive side of intelligence/information gathering in business. Gathering the right information or intelligence is what data analytics offered by IBM aims to reveal, providing, in the company's words, "actionable insights in your data…[finding out] what happened, and then explore why it happened. These insights can be used to chart or change the path of your business. The tools and technical products of IBM give you the power to collect, organize and analyze your data rapidly."[454] IBM touts its Watson software and consulting expertise to use business intelligence to improve results, or, as its slogan might put it, enable you to think smarter and create a smarter world.

12. Providing for ongoing updates of information and intelligence.

Clausewitz's point about the frictions of war is that kinetic engagement constantly changes the facts on the ground. Napoleon was a great commander as long he commanded a relatively small army and had line-of-sight over the movements made by all forces. Historian Andrew Roberts points out that

> "much of the art of warfare in the Napoleonic era depended not on the technology of weaponry… but upon the skilled interaction of the three main military elements of the day: cavalry, infantry, and artillery. When they were deployed in a coordinated way, complementing and supporting each other in attack and anchoring each other in

---

[454] IBM, "What is Business Intelligence? Transforming data into business insights," *CIO*, October 16, 2019: https://www.cio.com/article/2439504/business-intelligence-definition-and-solutions.html.

> defence, they could be a formidable, indeed campaign-winning juggernaut."[455]

Bonaparte was less adept at handling larger armies, as when he invaded Russia. The Russian misadventure is depressing even to read about. Movies portray attribute the debacle to the cold Russian winter trapping him. Certainly that hurt. But Napoleon lost the campaign before it even started, thanks to disorganization, lack of logistical preparation, and failure to think ahead.

At Austerlitz, he could see the order of battle. Commanding a disciplined, hardened, top-notch army, his aggressive pincer strategy was a masterpiece of rapid fire and maneuver. He attacked before his enemies could adjust. He exploited openings. The Russians and Austrians had a larger army. Napoleon triumphed by choosing the battleground and using disinformation that tricked the enemy into exposing their rear.[456]

His on-the-ground intelligence revealed that the allies incorrectly believed he wanted to negotiate, not fight. He duped them into initiating the battle he wanted. Relevant to business executives, he chose the time, place, and tactics to compete. He selected those that played to his strengths and exploited the other side's weaknesses. The parallels with Dollar Shave Club, Harry's Razors, and other innovative online retailers echo his mindset. As you think about marketing strategy and resources, get all the information you can on the competition. Figure out, in a shifting market in which the competition may not lie still while you eat away at their share, what they are likely to do, and then plan out the moves and countermoves.

The best modern military example of using information may be its brilliant use in Iraq during the 2003 Iraq War by General Stanley McChrystal. His "team of teams" concept enabled his team to aggressively collect and exploit intelligence. He flattened his organization, held 90-minute video sessions with vast numbers of participants, shared information, and kept ahead of the curve. His team adapted rapidly to new information in real time. His special operations task force alone accounted for perhaps 12,000 of the Al-Qaeda killed in Iraq.[457] The British had a similar team that accounted for 3500 Al-Qaeda deaths.[458] They created an

---

[455] See: Andrew Roberts, Waterloo: Napoleon's Last Gamble, (Harper Perennial, Kindle Ed), Kindle Loc. 589/1938.
[456] Frank McLynn, Napoleon: A Biography, (New York: Arcade Publishing, 2011) Kindle Loc. 6764/15,527.
[457] See: Stanley McChrystal, My Share of the Task, (New York: Portfolio/Penguin, 2013).
[458] Mark Urban, Task Force Black, (New York: St. Martin's Press, 2011).

iterative process that kept the Special Operations teams on top of where the enemy was. Today, McChrystal has moved his concept to the commercial world and earned tens of millions of dollars.

His approach works for executives, and you should think of ways to use it. The core precept of a "team of teams" is to devolve information sharing and decision-making to the lowest practical level and to capitalize on a flexible horizontal organization rather than a rigid hierarchical one.

13.   Addressing efforts to overcome language and cultural barriers.

Executives can deal with language barriers. Cultural barriers may present a larger obstacle. Global brands like Nike and Proctor & Gamble tailor narrative, themes, and messaging to local nuance.

Admiral Stavridis stresses the need to overcome these barriers in business.

> "Overcoming them is done the old-fashioned way. Study, learn, read, engage. Does your company have a reading list of recommended books? Does it detail its people to sit in on approved webinars? Do you take the time to educate your people? My daughter works at Google. Google partially funded her MBA at NYU. The Navy sent me to the Fletcher School of Law & Diplomacy for two years to work on a Ph.D. You need to study broadly, engage with people who know a foreign culture, take the time to dig beneath the surface, and really understand what makes cultures and their citizens tick. There are no short-cuts."[459]

---

[459] Interview with Admiral (Ret) James G. Stavridis, June 2, 2021.

14.   Citing helpful examples.

A communication plan should use examples to illustrate challenges and solutions which provide context and help the team make sense of the narrative, story, themes, and messages that drive strategies. Companies like to use creative briefs that parallel the military use of a written strategic plan. However you characterize the document, you need one.

15.   Budgeting the resources a campaign requires.

Define financial costs and the resources required: people, assets, technology, and transportation – everything a plan requires. Define communication requirements: know what is required to get the job done regarding physical assets, from cameras and recording devices to graphic artists, media placement experts, research, cyber capabilities, and people.

Discussion Questions

1. Who or what presents obstacles and what is their significance for your success? Are they mountains or molehills? How do you plan to identify and assess obstacles? What methodology will you employ to do so? How does each step in your strategy and action plan (SAP) connect to and surmount relevant or unanticipated obstacles or landmines?

2. How are you measuring to ensure success? Are you using performance or qualitative (outcome-based) metrics? Have you set up a baseline for judgments about the SAP's success? How will you determine what parts of your SAP work or don't work?

3. Are you willing to stand your ground against criticism or make appropriate adjustments to the SAP? Think about the cases of Coca-Cola's "Share a Moment" campaign and Moment's "suds" ad.

4. Has your SAP considered both the benefits and risks of the technology it employs? Think about Code's "Share a Moment" campaign and its 150-name list of names.

5. Are you fostering an atmosphere in which stakeholders can and do communicate to you all essential information – and does your SAP build in what's needed to do that?

6. How are you appealing to customer identity? The popularity of Coca-Cola Classic is an example of an identity-based success story.

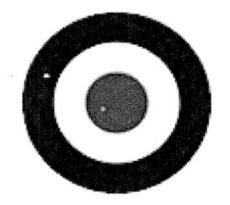

CHAPTER NINE

HOW VITAL IS STRATEGIC COMMUNICATION TO CRISIS MANAGEMENT?

Every executive faces a crisis sooner or later. How you handle it affects your career and your company's prosperity. Every crisis is unique. But what's common to handling them properly is smart strategic communication. That sounds like a "so what." Actually, more often than not, I've found that companies drop the ball. Their first reaction is usually denial. The second is looking for ways to shift blame or to excuse their conduct. The third is figuring out how to limit liability. At that point, they're caught up in a train wreck.

Bad facts make bad crises. But the right strategic communication can minimize the damage and avoid a debacle with long-term knock-on consequences.

A Military Example: Abu Ghraib

Abu Ghraib detention facility is a prison located twenty miles west of Baghdad. Brig. Gen. Janis Karpinski was commanding. In October 2003, Specialist (E-4) Joseph M. Darby, an MP, visited Abu Ghraib. He was shown a photo of a naked prisoner chained to his cell, arms above his head. In January, he made a report to the military's Criminal Investigation Division (CID) that included a CD with photos. CID opened a criminal investigation.[460]

The military announced its investigation. Seventeen U.S. soldiers were suspended pending the outcome. Maj. Gen. Antonio Taguba led an investigation. He reported that guards had placed bags over the heads of detainees, threatened them with rape, used dogs as intimidation and broken lightbulbs to pour their phosphoric liquid on detainees while grinning male and female American soldiers looked on.[461] Such conduct exposed a glaring crisis in management that severely damaged the reputation and credibility of U.S. and coalition forces, already struggling to win over the Iraqis. Most Iraqis were glad to see Saddam Hussein deposed. They were not happy to host what they viewed as an occupying force of infidels.

Scholars Carol Downing and Patricia Swann define crisis as "an unstable or crucial time or state of affairs in which a decisive change is impending, especially one with the distinct possibility of a highly desirable outcome."[462] This crisis rattled the military, as well it should have. The savage treatment of detainees violated this nation's values and the 1949 Geneva Conventions, the IMT Charter (Nuremberg), and other international accords, which forbid the ill-treatment of prisoners.[463]

---

[460] Carol A. Downing and Patricia A. Swann, "Situation: Abu Ghraib: A Comparative Study of Pedagogical Approaches to Faulty Communication," *Proceedings of the New York State Communication Association,* (2007): www.nyscanet.org/pdf/07proceedings/swann.pdf. For a more detailed discussion of the Abu Ghraib crisis, see James P. Farwell, Persuasion & Power, supra, Chapter Three, p. 37-39. The Abu Ghraib discussion draws on that book, which embraced the Downing/Swann model for dealing with crisis communication.
[461] Article 15-6, "Investigation of the 80th Military Police Brigade."
[462] Webster's Dictionary (1990), p. 307.
[463] Common Article 3 of the third 1949 Geneva Conventions explicitly prohibits "violence to life and person, in particular … cruel treatment and torture [and] outrages upon personal dignity, in particular humiliating and degrading treatment" with respect to persons taking no active part in the hostilities, including members of armed forces who have laid down their arms and those placed *hors de combat* by sickness, wounds, detention, or any other cause." Geneva III, "Geneva Convention Relative to the Treatment of Prisoners of War," August 12, 1949, 6 U.S.T., 75 U.N.T.S. 135. Article 6 of the IMT Charter (Nuremberg) defines "ill-treatment of prisoners of war" as a war crime. See: https://ihl-databases.icrc.org/customary-ihl/eng/docs/v2_rul_rule90_sectiona

Downing and Swann identified five specific strategies that the White House and the military employed to contain the damage: **preemption, commiseration, disassociation, shock,** and **rectification**.[464] Preemption seeks to get out in front of a story, control it, defuse controversy before severe damage is inflicted, or limit the damages that one could suffer. It recognizes that media stories exist today in a global environment in which radio, television, and print press come together in "one digital expression."[465]

The impact of that singularity is far-ranging. Social media such as Facebook, Twitter, Instagram, and YouTube are supplanting traditional newspapers, radio, and television. Social media empowers individuals to shape the discourse over emerging events, often almost immediately. Commiseration leads to expressions of empathy for the affected. Disassociation can separate the accused from responsibility for what transpired. Shock is a term that speaks for itself. Rectification seeks to redress the harm inflicted. The five strategies employed at Abu Ghraib are not exclusive.

Vietnam illustrates the consequences of failing to be transparent. Under the U.S. commander, General William Westmoreland, public affairs provided inaccurate, rosy reports about progress in the war. Westmoreland famously claimed he was seeing "the light at the end of the tunnel."

By the time North Vietnamese forces staged the Tet Offensive on January 31, 1968, the credibility of the U.S. command lay in tatters. The Communists suffered a stunning military setback with their failed offensive. Still, lack of credibility spurred CBS correspondent and anchorman Walter Cronkite to mistakenly believe and report that the Communists had won. Historians will long debate whether the South Vietnamese government could have prevailed. But it's evident that the U.S. military and political leadership's failure to get out in front with the truth hurt badly.[466]

The precepts for crisis communication apply pretty equally to military leaders and executives. W. Timothy Combs identifies additional strategies.[467] **Refutation** rebuts alleged facts. **Elimination** denies that a crisis exists.

---

[464] Carol A. Downing and Patricia A. Swann, "Situation: Abu Ghraib: A Comparative Study of Pedagogical Approaches to Faulty Communication," supra.

[465] Id.

[466] See: Neil Sheehan, A Bright Shining Lie, (New York: Random House, 1988); David Halberstam, The Best and the Brightest, (New York: Ballantine Books, 1993) (Anniversary Edition); and Lewis Sorley, (New York: Harcourt, 1993). Sheehan and Halberstam authored influential criticism of the war, while Sorley makes a compelling case for why the skeptics were misguided.

[467] See: W. Timothy Combs, Ongoing Crisis Communication, 4th. Ed., (Washington: Sage, 2015).

Avoidance acknowledges a crisis but seeks to justify what has occurred, pleading lack of intent to harm or that no laws were broken. **Justification** minimizes the seriousness or says the victims caused their own harm, i.e., "Our oil spill was a drop in the bucket compared to the Exxon Valdez," or faulting a car driver hurt in an accident he has not caused for failing to wear his seatbelt. In politics, the comparison used is "I got a speeding ticket. He committed murder." **Attachment** bolsters credibility by citing good things a company has done. Boeing has countered the hailstorm of bad publicity over the Supermax 737 crashes by touting itself as the industry leader in cutting-edge technology. **Transcendence** praises the victims for heroism, i.e., "The heroic efforts of those that helped clean this oil spill cannot be overstated."

The military has divided views on public relations. One school of thought argues that the military should avoid using it to express opinions to influence audiences. That's absurd, but Pentagon officials widely share the view. A second – embraced by Brig. Gen. (Ret) Mark Kimmitt – recognizes that all reporting has subjectivity. Just selecting what facts you discussed, neutrally presented, is a subjective choice. In crisis communication, executives and political players are generally smarter and faster on the uptake than the military. Thanks to Kimmitt, Abu Ghraib was an exception. The scandal was corrosively damaging and had to be contained.

Kimmitt led the military's public response. The key tactic was *to get ahead of the story so that the Coalition could shape the story.* At a March 30 press conference, he disclosed what had happened and advised that *Sixty Minutes II* planned to broadcast a story. The press asked tough questions. Kimmitt earned high marks for transparency. He invoked the strategy of disassociation, declaring that Abu Ghraib was an aberration. He gave assurances that the United States would treat prisoners with dignity.

On April 30, President George W. Bush denounced the abuses. He declared: "Yes, I shared a deep disgust that these prisoners were treated the way they were treated. Their treatment does not reflect the nature of the American people. That's not the way we do things in America."[468] He *commiserated* with the detainees although he erred in failing to apologize to the Iraqis. He *disassociated* the behavior at Abu Ghraib from what he deemed acceptable. He employed *rectification* in promising that justice would be done.

---

[468] President George W. Bush, "The President's News Conference With Prime Minister Paul Martin of Canada," April 30, 2007.

Secretary of Defense Donald Rumsfeld, State Department Spokesman Richard Boucher, Maj. Gen. Geoffrey Miller (commander of U.S. prisons in Iraq) and Kimmitt all maintained message discipline, echoing the president's message in their own media interviews, statements, and press conferences.[469] They drove the message that the U.S. stands for the right values and was helping, not hurting, the Iraqis. In August, the Pentagon issued public affairs guidance.[470]

The guidance offered the assurance that the "army is committed to ensuring all soldiers live up to the army values and the laws of land warfare regardless of the environment or circumstances." It may sound like vague military-speak, but the meaning was clear to the armed forces.

This guidance further defined the military's messages: the army investigation would "go where the facts lead." It held that the incident was caused by "misconduct by a small group of soldiers and civilians," "lack of discipline" by leaders and soldiers of the 205th M1 Brigade, and "failure of leadership by multiple echelons" within the Combined Joint Task Force (CJTF-7). The messages limited the scope of abuse, denounced them as a counter to US Army values, and, invoking the tactic of *attachment* that gives credit to the good aspects of an organization, stressed that this regrettable incident "should not blind us to the noble conduct of the vast majority of our soldiers."

Kimmitt notes that Abu Ghraib was an extraordinary situation, and he doesn't like to compare it to crisis management in the commercial world. "Due to the unique aspect of Courts-Martial," he notes, "the Commander may have to adjudicate the case, and any response may wind up prejudicing the legal process."[471] But his approach echoes tactics that executives employ. Kimmitt handled the situation like the top pro he is. His down-to-earth personality, open manner, and well-recognized integrity among the news media made a big difference for the U.S.

His interview with Dan Rather for *60 Minutes* resonated because he was upfront. My close friend Rich Galen, whom the White House had sent to Iraq to help with news media affairs, had kindly introduced me to Kimmitt some time ago. I was glad to be able to interview him for this book. He is a repository of wisdom and common sense.

---

[469] Downing and Swann, supra, p. 7.
[470] "Public Affairs Guidance Approved for Use Commencing 25 1500 AUG 04," www.aclu.org/files/projects/foiasearch/pdf/DOD045833.pdf.
[471] Interview with Brig. General (Ret) Mark Kimmitt, May 13, 2021.

As Kimmitt put it in our discussions,

> "Abu Ghraib was a gut-punch to the military. Speaking to the media – and a world audience – was grueling because the soldiers' action was indefensible. They let their fellow soldiers down. My focus was to acknowledge the transgressions but make it clear that they did not reflect the values of the Army or the 100,000 soldiers who were fighting a tough war honorably and ethically."[472]

While crisis management for executives is primarily about damage control, the military uses it proactively. I mentioned the tsunami earlier. The 2004 Boxing Day tsunami that killed an estimated 165,708 people presented an opportunity to blunt anti-American sentiment in Indonesia, the world's largest Muslim nation.[473] The U.S. deployed the hospital ship USNS *Mercy* to support the Indonesian government and navy with relief efforts. Coordinating with Indonesian naval officers, the U.S. Navy deployed an advance echelon team of five officers to prepare for *Mercy's* arrival.

Navy officials finalized arrangements with officials, hired contractors, identified local areas that would benefit from medical projects, and ensured achievable force protection goals. They capitalized on media opportunities to highlight positive stories about *Mercy's* visit. They pushed the theme of cooperation and interoperability, goodwill, and cross-cultural exchange. That helped Indonesians understand and aroused support for the U.S. Pacific Partnership mission.

The Navy team eschewed propaganda. It maintained open discussion of the mission with the Indonesian press. They produced press releases, images, and videos of medical events for the local media. It invited the local media to observe activities. The impact created a favorable image for the U.S. Navy among Indonesians.

How does the military's approach compare to the corporate world? Johnson & Johnson's celebrated handling of incidents involving Tylenol; Ashland Oil's response when a storage tank collapsed, dumping thousands of gallons of oil into

---

[472] Interview with Brig. General (Ret) Mark Kimmitt, May 13, 2021.
[473] D.L. Bernardi, P.H. Cheong, C. Lundry and S.W. Ruston, <u>Narrative Landmines</u>, (Piscataway: Rutgers University Press, 2012), Kindle Loc. 1604/2523, et al. The description of how the U.S. responded to the tsunami is drawn from this chapter in their book.

the river and affecting the drinking water of hundreds of thousands of people downstream; and other crises handled by Exxon, Toyota, Tide, and Boeing offer lessons for executive leaders.

Virgil Scudder is internationally renowned for counseling the CEOs of Fortune 100 companies on corporate communication and crisis management. Scudder argues that

> "most companies find themselves poorly prepared to deal with a major crisis. Crises cannot be avoided, but you can mitigate the damage. The key questions, all of which deal with strategic communication, and offer parallels to military problems discussed in this book, are not 'whether.' They are 'when,' 'how bad,' and 'is everything in place for a quick, effective response?"[474]

Scudder observes that a crisis crystallizes two qualities about a company: "its cultures and its level of preparation."[475] The Abu Ghraib case illustrates the same point. Scudder and Mark Kimmitt agree: how an organization *handles* a crisis is likely to significantly impact their reputation than the crisis itself.[476]

Disasters inflict damage on victims and organizations. But careful handling of them through action that communicates the organization's attitude towards itself and those affected, and a willingness to acknowledge the facts then solve a problem it may have created, can lessen damage. Conversely, mishandling a small crisis can inflict outsized adverse impact.

Tylenol

Early in the morning of Wednesday, September 29th, 1982, "a tragic medical mystery" began with a sore throat and a runny nose. It was then that Mary Kellerman, a 12-year-old girl from Elk Grove Village, a suburb of Chicago, told

---

[474] Interview with Virgil Scudder, May 3, 2021. Many of the insights in this chapter draw on my discussions with Mr. Scudder over the 33 years that I have had the opportunity to work with him as a colleague and friend.
[475] Id.
[476] Interview with Virgil Scudder, May 3, 2021; Interview with Brig. Gen. (Ret) Mark Kimmitt, April 30, 2021.

her parents about her symptoms. They gave her an Extra Strength TYLENOL® unaware that the bottle had been tampered with and the drug contaminated with potassium cyanide. Mary was dead by 7 AM. Within a week, there were six additional deaths, almost immediately attributed to contaminated Tylenol.[477]

Contrary to the anecdotal record, James Burke, the CEO of Johnson & Johnson, convened a meeting of his senior people the following day. He scheduled appointments the next week with the FDA, the FBI, and other agencies interested in the events. Chicago public authorities reacted instantly. They broadcast statements and sent rescue vehicles through neighborhoods, blaring announcements to set Tylenol aside until officials unraveled the mystery.

In a video biography produced by Harvard Business School,[478] Burke remarked that he and his entourage arrived in Washington, DC, and began meeting with the FBI. The Bureau urged J&J not to remove the product from the shelves for the fear that the FBI could not catch the perpetrators. The FDA also wanted to avoid panic or to create copycat events during Halloween, only thirty days away. Intelligence agencies feared it might be the work of a terrorist organization and removing the product might net terrorists a propaganda victory.

During the FDA meeting, Burke received a phone call from his office alerting him to a copycat crime on the west coast using a different poison, strychnine. Happily, the victim survived. At that point, nearly a week after the deaths of Mary Kellerman and six others, Burke instructed J&J to withdraw Tylenol from the market. In the Chicago area, aggressive warnings had deterred people from using it.

Burke's decision to accept responsibility helped protect the company's reputation, just as a decision by John Hall, the CEO of Ashland Oil, did for his company after a storage tank collapse.

The Tylenol account comes from an interview with Jim Lukaszewski, one of America's top corporate crisis managers who has advised over 400 major companies on crises. Says Lukaszewski: "Burke recalled 31 million capsules. More importantly, J&J established an extraordinary 24/7 global communications effort to tell the world to take no more capsules until the cause and extent of the tampering were determined. J&J stopped producing and advertising the product. A $100,000 reward for information – never collected – was posted.

---

[477] https://www.pbs.org/newshour/health/tylenol-murders-1982
[478] James Burke, "James Burke: A Career in American Business," videotape number 890-513, Boston: Harvard Business School Publishing Corporation, 2006

Lukaszewski also recalled another part of the incident that went largely unreported: the decade-long struggle between J&J and the survivors to get the cases settled. Jack O'Dwyer, a constant critic of the J & J response, reported in his October 1, 2012 newsletter that "it took eight years of wrangling in court to win a settlement out of J & J which family members say is far from munificent."[479]

Union Carbide

At Bhopal in the state of Madhya Pradesh, a plant that produced Sevin, a pesticide, experienced an accident that killed 3,800 people instantly, thousands more later, and injured at least 15,000 individuals. The tragedy affected 200,000 Indian citizens. It produced 145 class-action lawsuits against Union Carbide Corporation (UCC), got its CEO arrested in India, and wound up costing UCC over $470 million in settlement costs. Although the plant had experienced a history of problems, and maintenance was questionable,[480]

UCC protested that it did not design, build, or construct the plant. The plant employed 1,000 Indians. The only American employee had left two years before the accident, although critics argued that UCC monitored day-to-day operations from the U.S.[481] The Indian government considered the plant to be Indian, and the aftermath of the accident its responsibility.[482] Still, fingers pointed at UCC, throwing its back up against a wall and leaving it divided internally about what to do.

Journalist Dan Kurtzman has written an excellent account of the tragedy and Union Carbide's handling of it. This section draws upon his reporting.[483] India wanted foreign investment. It had asked UCC to build the plant. The

---

[479] https://www.odwyerpr.com/blog/index.php?/archives/5173-30th-Anniv.-of-Tylenol-Murders-Gets-Scant-Notice.html

[480] Dan Kurzman, A Killing Wind: Inside Union Carbide and the Bhopal Catastrophe, (New York: McGraw-Hill, 1987), Chapter 2, p. 37 et al. Kurzman argues that managers had short-changed safety and maintenance to save money, putting profit ahead of safety.

[481] Rajesh Chhabara, "Bhopal gas disaster: Corporate negligence has deadly consequences," *ethicalcorp.com*, January 3, 2010: http://www.ethicalcorp.com/supply-chains/bhopal-gas-disaster-corporate-negligence-deadly-consequences

[482] *In Re Union Carbide Corporation Gas Plant Disaster at Bhopal, India in December 1984*, 809 F.2d 195 (2nd Circuit, 1987), p. 7.

[483] Dan Kurzman, A Killing Wind: Inside Union Carbide and the Bhopal Catastrophe, (New York: McGraw-Hill, 1987).

government, not UCC, had selected the location. The government took a 22% stake in the company's subsidiary, Union Carbide India Limited (UCIL). It encouraged local investment, and 23,500 Indians invested. India considered the plant to be Indian and the disaster to be its problem.[484]

Widespread crop failures and famine that hurt farmers caused reduced demand for the pesticide, hence the plant experienced a drop-in in production. Plans were made to sell the plant. In the meantime, it continued operating, with safety equipment and procedures far below the standards found at its sister plant in Institute, West Virginia. The local Indian government knew the safety problems but insisted on keeping the plant going to avoid economic dislocation.[485]

One night, the chemical methyl isocyanate (MIC) was accidentally released from the plant. The incident became an explosive international story. The news media focused on events at the plant, loss of life, and rescue operations, cause of the accident, the economic impact on UCC, and UCC's response.[486] UCC officers and staff felt uncertain what to do.[487] The corporate communications staff strongly recommended transparency. But UCC was traditionally cautious in dealing with the media.[488] Concerned about liability issues, counsel urged management to say as little as possible.[489]

This issue comes up all the time in business. Disaster preparation needs to consider the correct business judgment that defines policy and strikes a balance between disclosure and non-disclosure. CEO Warren Anderson felt it essential to demonstrate commitment to the Indian government by making a personal appearance. His executives and the U.S. State Department cautioned he risked embroiling himself and UCC in deeper controversy.

UCC executives argued that Anderson could do everything needed from corporate headquarters in Danbury, Connecticut. They worried that survivors might kill him. They suspected that Indians would view the trip as a public

---

[484] *In Re Union Carbide Corporation Gas Plant Disaster at Bhopal, India in December 1984*, 809 F.2d 195 (2nd Circuit, 1987), p. 7.
[485] Edward Broughton, "The Bhopal disaster and its aftermath: a review," *Environmental Health*, Vol. 4, No. 6 (May 2005): https://www.ncbi.nlm.nih.gov/pmc/articles/PMC1142333/
[486] See: Lee Wilkins, "Bhopal: The Politics of Mediated Risk," in Lynne Masel Walters, Lee Wilkins, and Tim Walters, ed., Bad Tidings: Communication and Catastrophe, (Hillsdale: Lawrence Erlbaum Associates, Inc., 1988).
[487] Dan Kurzman, A Killing Wind: Inside Union Carbide and the Bhopal Catastrophe, (New York: McGraw-Hill, 1987).
[488] Id., p. 89.
[489] Id., p. 174.

relations stunt. Worried about a sharp drop in stock price, others insisted that he focus on convincing shareholders that the company would survive.[490]

Anderson consulted with a key Indian executive on the ground, Keshab Mahinda. Mahinda was skeptical but assured him – incorrectly – that Indians would welcome his visit. Anderson ignored the warnings and went to India. Arriving by private jet, what Anderson discovered was rattling. He realized he knew few details of the plant's operation.

Here we see essential lessons: know what is going on in your operations and who is doing what. Make certain clear lines of open communication exist. In any crisis, get and stay ahead of the curve. Anderson shouldn't have been taken by surprise.

At a meeting in Mumbai, Anderson impressed his team with his take-charge manner. He wanted to provide a relief check, perhaps presented to the Prime Minister after arriving in Bhopal, to show Union Carbide's concern for human suffering. He flew on the company jet to Bhopal. Authorities arrested him on his arrival for culpable homicide.[491] The state's Chief Minister, Arjun Singh, and his team had decided to show force and turn down any relief offered as a deal made with criminals.[492]

Here is a lesson in dealing with overseas operations. Make sure you have on-the-ground, trusted people who have the answers *and* know the score, as well as the guts to tell you the truth. Anderson let himself get blindsided.

Seeking to escape liability, the Indian government's strategic communication faulted UCC for lax safety and maintenance procedures. It wanted to show Indians it could handle the medical and disaster relief response. It sought to maintain the credibility of local government with its population.[493] No surprise that the government greeted Anderson with handcuffs, not flowers.

Despite its hands-off approach to operations, UCC faced other problems, especially after the U.S. Second Circuit Court of Appeal decided that Indian courts could handle litigation. Critics argued that "at every turn, UCC has attempted to manipulate, obfuscate, and withhold scientific data to the detriment of victims… [refusing to state]…exactly what was in the toxic cloud that enveloped the city on that December night." They charged that UCC failed to

---

[490] Id., p. 95-98, 114.
[491] Id., p. 108, 117.
[492] Id.
[493] Id., p. 118-120.

clean up the industrial site and that toxic chemicals continued to leak into local aquifers.[494]

UCC's strategic communication focused on the financial impact on the company, limiting liability, the company's future, stockholders, and Wall Street analysts. UCC found getting information difficult. It confronted conflicting interests, impairing its ability to define and rapidly drive messages.[495] Critics accused UCC of stonewalling.[496] Shrivastava argues that UCC had failed to prepare for a crisis, coming up short on information and an inability to articulate sympathy for victims.[497]

These problems undercut its crisis management. UCC lacked an incident response team. It failed to anticipate India's response. It had no way to communicate with the plant, complicating information collection. UCC took a severe hit. A hostile takeover effort forced it to divest itself of profitable divisions. It dwindled to one-sixth of its previous size.[498]

One bright note was that while UCC shelled out close to a half-billion dollars in accepting "moral responsibility," matters could have been worse. The Indian government had sought $3 billion.[499] Some believe that had UCC lost in trial, it might have faced a ruinous $10 billion judgment.

What struck me about this case is that the situation limited UCC's options. A lesson is that before a crisis occurs, assembling a solid security risk assessment team, and an incident response team, can pay off. The media will cover a breaking story. Executives are well advised to provide input into coverage. Otherwise, other parties, many of them hostile, will shape the story.

Former National Security Advisor, General (Ret.) Brent Scowcroft told me a story about what made President George H.W. Bush effective at national security. The lesson applies to Union Carbide's situation. The company's failure to establish strong media relationships was a problem in getting its message out. Scowcroft related that Bush often called foreign leaders. He forged personal

---

[494] Edward Broughton, "The Bhopal disaster and its aftermath: a review.
[495] Paul Shrivastava, Bhopal: Anatomy of a Crisis, (London: Ballinger Pub. Co., 1987).
[496] Id., p. 101.
[497] Id., p. 99.
[498] Edward Broughton, "The Bhopal disaster and its aftermath: a review," supra.
[499] Sanjoy Hazarika, "Bhopal payments from Union Carbide set at $470," *New York Times*, February 15, 1989: https://www.nytimes.com/1989/02/15/business/bhopal-payments-by-union-carbide-set-at-470-million.html. UCC had first offered $200 million, then raised its offer to $350 million.

relationships. It was why, during Desert Storm, he could assemble a broad international coalition to fight Saddam Hussein. Scowcroft's point was that when the time comes that you need friends, you will already have them. Warren Anderson hadn't thought of that, and the omission proved costly.

Boeing

People used to mouth a slogan at the Pentagon, where Boeing enjoyed large defense contracts: *If it ain't Boeing, it ain't going.*[500] On October 29, 2018, the attitude shifted after Lion Air flight JT 610 took off from Jakarta's Soekarno-Hatta International Airport at 6:20 a.m. Less than 13 minutes later, the Boeing 737 Max crashed into the sea, killing all passengers. In March 2019, a second Max crashed over Ethiopia. The final report on the Indonesian disaster pointed to flaws in Boeing's design of the plane and mistakes by the airline and staff.[501]

The flaw involved MCAS, an anti-stall software introduced on the Boeing 737-8 (MAX) to enhance pitch characteristics, flaps up, during manual flight in elevated angles. The flaw caused the plane's nose to point continually down, out of the pilots' control. The doomed planes nosedived to the sea or ground. The final report concluded that the design and certification of the software did not adequately consider the likelihood of loss of control of the aircraft. It stated that a fail-safe design concept and a redundant system was necessary.[502] A report on the Ethiopian air crash reached similar conclusions.[503]

Boeing's crisis management response was a Donnybrook. Tylenol and Abu Ghraib taught the value of transparency. Union Carbide showed that failure to prepare for disaster, including establishing good relationships with the media and

---

[500] David Schaper, "737 Max Scandal Cuts Boeing's Solid Image," November 26, 2019: https://www.npr.org/2019/11/26/783197253/737-max-scandal-cuts-boeings-once-rock-solid-image.

[501] Komite Nasional Keselamatan Transportasi Republic of Indonesia, *Aircraft Accident Investigation Report*, October 29, 2018: http://knkt.dephub.go.id/knkt/ntsc_aviation/baru/2018%20-%20035%20-%20PK-LQP%20Final%20Report.pdf

[502] For its part, Lion Air did not appear to have inspected a key sensor that turned out to be faulty. Id.

[503] Sinead Baker, "The full Lion Air Crash report hammers Boeing for design flaws that brought down a 737 MAX and killed 189 people," *Business Insider*, October 25, 2019: https://www.businessinsider.com/boeing-737-max-final-lion-air-report-design-crew-errors-2019-10

ensuring timely access to relevant information, can prove costly. Boeing offers a case study in obfuscation, denial, and a refusal to accept responsibility.

Pilots expressed outrage at Boeing's failure to alert them to the new software and suggest that the fault lay with pilot error.[504] Boeing CEO Dennis Muilenburg cut an unsympathetic figure. He explained why the company had installed MCAS and then defended not disclosing its existence to pilots. He challenged the media's characterization of MCAS as an anti-stall system, minimizing it as "not a separate system to be trained on."[505] After the crash report was released, Muilenburg said vaguely that the company was "addressing" the investigator's safety recommendations and "taking actions to enhance the safety of the 737 MAX" to prevent it from happening again.[506]

Instead of calming troubled waters, his statements roiled them. A March 12 statement asserted that "safety is Boeing's number one priority and we have full confidence in the safety of the 737 MAX," and that "The United States Federal Aviation Administration is not mandating any further action at this time…"[507] The assurance lacked credibility as Boeing delayed identifying and fixing the problems. The comment about the FAA was valid, but the implication was that the issues facing the MAX were minor.

The statement walked Boeing into a credibility trap. The impression conveyed was that Boeing put profits ahead of safety.[508] It failed to seize the narrative and guide it. As J&J's James Burke and General Mark Kimmitt showed, leaders must get ahead of the story. Boeing let others tell the tale, costing it control of the narrative. The media, regulators, the President, and the victims' families spoke up, muting Boeing's voice and further shredding its credibility.

Muilenburg was tone-deaf. Boeing's Twitter feed lit up after the Lion Air crash. Boeing did post press releases in a half-hearted effort to get ahead of the story, but it was too little. Forty countries grounded the MAX that night. Boeing asked the U.S. Government to keep it aloft. Muilenberg turned to President Donald Trump for support. That play backfired when news surfaced that he had donated

---

[504] David Schaper, "737 Max Scandal Cuts Boeing's Solid Image," supra.
[505] Id.
[506] Id.
[507] Boeing Statement on 737 MAX Operation, March 12, 2019: https://boeing.mediaroom.com/news-releases-statements?item=130403
[508] Michael Goldstein, "Boeing shows 'What Not to Do' in 737 Max Crisis Communications, Expert says, *Forbes*, March 18, 2019: https://www.forbes.com/sites/michaelgoldstein/2019/03/18/boeing-shows-what-not-to-do-in-737-max-crisis-communications-says-expert/#4884090140a7

$1 million to Trump's 2017 inaugural events. One lesson here is, be careful about making significant gifts to public officials, then asking for special favors under the glare of the media spotlight. It will undercut your credibility, and you risk alienating the officials you are cultivating.

Matters worsened when two employees exchanged messages, commenting: "This airplane is designed by clowns who in turn are supervised by monkeys."[509] Employees mocked federal rules, talked about deceiving regulators, and made jokes about potential flaws in the plane as it was in development. They bragged about limiting required pilot training time, which would increase company profits.[510] If your employees don't trust you, why should anyone else?

Boeing seemed unprepared to deal with this kind of situation. Aircraft mishaps are uncommon, but they do occur. Any large company needs a security risk and vulnerability assessment in place and a rehearsed incident response team to deal with crises. Boeing did fire its CEO but kissed him off with a $60 million golden parachute.[511] Here's another lesson: credibility sags when you pay failed CEOs excessive severance packages.

No surprise, a U.S. Congressional panel opened an investigation. The panel has indicated that its review of Boeing documents pointed to a "very disturbing" picture of commentary from Boeing employees. Boeing claimed that it "proactively brought these communications to the FAA and Congress as part of our commitment to transparency with our regulators and the oversight committees."[512]

As this book goes to press, a new book by Peter Robison takes a behind-the-scenes look that indicts Boeing for dysfunctional, poor management. It's a harrowing tale.

Boeing is a business-to-business operation. Generally, business-to-consumer companies like J&J seem better at handling crises. That does not excuse poor

---

[509] David Shepardson, "Boeing Releases Damaging Messages Related to Grounded 737 Max Fleet," *Reuters,* January 9, 2020: https://www.huffpost.com/entry/boeing-messages-737-max_n_5e17dcb7c5b6640ec3d1bb9d.

[510] Natalie Kitroeff, "Boeing Employees Mocked F.A.A. and "Clowns" Who Designed 737 Max," *New York Times*, January 9, 2020: https://www.nytimes.com/2020/01/09/business/boeing-737-messages.html.

[511] Jackie Wattles, "Boeing's fired CEO could walk away with golden parachute," *CNN.com*, December 24, 2019: https://boeing.mediaroom.com/news-releases-statements?item=130403

[512] David Shepardson, "New Boeing 737 MAX documents show 'very disturbing' employee concerns: U.S. House Aide," *yahoo.com*, December 24, 2019: https://news.yahoo.com/boeing-documents-under-review-point-175624265.html?guccounter=1

performance by what has been widely viewed as one of this nation's most excellent companies.

Starbucks

Starbucks is a legendary success story. But lack of racial sensitivity challenged it. Starbucks raced to address the problem. Any company could unintentionally face this one. Let's take a look.[513] After opening its first store in 1971, Starbucks established itself as an ethical company. It offered full health care and stock options to employees. It embraced diversity and inclusion, created a foundation to support its communities, and located stores in underserved areas. It promoted certified Fair Trade products, established ethical coffee-sourcing standards, and built farmer support centers in coffee-growing regions.

It is vocal about its progressive values. Unfortunately, the hashtag #RaceTogether – encouraging baristas to write "Race Together" on cups of coffee they served and to engage in conversations, generated a backlash.[514] In April 2018 in Philadelphia, two Black customers asked to use a store's bathroom. A White manager denied permission, stating that they made no purchase. Company policy was that restrooms were for customers only. The manager asked them to leave. They refused, explaining that they were waiting for a business associate. The manager called the police, who arrested the men on suspicion of trespassing. Protests, accusations of racial bias, and boycotts followed.[515] Melissa DePino, a customer, videoed the incident and posted it later that afternoon. The video went viral, racking up 9 million views.[516]

The incident raised stirred outrage. Mayor Jim Kenney tweeted: "I'm very concerned by the incident at Starbucks. I know Starbucks is reviewing it and we

---

[513] Rick Kelly, "The Starbucks Incident: a crisis management case study," *bernsteincrisismanagement.com*: https://www.bernsteincrisismanagement.com/the-starbucks-incident-a-crisis-management-case-study/

[514] Austin Carr, "The Inside Story of Starbuck's Race Together Campaign, No Foam," *Fast Company*, June 15, 2015: https://www.fastcompany.com/3046890/the-inside-story-of-starbuckss-race-together-campaign-no-foam

[515] Jonas Sickler, "Crisis Management Lessons Learned From Starbucks," *retailtouchpoints.com*, November 19, 2018: https://retailtouchpoints.com/features/executive-viewpoints/crisis-management-lessons-learned-from-starbucks.

[516] The video can be accessed at: https://abcnews.go.com/News/black-men-walked-starbucks-cuffs-trespassing/story?id=54470047

will be too. @PhillyPolice is conducting an internal investigation."[517] He asked the Philadelphia Commission on Human Relations to "examine the firm's [Starbucks'] policies and procedures" and would be reaching out to Starbucks "to begin a discussion about this." He added there would be a "thorough review" of police policies regarding "complaints like this."[518]

Starbucks CEO Kevin Johnson averted disaster through clear, direct communication. He took the lead as spokesperson. He was upfront and transparent. His message was that Starbucks had done the wrong thing and promised it would do better. He took personal responsibility and declared on Good Morning America, "The circumstances surrounding the incident and the outcome in our store on Thursday were reprehensible, they were wrong, and for that I personally apologize to the two gentlemen who visited our store."[519] He promised more training with store managers about unconscious bias. He reiterated that Starbucks stands against racial profiling and is a company that "creates a warm environment for all customers."[520] He declined to shift responsibility onto the individual employees and attributed fault to the company.

Johnson offered to meet with the customers, apologize in person, and open up a dialogue with them to ensure he understood the situation and to express empathy and compassion for what they had gone through. He invited the customers to join Starbucks to create a teachable moment. The GMA hosts praised his actions.

Starbucks recognized the explosive impact of the situation. Its action plan had four elements. It removed the store manager. It negotiated a fair settlement with the customers. It revised the customer restroom policy to allow anyone to use the restroom without making a purchase. It closed every Starbucks store for sensitivity training. As Reputation Manager Jonas Sickler observed, these rapid actions seized control over the narrative and showed a serious commitment to resolving the issue. They reduced the harmful content that could be published

---

[517] The Mayor's Tweet can be accessed at: https://abcnews.go.com/News/black-men-walked-starbucks-cuffs-trespassing/story?id=54470047

[518] M.L. Nestel, "Handcuffing of 2 black men in Starbucks in Philadelphia called 'reprehensible outcome' by CEO," *ABCNews.com*, April 15, 2018: https://abcnews.go.com/News/black-men-walked-starbucks-cuffs-trespassing/story?id=54470047.

[519] See Johnson's interview on GMA at: https://twitter.com/GMA/status/985848020011958272?ref_src=twsrc%5Etfw&ref_url=http%3A%2F%2Fkomonews.com%2Fnews%2Flocal%2Fstarbucks-ceo-apologizes-live-on-good-morning-america&tfw_site=SeattlePI

[520] Id.

and set the stage for favorable publicity with positive news stories about eliminating plastic straws, a new coffee brand, a partnership with McDonald's to save six billion paper cups a year from landfills, and the launch of a new juice brand.[521]

The Starbucks incident carries useful lessons. It echoed J&J's transparency and rapid response. It affirms that crisis management requires putting a team and strategy in place ahead of time. The Downing/Swann model applies well to corporate situations. Be accountable. Commiserate. Seize and control the narrative. Tell the truth. Communicate a solution and make it happen. Rectify the problem.

Exxon Valdez

The 1989 spill remains, Virgil Scudder states, "the definition of a botched response to an oil spill. The company stalled on its response, delayed clean up, and tried to dodge responsibility for the accident. Initially, it claimed the captain of vessel Exxon Valdez was drunk when it struck Prince William Sound's Bligh Reef, west of Tatitlek, Alaska, spilling 10.8 million gallons of crude oil. It ranks second to the Deepwater Horizon disaster among damage to the environment from an oil spill. The company's response was to stonewall reporters.

The incident provides a catalog of errors to avoid. Exxon's Chairman, Lawrence Rawl, sent underlings to Alaska but failed to go himself. His action communicated the message that Exxon failed to consider the spill important. Exxon did little to get its story out, holding briefings in a small town in Alaska (in an era before Twitter and social media). Executives waited a week to comment. As British Petroleum executives would later do during the Deepwater Horizon disaster, Exxon executives minimized the damage. That was ill-judged. Exxon's reputation took a severe hit for failing to get its facts straight.

Exxon's failures go back to the lessons this book has stressed: successful companies are rooted in strong values of integrity, transparency, hard work, commitment to excellence, and above all, improving people's lives. Exxon's performance merited an "F" on its report card, and it paid the price in litigation. The crisis cost Exxon over $7 billion, including $5 billion in punitive damages awarded by a jury in a 1994 federal jury trial.

---

[521] Jonas Sickler, "Crisis Management Lessons Learned From Starbucks," supra.

Key Lessons About Crisis Management

What lessons do these crisis management situations teach?

1.   Be prepared. Have a strategic crisis management plan.

Have a written strategic crisis management plan in place and get prepared ahead of time. It's the same rule as having a written plan for strategic communication for marketing.

Ken Scudder, a leading practitioner of corporate crisis communication, cautions against taking matters for granted. "Too many companies," he points out, "mistakenly believe a bad crisis can't strike them. They have no plan or, as bad, one that is out of date. Financial problems sometimes cause companies to skimp on crisis management preparation. That can prove costly when a crisis strikes. They lack a clear crisis organizational structure, putting the wrong people in charge or letting everybody call the shots. That's a recipe for disaster twice as worse. They fail to gauge the full impact on stakeholders, including the Board, company executives, shareholders, employees, and the media. You have to be prepared: wargame problems, assign responsibility, forge approaches that enable you to deal effectively with a crisis."[522]

Jim Lukaszewski suggests avoiding the term *crisis management.* In his view,

> "that's a PR term that irritates management, who are generally overconfident in their capacity to respond." The term is defensive. The core concept that emerged after 9/11 is *readiness.* Companies that deal effectively with crises prepare themselves. Their leadership is ready to take charge. They've put in place a response plan, assigned responsibilities, and hold people accountable. Leaders understand that the first strategic goal in crisis response is to prevent harm to victims. The second is to arrange for victim care. The first constituencies with whom company responders need to communicate are employees; those connected to the organization but indirectly affected; customers; shareholders; and the news

---

[522] Interview with Ken Scudder, May 12, 2021.

media. All these notifications should occur within
the first 120 minutes of crisis discovery."[523]

What comprises crucial elements of a crisis management plan? Surprisingly few companies have one, a serious risk in today's era of social media. Virgil Scudder, a top corporate counselor who advises Fortune 100 CEO's, argues that "few have current information about internal or external contacts – who's in what position, their email, phone numbers, etc."[524] He notes that "companies fail to update most plans after mergers or acquisitions."[525]

CEOs need to take charge ahead of time. They need to convene the response team's key members and solicit input from all employees to identify what crises are most likely to strike the organization. "The CEO must ask what the worst-case scenario is,"[526] Scudder notes. Former Pentagon official Dave Patterson adds: "Worst case means deaths, injuries, loss of public confidence, financial damage to the company."[527]

You must assess how prepared your organization is to deal with a crisis. Here are central questions: Who's in charge of crisis management? Who comprises the support team? Have outside counsel and public relations counsel been engaged? Outside PR and legal counsel are critical because if crisis planning and management fall under their purview, with good planning and execution, they *may* succeed in insulating the company from third-party, non-regulatory scrutiny under the attorney-client or work-product privileges.[528] The privilege matters because the first thing a third-party plaintiff will want to know is whether the company had a disaster prevention plan, what it contained, and how well execution of a plan compared to the desired implementation of one. Plaintiffs will hammer at discrepancies. Just as a plan has to be in place, so do members of the crisis management team.[529]

---

[523] Interview with James E. Lukaszewski, May 17, 2021.
[524] Interview with Virgil Scudder, May 13, 2021. He is Ken Scudder's father.
[525] Id.
[526] Interview with Ken Scudder, May 12, 2021.
[527] Interview with David Patterson, May 15, 2021.
[528] Legal privilege is a complicated topic and a detailed analysis of it lies beyond the scope of this book.
[529] For cybersecurity crises, one thinks in terms of the incident breach response team. The functions are parallel, although geared to a cyber incident. See: James Farwell, Geoff Elkins, Yvonne Chalker, and Virginia Roddy, The Legal Architecture of Cybersecurity (Lafayette: U. of Louisiana Lafayette/Sans Souci, 2017).

Outside PR and legal counsel are also valuable as they don't have the biases and "no-no" thinking that can cripple insider discourse. They provide objectivity, as the crisis does not threaten their employment or well-being.

Executives need to strike a balance between interest in legal protection and interest in protecting the company's reputation. Virgil Scudder cites the case of one set of corporate counsel whom he feels cost a company millions of dollars. He reports they also caused "years of distress when top management approved their *defiant* approach over the recommendations of public affairs counsel. Had they settled as we urged them to do, the insurance company was ready to pick up the $50,000 settlement. Four years later, the tab had run into the millions. The lesson is that you need public affairs/public relations and counsel at the same table and listening to the views of each carefully in reaching crisis management decisions."[530]

Virgil Scudder provides an interesting account:

> "A gay state official sued them for outing him, wanting $50,000 and an apology. The CEO was strongly anti-gay, saying "I will never apologize to that queer son of a bitch and he won't get a dime." They listened to their own aggressive chief legal officer and a TV-familiar DC lawyer who recommended taking a hard line. So, they fired me and kept them. Four years later, the problem was still in the newspapers, and they asked me to come back. I told them, "only if you will listen and follow my guidance." They said they would and did and ending up paying half a million dollars, but it stopped the deluge of media stories."[531]

Crisis simulations play an essential role in enabling executives to gain experience in dealing with crises scenarios. "We organized a three-day event for a mall in which the scenario entailed a hostage situation in which three people were killed," Virgil Scudder reports. "Soon after we did the exercise, the mall faced almost the exact same situation. They were able to bring matters under control with only one person killed. The CEO thanked us for getting them ready and stated that the training had kept a terrible situation from escalating into a

---

[530] Interview with Virgil Scudder, May 3, 2021.
[531] Id.

calamity. Local media praised the company for its quick and compassionate response to the shooting between the two gangs."[532]

2. The CEO's actions define the face of the company.

Commanders and U.S. political leaders provide the face for U.S. military action. Whether the outcome is positive or negative, that's who voters look to for information. Dave Patterson offers this insight:

> "The individual who is in charge and responsible for whatever outcomes are in play should be the face to the public. When the public affairs officer stands up and gives a briefing, it's interesting but not nearly as compelling as when the commander, or undersecretary, or secretary stands up and tells the press or any audience, for that matter, what has happened and what HE [or SHE] is going to do about it. If the crisis is ugly, never, ever let the flack do the talking. They are never able to adjust the actions to be taken or take responsibility if that is necessary. I've seen the very best do it, and the crisis is far more likely to be controlled."

The military generally puts its commanders out front only in special situations. Otherwise, it relies upon subordinates, although as we saw in the case of Mark Kimmitt in Iraq, that can mean a flag officer. In a major crisis, executives represent valuable assets if they present the face of the company. The key in all cases is to ensure that they prepare well for media encounters and get the truth out.

3. Be sensitive to the cultural climate in which a crisis occurs.

The military's handling of Abu Ghraib and the Navy's assistance efforts in Indonesia after the tsunami illustrate how the military achieves successful crisis communication. Dave Patterson has articulated a sound approach for how military leaders and executives should surmount this challenge: "It's like understanding any social system. Figure out who the decision-makers, influencers, and evaluators are. The challenge comes when you're faced with a crisis, and you are the decisionmaker. You need trusted confidants. By that, I

---

[532] Id.

mean someone who will tell you when you are wrong. Your job is to make clear you value that advice, solicit it, and listen."[533]

Renowned for goofball advertising, the fast-food chain Jack in the Box released a tone-deaf ad in which its mascot and fictitious CEO, Jack, bragged about the burger chain's new teriyaki bowls. It referred to "Jack's Bowls" and had co-workers saying, "There are some nice bowls" and "Everyone's gonna want to get their hands on Jack's bowls." Jack wears a fake clown-like head. Jack in the Box protested that it was poking fun at itself. Critics felt the play on words referred to private parts of a male body. In the #MeToo era, where sexual harassment in the workplace is a sensitive issue, you should tread carefully.[534]

In Iraq, searching homes without the presence of a male head of household, body searches by U.S. troops of women, and the use of sniffer dogs, proved culturally offensive.[535] The lesson is that what's acceptable in one culture may cause controversy in another.

4.   Taking care of victims is a priority.

"Victim management," Jim Lukaszewski declares, is the most crucial component of all crisis response, and it is missing from most responses. A perfect technical response means nothing if you fail to take care of victims – promptly, humanely, and empathetically. You need to see that their needs are met. Otherwise, the response will be remembered for any survivors, relatives, public officials, competitors, and always, the critics and the emotional voices of the victims."[536]

This is a tough challenge. Lukaszewski says that victim behavior is

> "emotional and often seems irrational, and businesses seem incapable of responding to emotion. Worse, management may be reluctant to take responsibility or blame, or even admit their errors. Management can be as emotional as victims. Too many business schools and American management culture seem to train leaders to

---

[533] Interviews with J. David Patterson, April 23 and May 3, 2021.
[534] Kelly McLaughlin, "Jack in the Box is under fire for a 'tone deaf' sexually charged commercial about teriyaki bowls," *Business Insider*, August 8, 2018: https://www.businessinsider.com/jack-in-the-box-teriyaki-bowls-commercial-criticism-2018-8
[535] Ali A. Allawi, The Occupation of Iraq: Winning the War, Losing the Peace, (New Haven: Yale University Press, 2007), p. 186.
[536] Interview with James E. Lukaszewski, May 17, 2021.

> appear tough instead of acknowledging the facts and accepting responsibility. An empathetic and prompt response makes them stronger, not weaker. Leaders fear appearing sentimental or soft. Too often, legal advice to remain silent ignores that a prompt, empathetic, apologetic response can repair a company's credibility and reputation. Executives can help themselves and their companies by showing humility and apologizing."[537]

Showing humility, being first out with the truth (echoing David Petraeus' mantra) and apologizing for errors are vital lessons that this top corporate crisis counselor urges.

5. Sexual or other harassment in the workplace is deadly.

Lukaszewski explains that harassment is the most grievous victim-producing act that a corporation or its leadership can commit, allow or overlook. "The personal pain of embarrassment or humiliation is permanent. It ruins lives. It taints the workplace. Leaders have a responsibility to lay down clear rules that prohibit it – and make clear that draconian, immediate public punishment will follow a breach of these rules."[538]

At this writing, the *Wall Street Journal* reported that Bill Gates, whom many have seen as a corporate role model, was forced to resign from Microsoft's board, the company he founded, over allegations of workplace harassment.[539] The United States military stands accused of violating its own guidelines in failing to achieve its zero-tolerance policy towards harassment. Hollywood and news media moguls have gained notoriety. But the problem affects small companies as well, and as an executive, watch out for it and move decisively if you detect it.

---

[537] Id.

[538] Interview with James E. Lukaszewski, May 17, 2021. He lays out in detail his views in "Managing the Victim Dimension of Large-Scale Disasters," *Leadership and Management in Engineering*, October 2012.

[539] Emily Glazer, Justin Baer, Khadeeja Safdar, and Aaron Tilley, "Bill Gates Left Microsoft Board Amid Probe Into Prior Relationship with Staffer," *Wall Street Journal,* May 17, 2021: https://www.wsj.com/articles/microsoft-directors-decided-bill-gates-needed-to-leave-board-due-to-prior-relationship-with-staffer-11621205803?mod=hp_lead_pos10.

6. **Using humor in crisis management can be a trap.**

The military should employ humor in dealing with adversaries, but certain humor, especially sexual humor, is a no-go. For industry, the experiences of Moment's "suds" tv ad and Jack in the Box noted above exemplify the trap. In today's highly charged climate of gender politics, that is especially true. One can misinterpret sarcasm or an innocent failed effort at humor, causing hurt, embarrassment or humiliation.

For the military, using humor to discredit enemies can be effective. Authoritarian figures are ideal targets for ridicule. Moliere built his formidable reputation as a playwright and satirist on this truth. Many mistakenly believe that Middle East media takes itself too seriously. Actually, most Arabs have a great sense of humor. They employ satire brilliantly. Saudi comedian Nasser Al Qasabi uses his wit – and a lot of courage – to challenge ISIS.

7. **Be Cautious about inviting consumer stories on the Internet.**

The military uses testimonials from victims of adversary abuse to discredit and de-legitimize the enemy. But what they post is carefully filtered.

McDonald's experience reveals the trap that humor can create. McDonald's created the hashtag, #McDstories. Although the company took down the initial Twitter posting within two hours, McDonald's discovered that crowd-sourced campaigns are difficult to control. Instead of supporting stories, ex-employees critical of the company flooded the Internet. They claimed sightings of rats in restaurants. One user declared, "One time I walked into McDonald's and I could smell Type 2 diabetes floating in the air and I threw up."[540] The hashtag became a bashtag.[541]

As Dave Patterson adds: "In the corporate world, consumer stories are not always controllable. The Pentagon has a better chance of controlling the message. Never depend on a favorable outcome."[542]

---

[540] Kashmir Hill, "#McDStories: When a Hashtag Becomes a Bashtag," *Forbes.com*, January 24, 2012: https://www.forbes.com/sites/kashmirhill/2012/01/24/mcdstories-when-a-hashtag-becomes-a-bashtag/#70f46225ed25

[541] Kashmir Hill, "#McDStories: When a Hashtag Becomes a Bashtag," *Forbes.com*, January 24, 2012: https://www.forbes.com/sites/kashmirhill/2012/01/24/mcdstories-when-a-hashtag-becomes-a-bashtag/#70f46225ed25

[542] Interview with David Patterson, April 23, 2021.

8.   **Social media requires a response within hours, not days or months.**[543]

Things happen immediately, online, often unpredictably, and everybody is a journalist. No longer do broadcast networks or major newspapers act as gatekeepers. Abu Ghraib and Starbucks illustrate how prudent action can make the Internet work for or against you. Boeing shows what happens if you fail to grasp social media's potential impact. Dave Patterson, again: "The propagation of a negative story is swift. You need to be ready to roll out a believable, persuasive, compelling response. There's no easy way to do it. Be prepared organizationally and keep a clear head about your narrative, theme, and message."[544]

9.   **Giving free information is one thing. Offering free products can backfire.**

The military gives nothing away for free. Companies do as promotions. Beware. McDonald's launched a campaign "When the US Wins, You Win" connected with the Olympics giving out scratch-off cards. They offered a small soda for a bronze, regular-sized fries for a silver, a Big Mac for a Gold. McDonald's gave away so many Big Macs that outlets ran short, causing a minor uproar. Still, the company *was* pleased with the visibility it received.[545]

Timothy's Coffee of Toronto offered to send fans four free 24-pack boxes of single-serve coffee for "liking" Timothy on Facebook. As the K-cup boxes for use in Keurig coffee machines sell at $17.95, customers rushed to take advantage of the offer. In three days, the stock was depleted. Overwhelmed, Timothy's had to backtrack. It waited three weeks to say the promotion was "first come, first served," apologized, and offered a coupon for a free 12-pack box.

There are two lessons. First, consider the downside of promotional giveaways before you start giving away. Second, if a problem crops up, act fast but prudently.[546]

---

[543] Paul Cubbard, marketing faculty, University of British Columbia. See: Kyle Schurman, "The untold truth of Jack in the Box," supra.
[544] Interview with Dave Patterson, April 23, 2021.
[545] Pamela G. Hollie, "Advertising; Big Mac's Olympic Giveaway," *New York Times,* August 10, 1984: https://www.nytimes.com/1984/08/10/business/advertising-big-mac-s-olympic-giveaway.html
[546] Jackson Wrightman, "Facebook promotion turns into PR nightmare for company," *Ragan's PR Daily*, January 20, 2012: https://www.prdaily.com/facebook-promotion-turns-into-pr-nightmare-for-coffee-company/

10. Empathy matters.

Military strategic communication needs to demonstrate a credible rationale to target populations for what the military does, how, and why. Showing that it cares about their well-being, health, and safety helps to neutralize opposition and shape the information environment. The U.S. success in wooing tribes in western Iraq turned, first, on our showing that our interests and theirs aligned, and second, that we would treat them with dignity, respect, and as equal partners. Those two lessons apply to executives: align interests, treat people with respect.

Uber provides a case study in failure. In March 2018, an experimental self-driving Uber car, a Volvo SC90 sport utility vehicle operating in autonomous mode, struck and killed pedestrian Elaine Herzberg. She was walking with her bicycle and carrying groceries. It was the first death of its kind. Uber said: "Our hearts go out to the victim's family. We are fully cooperating with the local authorities in their investigation of this incident."[547] Arizona prosecutors elected not to charge Uber,[548] but there was more to the story. The car had a backup driver whom they could have charged. The driver was watching "The Voice" on her cell phone when the collision occurred. Uber might have shown more sympathy. It needed to take and announce positive action to avoid a recurrence.

11.   Be careful about controversial political issues.

Military operations inherently embroil the US in controversy. Unless a company is trying to stir up controversy, companies are generally best advised to avoid politics, unless they want to make a strategic point that appeals to target audiences or to show corporate responsibility. American Airlines and United asked the government to stop using its planes "for transporting children who have been separated from their families due to the current immigration policy."[549] Flight attendants noticed children accompanied by federal agents. It caused a workforce backlash. Amazon employees have protested their

---

[547] Daisuke Wakabayashi, "Self-Driving Uber Car Kills Pedestrian in Arizona, Where Robots Roam," *New York Times*, March 19, 2018:
https://www.nytimes.com/2018/03/19/technology/uber-driverless-fatality.html

[548] Angie Schmitt, "Uber Got Off the Hook for Killing a Pedestrian with its Self-Driving Car," *Streetsblog.org,* March 8, 2019: https://usa.streetsblog.org/2019/03/08/uber-got-off-the-hook-for-killing-a-pedestrian-with-its-self-driving-car/

[549] Richard Fausset, "Airlines Ask Government Not to Use Their Flights to Carry Children Separated at the Border," *New York Times*, June 20, 2018:
https://www.nytimes.com/2018/06/20/us/airlines-transport-immigrant-children.html

companies' work in providing facial recognition to police agencies.[550] Equinox and SoulCycle triggered a backlash from customers when a high-profile company investor, Stephen Ross, held a major fundraiser for Donald Trump.[551] This heavily publicized political action prompted the company to distance itself from Ross and cost Equinox to lose members of its health clubs.

At this writing, bitter disputes over voting rights divide the country. Georgia's new voting law has been a flashpoint. Atlanta-based Delta Airlines made general statements in support of voting rights, although it did not mention the legislation. What opponents of the new law considered to be wishy-washy on Delta's position triggered criticisms, protests at Hartsfield-Jackson Atlanta airport, and calls for a boycott. CEO Ed Bastian then criticized the new law as "based on a lie" and proclaimed that the final bill "does not match Delta's values." That prompted Governor Brian Kemp to assert that Bastian hadn't piped up while lawmakers debated the legislation. Senator Marco Rubio branded him a "woke hypocrite."[552] One thing is clear: Bastian did Delta no favors by appearing to stand on both sides of the issue.

There are distinctions within distinctions. Patagonia's pitch is that its products improve people's lives with environmentally friendly clothing. By any reasonable measure, that's a good marketing posture. Innocent also stresses its environmentally friendly view. No one objects to that.

---

[550] Alexa Lardieri, "Amazon Employees Protesting Sale of Facial Recognition Software," *US News & World Report*, October 18, 2018: https://www.usnews.com/news/politics/articles/2018-10-18/amazon-employees-protesting-sale-of-facial-recognition-software; and James Vincent, "Amazon employees protest sale of facial recognition software to police," *The Verge*, June 22, 2018: https://www.theverge.com/2018/6/22/17492106/amazon-ice-facial-recognition-internal-letter-protest.

[551] Michelle Ye Hee Lee, "Trump scheduled to headline fundraisers in the Hamptons, where tickets run as high as $250,000," *Washington Post*, August 6, 2019: https://www.washingtonpost.com/politics/trump-scheduled-to-headline-fundraisers-in-the-hamptons-where-tickets-run-as-high-as-250000/2019/08/06/47698530-b855-11e9-a091-6a96e67d9cce_story.html; and Jordan Valinsky, "When Trump and Exercise Clash," *CNN.com*, August 15, 2019: https://www.cnn.com/2019/08/15/business/equinox-letter-stephen-ross/index.html

[552] Hannah Sampson, "Delta faces boycott threats for stance on new Georgia voting law," *Washington Post*, March 29, 2021: https://www.washingtonpost.com/travel/2021/03/29/delta-georgia-voting-law-boycott/; see also: Scott McKay, "Ed Bastian Keeps Digging," *American Spectator*, April 2, 2021: https://spectator.org/ed-bastian-delta-georgia-election-law/.

Yet Patagonia is also endorsing candidates for public office. I would think twice before doing that. What about sponsoring the 2022 Winter Olympics in China? Coca-Cola chairman James Quincey blasted Georgia's new election law, declaring: "We all have a duty to protect everyone's right to vote, and we will continue to stand up for what is right in Georgia across the US"[553] But Quincey has drawn criticism for Coke sponsoring the China-hosted Olympic games in light of its treatment of Muslim Uyghurs.

These cases pose this question: does a political controversy require or justify you to speak out on it? If you do, carefully think through the implications.

12. Communicate with shareholders and stakeholders what you are doing and why.

The military does this as a matter of course, although they defer to political leadership for policy. Clausewitz understood the will of the people was a center of gravity for conducting warfare. It is for political leaders to justify the military. Sometimes it matters more than at others. US efforts in Vietnam collapsed amid dissent at home.

France suffered defeat in Vietnam during the 1950s in no small measure for lack of support at home. Its leadership learned the lesson and applied it to defeat the FLN in the Algerian civil war. Special operations personnel and paratroops did most of the heavy combat. Conscription existed. But the army tried to send bachelors, not married soldiers, and these it deployed to less dangerous tasks, such as guarding the borders of Algeria.[554] The sensitivity of France paid off, and the French prevailed – temporarily. President Charles De Gaulle recognized that France could not sustain victory in deciding to give Algeria its independence.

Executives who fail to communicate with shareholders are asking for trouble. Internal memoranda explaining an issue coming before them and the Board are essential. J&J in the case of Tylenol and Starbucks did this right. Executive action bolstered management's ability to protect these companies.

During the COVID-19 pandemic, drug manufacturer Oxford-AstraZeneca took avoidable hits for a drug that scientists have blessed after critics lambasted the company for initially puffing optimistic news stories that proved inaccurate. Its

---

[553] Fred Hiatt, "Do companies really want to sponsor the Genocide Olympics?", *Washington Post*, April 4, 2021: https://www.washingtonpost.com/opinions/global-opinions/do-companies-really-want-to-sponsor-the-genocide-olympics/2021/04/04/6ce8144c-9315-11eb-bb49-5cb2a95f4cec_story.html

[554] See: Alistair Horne, A Savage War of Peace (NYRB Classics, 2011).

stakeholders were world populations, and health and government officials. The familiar precept reasserts itself: be truthful and get out there first with the truth.

13.   Pay attention to the timing of statements.

Inaccurate information can flaw first reports of a crisis. Secretary of State Hillary Clinton drew sharp criticism after insurgents murdered Ambassador J. Christopher Stephens in Benghazi, and UN Ambassador Susan Rice spoke on national news programs with inaccurate information. Crises require rapid response – but wait until you have the facts before speaking out.

President George W. Bush created a good photo opportunity when he co-piloted a plane onto the deck of the USS LINCOLN in May 2003, a few weeks after the invasion of Iraq, and posed below banners that proclaimed, "Mission Accomplished." He looked inept as former Baathists and Al Qaeda cropped up and renewed battle.

Industry has its failures. On July 29, 2017, Equifax discovered a massive data breach that affected the personal information of up to 143 million Americans, including their social security and driver license numbers. Hackers breached through a consumer complaint web portal. They used a widely-known vulnerability. Equifax should have patched it but hadn't. The company believed that the hack had taken place in mid-May. Equifax waited until *September* to make a public announcement.

The delay damaged management's credibility. Its whole response was a mess. It set up a site for victim information that looked like one phishers would use. Customers didn't trust it. It told every customer the breach affected them, whether or not it had. Initial language on the website implied to some that by merely checking to see if they were affected they waived their legal rights. Questionable conduct by some Equifax executives led to their exiting the company. Throughout, Equifax deserved an "F" on its report card for the timing of its actions and the content of its statements[555]

How does the military's approach compare to the corporate world? Johnson & Johnson's celebrated handling of incidents involving Tylenol, Ashland Oil's of

---

[555] Josh Fruhlinger, "Equifax data breach: What happened, who was affected, what was the impact?," *csonline.com*, February 15, 2020:
https://www.csoonline.com/article/3444488/equifax-data-breach-faq-what-happened-who-was-affected-what-was-the-impact.html. Lack of secure segmentation enabled access to usernames and passwords and to pull out encrypted data. Equinox's failure was to renew an encryption certificate on an internal security tool.

an oil pipe break, and other crises handled by Exxon, Toyota, Tide, and Boeing offer lessons for executive leaders. Virgil Scudder argues that

> "most companies find themselves poorly prepared to deal with a major crisis. One cannot avoid crises, but you can mitigate the damage. The key questions are not 'whether.' They are 'when,' 'how bad,' and 'is everything in place for a quick, effective response?'"[556]

Virgil Scudder observes that a crisis crystallizes two qualities about a company: "its cultures and its level of preparation."[557] As he and Mark Kimmitt agree,[558] how an organization *handles* a crisis is likely to impact their reputation more significantly than the crisis itself. Disasters inflict damage on victims and organizations, but careful handling of them with smart strategic communication can lessen the damage. Mishandling a minor crisis can inflict an outsized impact.

14. Corporations have more flexibility but having a CEO who can face the nation is important.

Well known for founding Tesla and for his vision for populating Mars, Elon Musk knows how to stir up controversy. Not all of it has helped him. The SEC sued Musk for securities fraud after he tweeted his intention to take publicly traded Tesla private and reported that he had secured funding. Other tweets suggested that mere shareholder approval was sufficient to de-list the company from the stock market.

Musk later said that Saudi Arabia's sovereign wealth fund might fund the effort. The SEC asserted that his tweets breached security laws.[559] Musk is the company's face, and when his credibility was shadowed, so was the company's.[560]

---

[556] Interview with Virgil Scudder, May 3, 2021. Many of the insights in this chapter draw on my discussions with Mr. Scudder over the 33 years that I have had the opportunity to work with him as a colleague and friend.
[557] Id.
[558] Interview with Virgil Scudder, May 3, 2021; Interview with Brig. Gen. (Ret) Mark Kimmitt, April 30, 2021.
[559] U.S. Securities and Exchange Commission v Elon Musk, Civ. Action No. 1:18-cv-8865 (S.D. New York, 2018)
[560] Sean O'Kane and Elizabeth Lopatto, "Elon Musk sued by SEC over 'funding secured' tweet," *The Verge*, September 27, 2018; and Jan Wolfe, "Elon Musk's defense of his Tesla tweet will get

Poor performances by Boeing's CEO made a bad situation worse. BP's CEO, Tony Hayward, was a bomb that went off in BP's face when he met the media. Exxon's CEO turned the *Exxon Valdez* disaster into a public relations fiasco.

What do you do with a CEO who's not naturally good at facing the media? *Prepare.* If preparation requires a week, so be it. The best example in the last couple of years that I've seen was Mike Bloomberg's disastrous appearances in two debates while running for President. Senator Elizabeth Warren unloaded on him for sexual harassment. Bloomberg is a brilliant man surrounded by brilliant advisers.

He flubbed the response and killed a promising campaign. Apparently taken aback when she jumped, he uncharacteristically temporized. Instead of letting her put him on the defense, he should have gone for Warren's throat over her spurious claim to be an "American Indian."[561] She used it in registering for the Texas bar. Association of American law school directories put her on the list of "minority law teachers" from 1986 to 1995.[562] The prestigious *Fordham Law Review* characterized Warren as Harvard Law School's "first woman of color."

Warren defends herself as vigorously as critics lambast her for that and other things.[563] I'll let voters decide the merits of all that. The strategic point here is that Bloomberg had ammunition to blow her away. Bloomberg surrounds himself with top talent. Why he wasn't better prepared to counter Warren confounds me.

15.   Understand the power and consequences of tweeting.

I haven't found that the US military does this well, although terrorists like ISIS excel at it. Elon Musk often discloses his intentions through tweeting. Former President Donald Trump dominated national narratives using Twitter.

SEC response," *Reuters,* March 12, 2019: https://www.reuters.com/article/us-tesla-musk-sec/elon-musks-defense-of-his-tesla-tweet-will-get-sec-response-idUSKBN1QT2N1

[561] That's how she explicitly described her race in filling out a Texas Bar registration card. See: https://www.bostonherald.com/2019/02/06/audio-elizabeth-warren-couldnt-recall-native-american-claim-apologizes-again/.

[562] Matthew Daly, "Warren: 'Never used' Native American claim to advance career," *Associated Press*, February 14, 2018: https://apnews.com/article/eb2d8595193843f6a6e14acf544ff48f.

[563] David French, "Elizabeth Warren: Progressive Fraud," *National Review*, November 28, 2017: https://www.nationalreview.com/2017/11/elizabeth-warren-native-american-heritage-harvard-fraud/. French claims she plagiarized a recipe for "Pow Wow Chow" from French chef Pierre Franey and falsely claimed to be the "first nursing mother" to take the New Jersey bar exam.

Lawyers or executives who tweet carelessly can open themselves and their companies to lawsuits. Trump claimed that the voting machine company Dominion had helped rig the outcome of the 2020 election. His attorney, Sidney Powell, and Fox News, whose opinion shows were generally pro-Trump, have found themselves in actual or potential lawsuits for defamation.

16.   **Influencer marketing.**

Choose influencers carefully and subject all of their work for pre-approval. Military target audience analysis aims first to identify the influential voices. That is a complicated process. It is not about sentiment analysis – whether someone "likes" a social media post. Often, the most influential voices are singular and heard only occasionally.

Let's return to President Franklin Roosevelt's actions to unify the nation before entering World War II. Roosevelt conceived and executed a delicate strategy that maneuvered the U.S. into a posture from which it could enter World War II merits a closer look. Roosevelt understood the power of influencers. He faced a nightmare in getting Americans engaged in World War II. He knew war was imminent. His goal was to enter it with a nation united. He carefully maneuvered to ensure that someone else fired the first shot. Pearl Harbor took care of that problem.

Roosevelt anticipated that Japan would act after he placed an embargo on oil exports to them. Yet in September 1942, ten months after the surprise attack, although isolationism had receded, many Americans lacked intense feelings about going to war. Those ready to fight wanted payback against Japan, not Germany. One might expect Douglas MacArthur to own that view. But George Marshall, Dwight Eisenhower, and the military chiefs felt the same way. We think of Roosevelt as a political master. He was an equally superb military strategist.

Roosevelt grasped that Japan had regional aspirations. Pearl Harbor aimed to force a settlement that satisfied Japanese interests in Asia. The Nazis posed a *global* threat. Hitler's force might well have seized control of West Africa, march south, and hopped from Dakar to Brazil. From there, the US beckoned. Fortunately, despite his diplomatic success in the 1930s in bullying hapless European leaders, most of whom were despots, Adolph Hitler proved an incompetent military leader. Many presumed that American resources would ultimately carry the day. This is not the venue to argue World War II. But, as

Oxford historian Richard Overy details in his excellent book, Why the Allies Won, that view is a myth.[564]

Roosevelt understood that demonizing Adolph Hitler required personalizing the conflict and portraying him as a devil with a forked tongue. Many Americans would have found the scale of German atrocities hard to believe. A widely shared school of thought held out for a compromise peace. In this fairy tale, the German Army would toss out Hitler to stop the war.[565]

How did Roosevelt use strategic communication to sway skeptical minds? The Nazis' brutal retaliation for Reinhard Heydrich's 1942 assassination in Lidice, Czechoslovakia provided the opportunity.[566] FDR spotlighted the voices of prominent figures, including Albert Einstein, Thomas Mann, and correspondent Rex Stout, to decry German barbarity. They helped to expose the truth. Roosevelt also used experts who discussed how the Nazis were desecrating religion and exploiting slave labor. It was a clever use of influencers. These voices helped to change the war's outcome. Even then, popular views forced Roosevelt to demonize Hitler throughout the war and pinpoint the Nazis as the true enemy rather than the German people.

Americans naively believed the average German was incapable of industrialized evil. Movies often portray German generals as decent and patriotic. Producers habitually dramatize the *Waffen SS* as the evil-doers who overrode the military. That's absurd. The German army was complicit in Hitler's war crimes.

Industry has a more straightforward task. Celebrity endorsements are a staple, as witness Nike, Under Armour, Adidas, and Dodge. In crisis management, Cadbury's chocolate deployed East Indian movie star Amitabh Bachchan as a brand ambassador to revive its reputation when worms found in chocolate made in India rattled consumers.

The essential point is to select influencers whom you rely upon to raise awareness and drive a narrative, theme, and message prudently, and to utilize them in ways relevant to a service or product. A TV ad for a pharmaceutical drug featuring an endorsement by Natalie Portman or Ashton Kutcher wearing a white physician's coat is more likely to elicit groans than purchases. The savvy of Roosevelt and the companies above paid off. Lesson: choose wisely and use influencers relevantly.

---

[564] See: Richard Overy, Why the Allies Won, (London: W. W. Norton & Co., Inc. 1996).
[565] Steven Casey, Cautious Crusade, (Oxford: Oxford University Press, 2001), p. 76, Kindle loc. 2082/8464.
[566] Id, p. 68-70, Kindle Loc. 1819-1832/8464.

17. Media training is essential.

Politics offers two more great examples. In a TV appearance in 1992, President George H.W. Bush kept looking at his watch and could not tell audiences the milk price. It boosted the populist Bill Clinton and made Bush look elitist. In 2012, Mitt Romney went from being one of the worst debaters imaginable to one of the best by the Florida primary. Newt Gingrich had trounced him days before in South Carolina. Romney's sterling performance on the eve of the Florida primary, the result of excellent training, saved his nomination fight. It also enabled him to best President Barack Obama in the first of their three debates. Luckily for Obama, he was prepared for the next two, and each candidate held his own.

In business, a major reason the tobacco companies maintained their edge was their knack for selecting and training able spokespeople. I don't know what training J&J's James Burke or Starbucks' Kevin Johnson had, but their performances in interviews strongly suggest they went into the interviews well-prepared.

18. Consistent messages.

Returning to Abu Ghraib, mistreatment of detainees damaged our credibility because the guards' behavior was inconsistent with our message that we were fair-minded, noble, and had invaded Iraq to improve the lives of its citizens. In contrast, top brands like Nike, Apple, IBM, and Dove flourish partly by maintaining message discipline.

19. Allow sufficient question and answer periods in news conferences.

This is a nuanced question. Remember that a news conference is not a deposition. You, not the news media, can and must control their duration. Former CBS correspondent Dan Rather demonstrated one approach. Caught in a controversy over George W. Bush's military service, he stepped outside his Manhattan apartment building and found a sea of reporters confronting him. If you have never experienced that, it is like being trapped on a small boat amid the swells of a raging ocean. It's easy to get thrown off balance.

Rather took control by raising his hands for silence, then telling the reporters he did not want to impose on his neighbors. He offered to meet them at CBS, where he would be happy to take questions. It bought him time to get his thoughts straight and gave him control over the narrative. The lesson is to think ahead so that if you are "ambushed" by the media, you know what steps are in order to seize control of the situation and the narrative.

Rather's response demonstrates an additional lesson. *Never meet with the news media in a place from which you cannot retreat.* If you invite the media to your offices, meet them in a conference room or appropriate place, but not your personal office. Failure to do that will open you to potential problems.

20.   Acknowledge the problem.

Starbucks, J&J, and General Kimmitt did that. It made a positive difference in preserving or strengthening credibility.[567] Jim Lukaszewski feels immediate acknowledgment of the problem prevents the inevitable criticism of the victims and bellyachers that the company could have acted sooner and done important things – like reducing the number of victims – more quickly. Today's reality is that we are 280 characters away from this corrosive criticism that, if allowed to fester, will haunt the perception of the most technically perfect response.

21.   Apologize for errors.

Starbucks' swift apology reduced the volcano of criticism that erupted in Philadelphia. Kimmitt's handling of Abu Ghraib fits under the same category. He wasted no time in getting out a positive story about the US response to detainee abuse.

22.   Share the solution.

Starbucks closed all its stores for training, showing commitment to making things right.[568] J&J and General Kimmitt also showed commitment.

23.   Keep employees informed.

This is critical to making sure everyone is on the same page. Boeing's failure to enlist the support of its workforce led to embarrassing news stories.

The same applies to the Board of Directors, which legally, in most states, is the party with the authority and duty to manage the company.

24.   Communicate with customers and suppliers.

Cadbury illustrates the point. Cadbury makes chocolate. It faced a crisis when worms were found in its Dairy Milk chocolate in India. Customers complained they had found worms in packets just before the festival of Diwali, a season of high sales. The company moved fast and effectively. Maintaining the confidence of its retailers, suppliers, and customers was paramount. Initially, it issued a

---

[567] Id.
[568] Id.

statement that infestation was not possible at the manufacturing stage. It pointed to poor storage by retailers as the likely cause.

When denying responsibility failed, it launched project "Vishwas," an education initiative directed at 10,000 retailers in key states. This quick action backed its earlier statements. It also acknowledged that responsible companies had to earn customer trust. It revamped packaging to make it tamper-proof.

This made its product costlier to manufacture, but Cadbury ate the cost and kept prices the same, treating the expense as an investment for the future. Cadbury recruited movie star Amitabh Bachchan as a brand ambassador. The actor put his personal equity on the line. The strategy regained customer confidence and market share.[569]

The lesson is that everything possible to protect brand reputation requires active engagement with your target audience.

25.   Update early and often.

Better to over-communicate than to let rumors fill the void. We live in a 24/7 news cycle.

26.   Establish a social media team that monitors, posts, and reacts to social media activity throughout a crisis.

This is an important step in maintaining control over the narrative. You can be sure that companies that emerge successfully from a crisis have done that.

---

[569] Achyut Telang and Amruta Deshpande, "Keep calm and carry on: A crisis communication study of Cadbury and McDonalds, *De Gruyter Open*, uploaded by Achyut Telang on October 1, 2017. The example is drawn from their analysis.

Discussion Questions

1. Is a problem you're dealing with actually a crisis? How do you describe or define a crisis?

2. Thinking about the Downing and Swann categorization of responses, preemption, commiseration, dissociation, shock, and rectification, do any apply to your response and, if so, how?

3. Thinking about Combs' characterization of responses, refutation, elimination, avoidance, justification, attachment, and transcendence, do any apply to your response, and if so, how?

4. What channels of communication are you prepared to use internally and externally to deal with a crisis, and why?

5. How are you prepared to deal with the news media? Have you selected a spokesperson or persons? Are they media-trained? Will your CEO be the face of the crisis? What governs that decision?

6. Do you think public affairs should be used to push a narrative or just to get out what you believe are the facts? This question goes to the debate that rages within the Pentagon but can apply to executives. What is your reasoning?

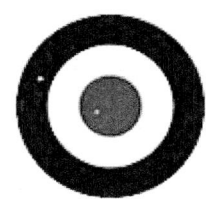

CHAPTER TEN

CYBERSECURITY RESILIENCE

Former FBI Director Robert S. Mueller, III summed up the cybersecurity crisis confronting executives. He declared: "There are only two types of companies: Those that have been hacked and those that will be hacked."[570] Journalist Stephen Barnes added a shrewd third example: companies who don't know they've been hacked." The situation is worsening every year, as technology advances and hackers grow more sophisticated. The advent of artificial intelligence, 5G Internet, and quantum computing will seriously worsen the crisis.

Your strategic communication plays a vital role in preventing breaches and responding to them. An incident breach can cause serious damage to your reputation with customers and shareholders, stock price, business operations, systems and networks, and can result in loss of data. It's important to understand the challenge and what needs to be done to protect your company's interests.

Cybersecurity breach incidents afflict nearly *half* of US companies.[571] Hackers who breached the Target stores cost the company $200 million in losses to credit unions and community banks for reissuing 40 million stolen credit cards. Criminals sold **three million cards** on the black market for a mid-range price of

---

[570] Quoted by Stephen Barnes in "There are only two types of companies: those who know they've been hacked and those who don't," *dynamicbusiness.com*, March 29, 2018.
[571] http://www.networkworld.com/article/2996639/security/talktalk-had-no-legal-obligation-to-encrypt-customers-sensitive-data.html

$26.85 per card. Hackers stole 70 million records that included the name, address, email address, and phone number of Target shoppers. The company was hit with 140 lawsuits. Target experienced a 46% drop in profits. The company said it would also spend $100 million to upgrade security at their payment terminals.[572]

Those two incidents ranked among the most visible. Neiman Marcus, Home Depot, TJ Maxx, Marshalls, Sony PlayStation Network, Google, and Yahoo, all large companies with enormous resources to provide protection, have also suffered data breaches.[573]

The cybersecurity challenge threatens every company. Each year it worsens. In 2013, there were 62% more data breaches than in 2012.[574] In 2014, there were 27.5% more data breaches than in 2013. In 2015, data indicates the numbers climbed again.[575]

In 2021, at this writing, breaches exposed 18.8 billion records.[576] Compromise has hit over 160 million victims in the third quarter, higher than the first two quarters combined. The number of breaches is up 27% compared to 2020.[577]

A few examples tell the tale. The cyber breach involving SolarWinds' Orion platform in early 2020 affected private industry and the military. Russian infiltrators – this was classic espionage, not an attack, a virtual invasion, or an act of war[578] – exploited a software update by a private company called

---

[572] "After a data breach, who's liable?", *Duo.com*, September 17, 2014: https://duo.com/blog/after-a-data-breach-whos-liable; and "The Target Breach, by the Numbers," *Krebs on Security*, May 14, 2014: http://krebsonsecurity.com/2014/05/the-target-breach-by-the-numbers/

[573] Kramer, Levin Naftalis & Frankel LLP, "Beware the breach: data breaches, notification duties, and legal liability," August 29, 2012:
https://mail.google.com/mail/u/0/?shva=1#inbox/153f4046540dabd3

[574] Symantec Corp., "Internet Security Threat Report 2014," at 5.

[575] Robert P. Hartwig & Clarir Wilkinson, Inc. Info. Inst., Cyber Risk: Threat and Opportunity 3 (2015).

[576] 2021 Mid Year Data Breach QuickView Report, August 4, 2021:
https://www.securitymagazine.com/articles/95793-data-breaches-in-the-first-half-of-2021-exposed-188-billion-records.

[577] Source; Identity Theft Resource Center: https://www.idtheftcenter.org/identity-theft-resource-center-to-share-latest-data-breach-analysis-with-u-s-senate-commerce-committee-number-of-data-breaches-in-2021-surpasses-all-of-2020/

[578] The Law of Armed Conflict does not treat espionage as an act of war. See: David Turns, <u>The Law of Armed Conflict</u>, Ch. 27 (London: Oxford University Press, 2018). Although LAC doesn't

SolarWinds. Infiltrators entered through "back doors" to access the networks of dozens of companies, government agencies, and think tanks. The attack gained them "persistent access." A year elapsed before detection.[579] Another private company, FireEye, founded with CIA support, discovered, and reported the attack.

At this writing, the effects remain unknown, but they are widespread. SolarWinds counts all five military services, the Pentagon, and the National Security Agency among its clientele. The March-June 2020 hack affected 18,000 customers – government agencies, the military, and businesses. Apparently, the perpetrator is Russia, which mobilized perhaps 1,000 engineers to launch the attack. The Biden administration has promised payback, although whether it will disclose details of action taken is unclear.

In the Navy, Admiral Michael Brown became a distinguished expert in cryptology and cyber warfare. Today he is a senior advisor with a large cybersecurity company, Palo Alto Networks. Admiral Brown observes that the Solar Winds hack provides a window that CEOs need to study through to grasp current cybersecurity challenges.

> "Solar Winds demonstrates how wide and deep the adversary – almost certainly Russia in this case – will dig in exploiting the supply chain as an attack vector. If you can defeat cybersecurity vendors and gain access to their clients' networks and capabilities and their intellectual property, as happened with Solar Winds, you've got a pretty good idea of how to defeat governments and critical infrastructure companies. That Russia instigated this illustrates the nature of today's cyber threat environment."[580]

---

prohibit espionage, the laws of nations in which it is conducted may, which is why during times of war, spies out of uniform are often shot.
[579] Major Juliet Skingsley, "The SolarWinds hack: A valuable lesson for cybersecurity," *Chatham House*, February 2, 2021: Bob Giesler served as the Director for Strategy Coordination for the Secretary of Defense.
[580] Interview with Admiral (Ret) Michael Brown, March 23, 2021.

Defending Against Attacks

Joe Biden appointed Chris Inglis, the former deputy chief of the National Security Agency, as the National Cyber Security Director. Inglis ranks among the nation's top experts on cybersecurity. I've had the pleasure of knowing him through Pentagon work. He advises companies to focus first on constructing a strong defense.

> "The goal isn't absolute security. That's an irrational goal. You can't get there. You'll spend your precious capital beating your head against the wall. The goal is a defensible enterprise. Defensibility, not security, is the keyword. That means devising a digital infrastructure in a way that one can defend it. You then have to use operational initiative, agility, and maneuver to defend it. That requires understanding fully how your defenses operate. The goal is to interdict attackers as early as possible."[581]

Inglis stresses that companies need to set priorities. "You can't defend all things against all hazards, right? You start with a strategic purpose. Prioritize the components that define that purpose, then allocate resources to fulfill it best. That enables you to hierarchically choose what to defend and horizontally to allocate time and attention that creates an integrated defense to achieve maximum impact."[582]

Inglis identifies three parallel concerns to achieve the desired goal. First, people, or what in the cyber world, we term "cyber hygiene." You need to train and supervise the workforce to create a culture conscious of security issues. Train them to be on the lookout for phishing or fake emails that open the door to malware. Second, building digital architecture that is inherently defensible. A key element is patching software. This is not always as straightforward as it may seem because IT people may argue that a patch has adverse knock-on effects that change software behavior and hurt efficiency elsewhere in a computer network or system. Nevertheless, the better view is to patch. If you don't patch, you open the door to malicious actors, and the statistics tell a lot: those actors will walk straight through it. Finally, is what Inglis terms "the doctrinal piece." In that

---

[581] Interview with Chris Inglis, April 19, 2021.
[582] Id.

dimension, you need to properly define roles and responsibilities, be aware of what your people are doing, and stay ahead of the curve to ensure that the company functions as a coherent team.[583]

Both Maj. Gen. (Ret) John Davis, who served as the Principal Adviser to the Secretary of Defense on cyber and held a high-ranking post at US CYBERCOMMAND, and Inglis, caution against the cyber challenges that Russia, China, Iran, and North Korea pose to national security and industry. Like Inglis, Davis focuses on defending against attacks.

> "Fast evolving technology complicates the challenge. The change is so fast that shortening time horizons make it tougher to get the strategy to counter the challenges right. You don't have three years to develop a strategy and the cyber infrastructure to execute it."[584]

Inglis adds that Russia and China tend to have different goals. "Russia sees cyber as a tool used to diminish the confidence of its Western competitors in their political and social institutions and to disrupt their stability. China's focus is on the theft of intellectual property. Although as Sony Pictures discovered, North Korea poses a challenge, its activity is often focused on disruption and vandalism."[585] The infamous Sony Pictures hack, motivated by Kim Jong-un's irritation at a Seth Rogan film that satirized him, cost its top executives their jobs.

Davis continues:

> "While some people favor the idea that the best defense to cyber-attack is a strong offense, any solid offensive capability needs strong cyber defenses as a foundation against adversaries who attack with increasing speed and scale. They're doing that deliberately below the threshold of traditional acts of war to create confusion and fear. They know they can't defeat us using traditional military capabilities. So they're turning to cyber to undercut our defenses, steal secrets,

---

[583] Id.
[584] Interview with Maj. Gen. (Ret) John Davis, March 18, 2021.
[585] Interview with Chris Inglis, supra.

> give themselves a strategic advantage. Our strategic cyber thinking needs to grasp that and deal with it."[586]

Davis believes we must "increase their pain and lessen their gain by applying continuous pressure with sustained counter information warfare that deters adversaries."[587] He recognizes that a bright line separates what the military and industry can do. The Computer Fraud and Abuse Act[588] makes inflicting $5,000 or more in damage on another party's computer a felony. It's a conundrum. He and Inglis point out that allowing industry to strike back on its own against a cyberattack is risky because of "the risk of unintended consequences. A cyberattack that can inflict damage in minutes or even seconds is huge and long-lived, especially as each side engages in attack and counter-attack. Escalation can happen in a flash." [589]

Equally, Davis points out that:

> "[adversaries] are leveraging surrogates, front companies, research institutions, moonlighters, patriotic hackers. You don't know their skills, capabilities, or intentions. That was what I worried about most at the Pentagon. An attack by a loosely controlled state proxy or third party could make a mistake that got quickly out of control and escalated. Imagine a situation in which that took down our power grid, shut down hospitals or airports, froze communication, and brought transport to a halt."[590]

Technology is advancing by leaps and bounds, carrying greater risks every year. The situation is dire enough that even the National Security Agency operates in what it deems to be an insecure operating environment. If the NSA feels its environment is unsafe, how would any company rate its chances of avoiding a cyber breach?

---

[586] Id.
[587] Interviews with Davis and Inglis, supra.
[588] 18 U.S.C.A. 1030 (1986).
[589] Id.
[590] Id.

Looking at Industry

The military doesn't always disclose its problems. Industry does so to understand how information warfare and strategic communication affect companies. Let's look at a celebrated – or infamous – incident involving Sony Pictures. Although management tried to minimize the attack by characterizing Sony as the victim of *uber-sophisticated* adversaries, this was the *third* breach the organization had experienced within a few years. In 2011, a group calling itself *We Are Legion* had hacked the company's PlayStation and Qriocity networks, stealing the billing information of up to 77 million people. Other hackers had earlier breached Sony's Online Entertainment Site.[591] The failure of management to handle its problems, and flaws in the company's strategic communication, cost executives their jobs and the company hundreds of millions of dollars.

Amy Pascal had risen from secretary to co-Chairperson of Sony Pictures Entertainment and ranked among the most potent people in the hardball movie industry. The business of movie-making is rough and tumble. Hundred-million-dollar budgets put a lot of risk at stake. On November 24, 2014, she discovered hackers had installed malware that froze computers. A neon red skeleton featuring the words *#Hackedby#GOP,* for Guardians of the Peace, not the Republican Party, contained a directive mandating obedience. A series of messages followed. The messages provided links to download data files.[592]

Hackers posted four movies awaiting release on pirate websites. They stole 38 *million* files. The haul included sensitive personally identifiable information and confidential materials: Social Security numbers, profit-and-loss statement, pilot scripts for films, including the new James Bond flick, *Spectre.* Gossip from 5000 of Pascal's emails got posted. These included hostile blasts between Pascal and producer Scott Rudin, who denounced Angelina Jolie as a "rampaging spoiled ego."

The crime cost Sony $100 million. The loss would have been steeper had Courts failed to dismiss lawsuits from customers on grounds they could show no damage. But Sony's operations were disrupted. Productivity dropped. The financial viability of films like their controversial *The Interview,* satirizing the

---

[591] Hayley Tsukayama, "Cyber-attack was large-scale, Sony says," *Washington Post*, May 4, 2011: https://www.washingtonpost.com/blogs/faster-forward/post/cyber-attack-was-large-scale-sony-says/2011/05/04/AF78yDpF_blog.html?itid=lk_inline_manual_33.

[592] Andrea Peterson, "The Sony Pictures hack, explained," *Washington Post*, December 18, 2014: https://www.washingtonpost.com/news/the-switch/wp/2014/12/18/the-sony-pictures-hack-explained/

North Korean leader, took such a hit that Sony was forced to release it directly to cable.[593]

The FBI concluded that the hackers were a North Korean front.[594] They had penetrated Sony's flimsy cyber defenses through a phishing attack. Emails received by employees captioned *igfxtrayex.exe* looked like a legitimate Microsoft Windows program. An employee downloaded what contained wiper malware. The malware infected that employee's computer and created a file share that enabled that computer to communicate with other computers on Sony Pictures' network. Every computer at headquarters got infected. The hackers posted confidential documents online, exposing them to cybercriminals, journalists, investors, employees, and actors.

As cyber expert Josephine Wolff pointed out,[595] huge gaps plagued Sony's defenses. Segmenting its networks to keep compromise of one computer from opening the door to other portions of the network would have limited damage. The hackers' aim wasn't to ransom Sony; it was to shame and embarrass executives. Using relatively unsophisticated malware, they deleted data on 3,262 of the company's 6,797 personal computers and 837 of its 1,555 servers.

Sony could have monitored the exfiltration of data, with systems that raised a red flag for unusual amounts of data exfiltrated to one location, especially at off-hours. Sony could have conducted vigorous employee training to guard against social engineering. It did neither.

No defense is foolproof against cyber hackers. Sony could have limited its damage. It should have been open, and urgently corrected its mistakes. Instead, management postured itself as a victim of the cybercrime of the century.

As noted earlier, cyberattacks generally can inflict at least five types of damage. Sony was vulnerable to all of them:

- **Damage to reputation.** People lost faith in management's ability to protect confidential data. Pascal lost her job after the breach. Almost certainly, it was a factor. The hack exposed Sony to the poaching of stars,

---

[593] Lisa Richwine, "Sony's Hacking Scandal Could Cost The Company $100 Million," *Reuters*, December 9, 2014: https://www.google.com/#q=Sony+hack+damage; and Mark Seal, "An Exclusive Look at Sony's Hacking Saga," *Vanity Fair*, March 2015: http://www.vanityfair.com/hollywood/2015/02/sony-hacking-seth-rogen-evan-goldberg.

[594] Sony Pictures had produced a movie satirizing Kim Jong-un, The Interview, which irritated the Korean leader. Sony was forced to cancel its theatrical release and streamed it.

[595] Josephine Wolff, You'll See This Message When It Is Too Late, (Cambridge: MIT Press, 2018), p. 168.

writers, and executives. It embarrassed Sony by revealing that it paid women far less than men.[596]

- **Damage to value.** Sony shares fell 6.6 percent on the New York Stock Exchange, more than twice the S&P 500 decline during the same period. Stock analysts were reluctant to attribute that solely to this hack. The April 2011 hack of Sony PlayStation did inflict a prolonged hit on its stock.
- **Financial Damage.** Sony had forecast a $2.15 billion loss for 2014, although restructuring costs at its mobile phone division caused part of that.[597] But the hack cost it substantial monetary damage. The 2014 hack cost $35 million just in IT repairs.[598] Although third parties lost their lawsuits, the incident cost hundreds of millions of dollars in the investigation, lost productivity, and in defending suits by company employees.[599]
- **Operational Damage.** The disruption to operations, business interruption, loss of time and resources, and lessened efficiency can be catastrophic. Taking computer systems off-line costs time and adversely affects operations.
- **Legal Liability.** Such liability may stem from contracts, federal and state law, regulatory proceedings, sanctions, and litigation.

---

[596] Annie Lowrey, "Sony's very, very expensive hack," *New Yorker*, December 16, 2014: https://nymag.com/intelligencer/2014/12/sonys-very-very-expensive-hack.html

[597] Gavin J. Blair and Paul Bond, "Sony Stock Price Hit by Hacking Problems But Worst May Be To Come," *Hollywood Reporter*, December 16, 2014: https://www.hollywoodreporter.com/news/sony-stock-price-hit-by-757610#:~:text=Shares%20of%20Sony%20have%20fallen,fall%20to%20the%20computer%20hack.

[598] Tom Hornyak, "2014 cyberattack to cost $35M in IT repairs," *Computer World*, February 4, 2015: https://www.computerworld.com/article/2879480/2014-cyberattack-to-cost-sony-35m-in-it-repairs.html.

[599] Sony paid $8 million over employees' lost data. See: "Sony pays up to $8M over employees' lost data," *BBC News*, October 21, 2015: https://www.bbc.com/news/business-34589710.

The Broader Implications

Here are some alarming facts you need to know about cybersecurity breaches:

1.   A risk you cannot eliminate.

Even in *its most highly classified and protected institutions*, the US Government recognizes that cyber threats cannot be eliminated. Your strategic goal is to *manage* and *mitigate* risk.[600] If the US Government cannot eliminate the risk with its resources, it's doubtful any private company can.

2.   The skyrocketing cost.

An American Bankers Association (ABA) survey found that for Target, the loss for each fraudulent debit card costs banks an average of $331 and for each credit card $530.[601] For smaller banks, ABA found that the cost of creating and mailing a new debit card is about $11, and for credit cards, $12.75.

3.   Costs beyond remediation.

A study by the Ponemon Institute and IBM in 2021 revealed that the average total cost of a data breach has climbed to $4.24 million, a 10% rise from 2019. The average cost per record of a data breach rose to $161, up from $146 in 2020.[602]

4.   Regulatory Costs.

The Federal Trade Commission and other regulatory bodies will vigorously enforce deceptive or unfair trade practices and other applicable rules. As the Wyndham Hotel Chain found, to its horror, merely the *legal fees in the investigatory phase* of an FTC proceeding involving breaches of more than 619,000 consumers leading to over $10.6 million in fraudulent charges, plus millions of dollars in legal fees.[603] In moving to quash an FTC request for

---

[600] "The DoD Cyber Strategy," U.S. Department of Defense, April 2015: http://www.defense.gov/Portals/1/features/2015/0415_cyber-strategy/Final_2015_DoD_CYBER_STRATEGY_for_web.pdf
[601] Penny Crosman, "How Much Do Data Breaches cost? Two Studies Attempt a Tally," *American Banker*, September 11, 2014: http://www.americanbanker.com/issues/179_176/how-much-do-data-breaches-cost-two-studies-attempt-a-tally-1069893-1.html.
[602] "Cost of Data Breach Report 2021," Ponemon Institute and IBM: https://www.ibm.com/downloads/cas/OJDVQGRY
[603] Colin Lecher, "FTC Settles Data Breach Lawsuit with Wyndham Hotel Chain," *The Verge*, December 9, 2015: http://www.recode.net/2015/12/9/11621330/ftc-settles-data-breach-lawsuit-with-wyndham-hotel-chain.

documents and answers to interrogatories, Wyndham's counsel estimated that responding to them would require *two years* and *$3 million in attorney's fees.* Chris Inglis argues that companies need to develop close contacts with regulators, to foster smooth relationships essential in dealing with incident breaches.[604]

5. Loss of Customers.

Customers don't necessarily announce they're leaving because of a breach. But research by Kaspersky Lab found that 43% of businesses changed banks following fraud on their account. Another 33% moved their primary cash management services elsewhere. And 62% say they would consider leaving an institution after a breach. Why would one question that hotel guests and retailer customers would harbor similar doubts?

6. Damage claims cover a broad spectrum.

After it was hacked, the TJX companies provided consumers with three years of credit monitoring, compensated customers who could show actual losses, and paid $6.5 million in attorney fees. One court estimated that a full settlement would cost the company $200 million.[605] As insulation from further liability, TJX paid $9.75 million to settle claims by 41 state attorneys general in a multi-state comprehensive information security program.[606]

7. Evolving case law creates uncertainty.

Private class actions have encountered difficulty in showing actual damages, causing the dismissal of many claims.[607] Thus far, courts have required plaintiffs both to allege and show tangible harm. Increased risk of future identity theft is not actionable. Mere danger of future injury, absent present damage, has not supported a negligence action. Claims failed where plaintiffs failed to show that a hacker who stole confidential customer and employee information (i) read, copied, and understood the information, (ii) intended to illegally misuse the information, or (iii) was able to make authorized transactions in the affected individuals' name.

---

[604] Interview with Chris Inglis, supra.

[605] *In re TJX Cos. Retail. Sec., Breach Lit.*, 584 F. Supp.2d 395, 401 (D. Mass. 2008).

[606] Jaikumar Vijayan, "TJX reaches $9.75 million breach settlement with 41 states," *ComputerWorld,* June 24, 2009: http://www.computerworld.com/article/2525965/cybercrime-hacking/tjx-reaches--9-75-million-breach-settlement-with-41-states.html.

[607] *Piscotta v Old National Bancorp*, 499 F.2d 629, 635 (7th Cir. 2007); *Krottner v Starbucks Corp.*, 406 Fed. Appx. 129 (9th Cir. 2010); *Caudle v Towers, Perrin, Forster & Crosby, Inc.*, 580 F. Supp. 2d 273 (S.D.N.Y. 2008); and *Reilly v Ceridian Corp.*, 664 F.2d 138 (3d Cir. 2011).

However: where a plaintiff alleges and shows that actual fraud occurred, plaintiffs have recovered costs to mitigate damages caused by negligence.[608] We expect to see more sophisticated pleadings by class action and individual plaintiffs. The cost of merely defending these actions can be enormous.

8. **Employee negligence and malicious intent pose a grave threat.**

A 2021 study by Securonix found about half of data breaches resulted from criminal or malicious acts.[609]

Strategic Communication to Protect Companies

Preventing cyber breaches and responding to them requires a holistic approach that embraces conducting regular information security response assessments, establishing an information security management system, and putting in place both an incident breach response team and plan. Strategic communication plays a central role in responding to cyber breaches. What you say to insiders and outsiders, including law enforcement, can affect reputation, forensics, the ability to catch lawbreakers, and protecting the company's operations. Understanding what to say lends itself to no formula. One has to understand the keys to dealing with incident breaches.

What are the critical communication considerations?

1. **Be prepared.**

From the board and management down to the lowest ranking employee, the company's entire team needs to understand and buy into a **culture of security.** That requires a disciplined strategic communication plan that informs the whole company team of the threats, risks, and vulnerabilities and the individual responsibilities that each member must be aware of in preventing and responding to a breach. Admiral Brown argues that preparation requires a minimum of three parallel steps. He counsels:

> "First, you need to inventory your information assets and understand their risks and vulnerabilities against which a strong cybersecurity posture can protect. Second, you

---

[608] *Anderson v Hannaford Bros. Co.,* 659 F.3d 151 (1 Cir. 2011).
[609] 2020 Securonix Insider Report: https://pages.securonix.com/rs/179-DJP-142/images/Insider-Threat-Report-May-2020-Securonix.pdf

need to understand your infrastructure to know where the risks are and mitigate them. That goes not only for your company but also for third-party supply chain vendors. Finally, you need to put a business continuity, disaster recovery, and incident response plan in place before an incident breach. People need to know their roles and responsibilities. You need to have the incident breach response team in place *before the fire breaks out, not when the house is burning down.* You need to know who you can call on for help and have the relationships already in place that surmount the challenge."[610]

2. Outside counsel should lead in formulating this plan to bring it under the attorney-client or work-product privileges.

Regulators have the authority to investigate what you do, but third-party plaintiffs do not necessarily have the same right. One of the first actions any plaintiff will take in litigation or pressing claims is to ascertain how you assessed your risks and what actions you envision for protecting the company. A plaintiff will want to compare that assessment, and your breach response plan, to what you did if a breach occurs to identify gaps between the two. These gaps can increase legal vulnerabilities that you can do a lot to minimize.

3. Should a breach occur, state laws prescribe requirements for notifying stakeholders.

Each state has its approach. Europe uses a unified approach. The United States allows each state to define its own breach notification requirements. That requires knowing what rules each state prescribes. For example, California's law is broad and may well affect companies in the other 49 states. John Davis underscores the importance of this step: "You need to know what laws govern your conduct. You can pay sorely for ignorance. Handling this correctly requires close coordination between the Board, C-Suite, IT, company security, and outside counsel."[611]

Consult with counsel to understand and comply with the requirements to notify affected parties of a breach. States are not consistent in their requirements. That

---

[610] Interview with Admiral Michael Brown, supra.
[611] Interview with Maj. General Davis, supra.

requires knowing the requirements and exercising prudent legal and business judgments, as failure to comply can result in significant liability.

4.   Protect your credibility.

Critics like Rep. Mary Bono Mack (R-Calif) blasted Sony for "half-hearted, half-baked" efforts to do so. She was harshly critical of Sony's decision to notify customers through its company blog, forcing customers to search for information on the breach.[612] What you tell your customers needs to be cleared with counsel and easily accessible.

Cybersecurity incidents are by nature complex. In 2017 Equifax announced a massive breach that could impact at least 143 million US consumers – 44% of the US population. Too often, company statements report that a breach occurred but take pains to absolve itself of blame. A frequent excuse is that the attackers were super-sophisticated and that no reasonable company could be expected to turn back their attacks. That's an inadequate response, as a matter of business judgment and in preparing a legal defense. Such statements offer general explanations about what the company is doing and show their very basic coverage to protect credit scores. That is weak strategic communication.

Equifax made some good steps in responding as well as some fumbles. It issued a **clear statement** that described the scope and depth of the breach. It defined specific actions being taken to gather more information. It made clear how that information was being communicated to affected consumers. It identified who Equifax was working with to deal with the situation. It described what Equifax had already set up to help consumers. Critically, it accepted ownership of the problem through a statement by its CEO and Chairman Richard F. Smith. Instead of avoiding blame, he apologized for the data breach that enabled the theft of private financial information owned by 143 million people. He focused on Equifax's commitment to solving the problem and protecting customers.[613] The company's board found that insufficient and ousted him.

That was on the plus side. Still, within two weeks after the apology, Equifax stock had fallen 30%. Two executives were fired. Congress opened an investigation. Class action lawsuits were filed. Taking six weeks from the discovery of the breach to alerting the public undercut public confidence in the company. Worse, Equifax customer service had directed victims to a fake

---

[612] Hayley Tsukayama, "Cyber attack was large-scale, Sony says," supra.

[613] See: Mark Nunnikhoven, "Equifax Breach – an Example of Good Communications," *Trend Micro.com*, September 8, 2017: https://blog.trendmicro.com/equifax-breach-example-good-communications/.

phishing site for several weeks. Worse, insider dealing reared its ugly head. Three senior executives sold $2 million worth of stock in the days after the breach was discovered.[614] Lesson: apologies help but action helps a lot more. You must do more than acknowledge the problem and mistakes. You have to show empathy and take actions that show you are rectifying the problem and preventing recurrence. Effective strategic communication requires that.

In the military, Brig. General Mark Kimmitt's interview with Dan Rather acknowledging the problems at Abu Ghraib, the military's transparency in dealing with the crisis, and the actions taken that included firing the General in charge of the prison illustrates what wiser action looks like. Johnson & Johnson's handling of the Tylenol crisis offers an excellent corporate parallel.

5.   Forge and put in place a communications plan for responses to a breach and create a war room to execute it.

This is internal. It should lay out what procedures and processes the company will follow in responding and informing the public. The last thing you want is for investors and other stakeholders to learn about the breach in a media story. One key aspect is to set up a secure channel of communication so that the company team members can communicate with one another in planning and executing the team's actions.

6.   Rehearse and conduct drills and exercises to test and refine the communication plan before a breach occurs.

Once a breach occurs, you have 24 to 72 hours to conduct most forensics to identify the source and cause of a breach and identify the attackers. You need to be ready to move when a breach occurs. You will improvise to deal with shifting circumstances, but the team needs a clear understanding of its communication strategy.

Admiral Brown cautions that,

> "if you've got a strategic communication and incident response plan, that's vital. But it's not sufficient. You have to conduct exercises at least twice a year to ensure that people are clear about roles and responsibilities and execute an incident

---

[614] The Equifax Effect: In **Corporate Apologies, Words Are Often Not Enough,"** *The Strategist*, October 26, 2017:
https://apps.prsa.org/Intelligence/TheStrategist/Articles/view/12075/1149/The_Equifax_Effect_In_Corporate_Apologies_Words_Ar#.YJAqzGZKhBw.

breach response. We did that in the Department of Defense. Companies need to be just as vigorous on this front. Doing this properly will create a battle rhythm that focuses minds and keeps teams working efficiently. If you don't have that regular battle rhythm, you're in terrible shape."[615]

7.   Develop a clear comprehension of industry best practices for the best communication strategies in *your industry*.

You don't need to reinvent the wheel. Learn from the experience of others. As the CEO of the SecDev Group based in Ottawa, Rafal Rohozinski has long served as a recognized top cyber consultant to the Canadian, British, and US military, as well as multi-national corporations. "The militaries have their own rhythms," he says. "But companies are well-advised to ferret out and implement security practices that meet best practices for industry."[616]

8.   Root communication in the facts.

About the worst mistake you can make is to put out inaccurate information. That will undercut your credibility and increase legal exposure. Consider the 2010 Deepwater Horizon disaster in the Gulf of Mexico. The executives of British Petroleum were led by its hapless CEO, Tony Hayward, best known for his response that "There's no one who wants this thing over more than I do. You know, I'd like my life back."[617] And Hayward lied in assuring the public that the environmental impact would be modest. When the facts revealed that he was lying, he suggested that the Gulf would heal itself. The spill cost the company $61.1 billion.[618] As an Advisory Member of the New Orleans Business Council, I engaged with BP executives directly on the spill. They lied through their teeth, failing to carry through on any promises made. Worse, it was evident in the meetings that they *knew* they were disingenuous.

---

[615] Interview with Admiral Brown, supra.
[616] Interview with Rafal Rohozinski, April 30, 2021.
[617] "Gus Lubin, "BP CEO Tony Hayward makes idiotic statement: 'I'd like my life back,'" *Insider*, June 2, 2010: https://www.businessinsider.com/bp-ceo-tony-hayward-apologizes-for-saying-id-like-my-life-back-2010-6
[618] See: "11 Facts About the BP Oil Spill," *Do something.org*: https://www.pagecentertraining.psu.edu/public-relations-ethics/ethics-in-crisis-management/lesson-1-prominent-ethical-issues-in-crisis-situations/case-study-tbd/ *Arthur W. Page Center/Public Relations Ethics*: https://www.pagecentertraining.psu.edu/public-relations-ethics/ethics-in-crisis-management/lesson-1-prominent-ethical-issues-in-crisis-situations/case-study-tbd/.

The BP Deepwater Horizon disaster spill offers a vital lesson underscoring the need that David Petraeus stresses in a military context that also applies to a corporate one, for honesty, telling the truth, *and doing so first*, as well as behaving with integrity.

9. **Communicate rapidly**.

Update stakeholders. These steps will bolster credibility and protect it. Johnson & Johnson did that in the Tylenol disaster. The 1988 oil tank collapse in Pittsburgh reinforces the Tylenol lesson. A giant oil storage tank owned by Ashland Oil Company split apart vertically at the company's storage yard in Floreffe, Pennsylvania, dumping 3.85 million gallons of diesel fuel into the Monongahela River. It ranks among the worst inland oil spills in our history.[619] As Virgil Scudder notes in praising the response, the "company was upfront, apologized, took responsibility, explained questionable decisions, and wasted no time on cleanup. Praised for its response, the company's protected and even strengthened its credibility."[620]

10. **Monitor social and traditional media to stay ahead of the curve in what people are saying about the breach and the company's response**.

Starbucks did that in dealing with complaints of racial insensitivity and its decisive action helped protect the company's reputation. "The US military ignored it in the Jessica Lynch fiasco, and that made a bad situation worse," notes Dave Patterson.

11. **Communicate rapidly and accurately with relevant regulators**.

Such communication should be done under the oversight of outside counsel. This is a legal requirement whose discussion lies beyond the purview of this book. The Equifax and Ashland Oil disasters illustrate the need to quickly minimize fines and penalties and work out corrective action plans. When the Federal Trade Commission or other regulator mandates a company to put in place a corrective action plan, which can require two to three years of monitoring and reporting, *that* punishment can be far more expensive than the actual fine imposed. Blue Cross of Tennessee got slapped with a $1.7 million fine for the loss of data on disks, but the three-year correction action plan cost it $17 million.

---

[619] Jack Doyle, "Disaster at Pittsburgh," *pophistorydig.com*: https://www.pophistorydig.com/topics/ashland-oil-tank-collapse-1988/.

[620] Interview with Virgil Scudder, May 3, 2021. Mr. Scudder also noted the incident in his book written with his son, Ken Scudder, World Class Communication (New York: John Wiley & Sons, Inc., 2010), p. 168.

Infectious Disease Pandemics

The 2020 COVID virus has disrupted the economy and forced companies to deal with unprecedented challenges in corporate communication. Remote communications using Zoom, Microsoft Teams, Blue Jeans, and other forms of video conferencing have replaced face-to-face engagements in the interests of protecting health. Email, texting, and telephone communication have all assumed a more significant role. Protocols, rules, and training that govern the use of each channel of communication are needed. Security in each of these poses a challenge. All communication in a crisis environment poses policy and legal implications.[621]

Key considerations that apply equally or almost so to the military and industry for communications include:

1.   Define communications goals.

How do you define success? What metrics will you use to do so?

2.   Identify target audiences.

Which audiences are indispensable to articulating your narrative, theme, and message? Which ones are simply important? Which ones are not important? What channels of communication do you plan to employ? At this writing, President Joe Biden's administration has enjoyed success in getting Americans vaccinated. But it still faces challenges from those who refuse to be vaccinated.[622]

---

[621] See: Alicia Whittlesey, "Communication during a pandemic," *raps.org*, April 24, 2020: https://www.raps.org/news-and-articles/news-articles/2020/4/communication-during-a-pandemic.

[622] Apoorva Mandavilli, "Reaching 'Herd Immunity' is Unlikely in the U.S., Experts Now Believe," *New York Times*, May 3, 2021: https://www.nytimes.com/2021/05/03/health/covid-herd-immunity-vaccine.html?action=click&module=Spotlight&pgtype=Homepage; and Isaac Stanley-Becker, "Many police officers spurn coronavirus vaccines as departments hold off on mandates," *Washington Post*, May 2, 2021: https://www.washingtonpost.com/health/2021/05/02/police-low-vaccination-rates-safety-concerns/.

3. **Designate a communication spokesperson and coordinator.**

Your team needs to speak with one voice. Otherwise, message discipline will collapse, and the consequences could be enormous. The military has proven adept at that, using public affairs to guide communication with the public. Public affairs officers use comments from commanders selectively. During the 1991 Gulf War, General Norman Schwarzkopf, Jr.'s news conferences became iconic. In other conflicts, generals remained less visible. The highly respected commander, General Stanley McChrystal, found out the hard way that while no one gets fired for refusing to speak to the media, doing so can backfire.

Companies generally do well, although which official to designate as a spokesperson is a strategic decision. Johnson & Johnson handled the Tylenol crisis adroitly by deploying its CEO to speak for it. I find some CEOs may overestimate their ability to handle media; each situation requires a tailored judgment call.

4. **Forge and execute a communication plan with a clear story, narrative, theme, and messages tailored to each targeted audience.**

I have discussed this earlier in this book. For pandemics, that includes steps to protect the safety of employees, customers, and the workplace. It includes reporting duties for employees and the company for those suspected of contracting a virus – or who contract one. It also should address protocols for internal communications among employees who work remotely.

5. **Define communication channels that you will employ to reach different target audiences.**

Pandemics stand apart because of the rapid spread of infections and the role in fighting them that local, state, and federal authorities play.

6. **Prepare talking points.**

These provide a pre-approved narrative, theme, and message to deal with the media and stakeholders. You also need to identify and prepare supporting materials, including fact sheets, charts, maps, and relevant background information that journalists will find relevant and valuable. Most critical is establishing and maintaining credibility with the media and in social media. Once lost, credibility is almost impossible to regain. Post all relevant statements and information immediately on your website.

7. **Establish updated procedures for talking points.**

There's no formula here. Tailor it to the size, nature and complexity of your business. The military does this naturally, as commanders constantly seek battlefield updates.

8. **Making your first public announcement.**

It bears stressing: make sure of your facts and that your sources are credible. Avoid vague statements that could be misinterpreted. As Equifax did, express empathy, what you know, what you don't know, and how you approach the problems that an infectious disease poses for your employees, their families, customers, and other stakeholders. Kimmitt employed a similar approach in discussing Abu Ghraib.

9. **Be Careful with emails.**

Military and government officials need to be especially careful because emails have a way of leaking, and they may be subject to public information disclosure proceedings. Tone and context matter. It is easy to miscommunicate your intentions by using the wrong language. I learned this the hard way in pre-production for a stage play I wrote, produced in London. Tension and misunderstanding result from imprecise language.

Read and re-read emails before sending. Don't rush to hit "reply" or "reply all." Emails create a record that may carry profound legal and business implications.[623] Write them so that people understand your intention.

10. **Different narratives for different audiences.**

An important theme of this book has been to emphasize the need to tailor your messaging to individual audiences. In a crisis atmosphere, with hysteria and doubts about whom to trust with what information, understanding audiences and communicating in language they will understand is vital. This has always been true. For example, my late friend Karen Duncan, a tragic victim of breast cancer, served as counsel to a medical insurance company. She related that one reason physicians get sued for medical malpractice is the *manner* in which they dealt with patients. Empathy establishes bonds. A brusque manner can provoke litigation.

---

[623] Id.

11. Stay in touch with public health authorities at the local, state, and federal levels as appropriate.

Remain ahead of the curve on the risks to employees, customers, and other stakeholders and their recommended courses of action.[624] This precept is fundamental in dealing with municipalities and governors, who have the lead in protecting public health during the outbreak of an infectious disease pandemic. This affects every aspect of operations in the health sector and food security, livelihoods, logistics, and mobilization of resources.[625]

12. Make sure that legal counsel reviews all communication to regulators.

Every word may have legal implications. The Office of Civil Rights governs the Health Insurance Portability and Accountability Act (HIPAA)[626] and the Federal Trade Commission prohibits companies from false or misleading claims. These regulators employ a loose standard that requires "reasonable and adequate" steps to protect private or confidential data. Due diligence and good faith are factors they take into consideration. Carefully weigh every word of communication with them.

13. Social media communications are subject to the same protocols used in any other channel of communication.

People often seem laxer when dealing with social channels like Facebook, Instagram or Twitter. Laxness is not a virtue in dealing with pandemics.

---

[624] ASTHO, "Addressing communication challenges during an Infectious Disease Emergency Response:" https://www.astho.org/Programs/Infectious-Disease/Addressing-Communication-Challenges-During-an-Infectious-Disease-Emergency-Response/

[625] See: "Communications Plan Implementation for A Severe Pandemic," *Paho.org*: https://www.paho.org/disasters/index.php?option=com_docman&view=download&category_slug=tools&alias=540-pandinflu-leadershipduring-tool-13&Itemid=1179&lang=en

[626] Pub. L. 104-191.

14. Be careful in disseminating information.

In particular, about the latest science or opinions that government bodies like the Center for Disease Control (CDC) or public health/medical experts put out about protecting oneself from a virus. You don't want to own responsibility for the accuracy of statements from other sources, so be sure you attribute them to your source. You do not want to vouch for the accuracy of regulatory public health opinions that may change as new information emerges.

15. Conduct regular conference calls or video conferences with stakeholders.

Whether employees, industry associations, or others. Keep them updated on the company's status and developments about any infectious disease affecting business operations.

16. Conduct thoughtful media outreach to enhance credibility.

Apprise the media of steps the company is taking to protect the health of employees, their families, customers, and other stakeholders.

17. Maintain consistency and message discipline in communication.

This is critical in nurturing and maintaining credibility.

18. As necessary, communicate rapidly.

This can be vital in heading off or neutralizing rumors that are inevitably a characteristic of pandemics.

Discussion Questions

Note: *Cybersecurity is a complex, nuanced area. This chapter and these questions focus mainly on strategic communication in defending against and responding to cyber breaches but touch on the National Institute for Science & Technology (NIST) framework for defending against and handling cyber breaches.*

1. Have you been hacked? What was your experience and what lessons did you learn?

2. What steps are you taking to detect, prevent, respond to, communicate, and remediate a hack?

3. How are you engaging with key stakeholders inside and outside of the company, including law enforcement and regulators?

4. Has your plan considered potential damage to reputation, shareholder value, finances, and operations, business interruption, and loss of customers? Has your plan considered legal liability? Does your communication plan balance protection of reputation against legal liability? What role does outside counsel play in formulating your communication plan?

5. Does the communication plan take into account the channels of communication you'll use in dealing with cyberattacks?

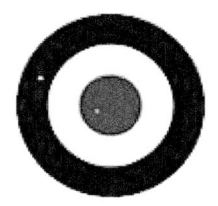

CONCLUSION

The Corporate Warrior draws upon my own experience as an advisor to companies, Special Operations, the Pentagon, and as a political consultant who has advised in seven Presidential campaigns around the world and as an attorney advising companies. I learned a lot from admirals, generals, senior officers, and corporate leaders who moved to the business world and applied their expertise to industry.

The lessons I describe to position and market a service or product apply to individuals and small or medium-sized organizations, not just big ones like Nike or Apple. Humans are innovative and flexible. That sets us apart. I believe strongly in respecting other species. They're far more intelligent than too many people recognize. Still, none of them have put a human into space.

Character and Leadership: Learning from the Best

Few precepts are universal. Here's one that is: *culture is character*. A company's culture defines its character and its identity. Successful companies need credibility, and their products or services need credibility. That stems from their character. Companies that aim to improve lives, that respect values of integrity, hard work, fair play, discipline, excellence, and loyalty are more likely to succeed.

That trait is about *leadership*. Leadership at the top, the middle, the bottom. Successful leaders lead teams, not subordinates. Great leaders espouse the values just noted. The great Arkansas and later Notre Dame football coach Lou Holtz influenced my thinking about what we need in order to succeed in life. He said that all of us need four things: something to do, someone to love, something to hope for, someone to believe in. You'll find most outstanding generals and executives exude these traits.

These outstanding leaders surround themselves with able people. They exchange ideas. They listen. They *hear*. For these leaders, collaboration is a loop, from the bottom up to the top down. People follow those they admire and respect.

A lot of executives I've dealt with talk about getting input from their team then lash back the first time anyone contradicts or challenges them. Arrogance is a killer. What gets me about these types isn't just that they're fools, but stupid, blundering fools. Arrogance afflicts a lot of CEOs, especially in large organizations. Ring kissers fill these places. They laugh at unfunny CEO jokes as if in Stephen Colbert's audience. They nod sagely at a CEO's imprudent ideas. They feel intimidated against standing up.

One lesson every flag officer I interviewed noted was the absolute necessity to avoid arrogance. You also have to avoid reading your own press releases. One of my favorite humorists, P.J. O'Rourke said it best: Hubris is one of the great renewable resources. Arrogant CEOs see themselves as indispensable. They choke off innovation, kill ideas, demoralize employees, and have a knack for running their organizations off the tracks.

I read a lot of biographies because I learn a lot from what other people have experienced or achieved (or failed at). Along with Dwight Eisenhower and Turkish leader Mustafa Kemal Ataturk, Charles de Gaulle was one of three generals who successfully transitioned to politics and cut it as a head of state over the last hundred years. De Gaulle stands out for his good judgment, the quality I most prize in leaders.

He was a difficult personality for Franklin Roosevelt and Winston Churchill. They thought him arrogant. In this case, the French leader probably needed full self-confidence to weather the storms that beset himself and France. But Charles De Gaulle didn't let his self-assurance cloud his judgment. After World War II, he realized political infighting was polarizing France. Today's political leaders would double down on cable news to argue their point.

De Gaulle recognized paralysis among competing egos and agendas. He dropped out of politics for over a decade until called back to save his country. He served as President when finally France prevailed in a bloody, hard-fought civil war in Algeria. The French are proud people; De Gaulle was the proudest, yet he maintained cold objectivity in looking over the horizon. He knew the victory could not hold. Hubris did not obstruct his judgment. He was equally cool-headed in ceding independence to Algeria rather than making it a Department of France, an outcome many Algerians might have liked. Strength is foundational to leadership. But there's a fine line between strength and egotism. Each of us can fall into the trap, especially if the responsibility for running an organization falls on our shoulders. You need to be observant and avoid landmines.

Meeting Goals in a Changing World

The world has changed more in the last 30 than in the prior 300 years. I have no doubt it will change that much again in the next 30. I can still remember the days years ago when I joined a large law firm as a young associate. My secretary (remember secretaries?) banged out legal briefs on a manual Royale typewriter. I felt like a character on *Star Trek* when science and engineers produced the IBM Selectric II. I realized it was great to be part of a modern world. Then the original consumer computers arrived. I still remember an AT&T (yes, AT&T once manufactured computers) salesman showing me their three models and how advanced the most expensive one was. My eyes glowed. That one seems medieval compared to what we have today. What really hit me was when somebody pointed out that today's cell phones pack more than the original technology for a Boeing 747.

Realizing your goals requires an understanding of the world you operate in. Let's face it – the place can prove scary. Getting blindsided at right angles is part of life. As business executive Leonard Tallerine put it, a lot of people have all the answers, but they don't know the score. *Savvy* and *smart* are different words. Intelligence manifests itself in different forms. Each requires respect. In dealing with people, the core question isn't necessarily whether you trust a person, but with what. Excellent leaders see that distinction and judge accordingly.

Competition is a fact of life. It used to be that Berliners competed, say, against workers in Cologne. Or South Carolinians against Californians. Now everybody competes against people in other countries. For a long time, Americans complained that workers in South China could win on price point. Now Vietnamese or Malays worry executives in China. The world turns.

Technology has taken off like a shot. It's evolving so fast that figuratively, we're maybe thirty seconds post-liftoff. Artificial intelligence, machine learning, virtual or enhanced reality that lands us into a metaverse, not unlike the one Stephen Spielberg created in his film READY PLAYER ONE, weaponized and medical neurotechnology, and other technologies will radically change how we live, what our expectations are, and how we manage all of that.

Importance of a Written Strategy

This changing world is the reason that *having a strategy and writing it down, reviewing it regularly, and adapting it with an innovative, flexible approach*, is so important. You need to know where you want to go, how you'll get there, and by what means:

1. Ends
2. Ways
3. Means.

Mountains of books exist to explain strategy, but those three words, used by the military, get at the core. It's not just a Western way of thinking. China's doctrine *Science of Military Strategy* is complicated, but at heart advocates the same idea. The ends define the other two. As my good friend, former Major General John Davis says, if you don't know where you're going, any road will take you there. Despite endless resources, a *lot* of executives and organizations fail the ends, ways, and means test. Pay attention to it. Use it. It's broad but describes the three vital milestones to your success.

Understand what obstacles block the achievement of success. The best strategic plan is useless unless calibrated to surmounting whatever blocks your success. Good strategic communication uses information to overcome the specific obstacles that stand in the way of your particular objective or end-state. As you think about using communication and information, put in front of you the notions of story, narrative, theme, and message. Tie these into a broad strategy for success. You need to integrate tactics into that framework, not just, as too often happens, focus on tactics.

Obstacles vary. Life is full of them. Marcus Aurelius insisted that we "accept the things to which fate binds us." I believe in making our own success in shaping our fates. You should all want to be the hero of your own life stories. The Emperor was closer to the mark in suggesting that we love the people with whom fate brings you together, and to do so with all your heart. Of course, epigrams run up against limits.

When you're fighting a tough adversary, especially one you don't respect, I come down with Heinrich Heine, who said "one must, it is true, forgive our enemies, but not before they have been hanged."[627] My dad, a great guy, a

---

[627] https://www.goodreads.com/quotes/408474-mine-is-a-most-peaceable-disposition-my-wishes-are-a

respected physician, held an incredibly optimistic view about people and life. He gave me this advice: "Son, just remember this. If it's not one damned thing, it's another. Stay strong and don't give up."

Technology is exciting. It has defined the new global environment for competition. Connectivity and networks are characteristics of that environment. Today's marketplace for ideas, services, and products is global. That unveils opportunity and challenge, for executives and the military. No formula describes how to prevail over the competition. I personally buy into the Blue Ocean theory: beat the competition by entering an uncontested space.

There's a reason innovative *new* products or services can do so well. There was a time when manufacturers competed to make the best buggy whip. They went out of business once people manufactured the automobile. Today innovation happens far more rapidly. Historically, less so. Nobody knows exactly who invented the first automobile, but Leonardo da Vinci gets credit in the 15th century for creating designs and models for transport vehicles.

Before you lose your breath from excitement over anticipated developments, I say *whoaaa!* Let's pause for a moment. Technology is about *means*. Unless you manufacture technology, it's not a strategic end in itself. It doesn't change the *nature* of what drives strategic communication, or story, narrative, theme, or message.

For a while, new technologies gave rise in the military to what was termed a "revolution in military affairs." The theory concerned the future of warfare. Advocates felt that advances in technologies changed the *nature of warfare.* The theories propounded by Carl von Clausewitz that view the frictions of war through his holy trinity of will, chance, and purpose have remained fundamental to warfare and will continue to do so.[628]

---

[628] Scholars more often refer to the trinity as passion, chance, and reason. Writing nearly two hundred years ago, Clausewitz talked about passion in terms of hatred and animosity, which he saw as a characteristic of the people. I feel a better interpretation of passion as the will of the people. The will of the people is essential for both offense and defense. Indeed, Clausewitz viewed war – a violent collision between conflicting political entities – as about defense first. He wrote that the objective is not necessarily the destruction of the enemy but also its resolve – its will – to fight. Clausewitz, On War, supra, Kindle Loc. 808/4381. In his words, "hostile feeling and action of hostile agencies, cannot be considered as at an end as long as the will of the enemy is not subdued, also." Id., Kindle Loc. 662/4381. That becomes notably relevant as one

Understanding Success and Winning

Technology has changed the way you can market services and products. The means to an end have evolved. But what made the unicorns a success hasn't changed – the fundamentals persist. Companies that have the right values, led by executives who think clearly, define ends clearly, and apply imagination, savvy, hard work and discipline are still most likely to succeed. The Internet merely provided a new tool – a new way or means – to enable success.

The notion of winning hasn't changed. In the military or politics, winning has different meanings depending on the players, the strategic situation, the desired end-states, and understanding how you define it all. Thus, the war in Afghanistan proved a failure for the West partly because no one defined or executed a coherent grand strategy that took into account both political and military considerations. Set aside our 2021 exit, which illustrates the notions of poor planning and poor judgment.

Afghanistan did not represent a defeat for the West. The Government of Afghanistan lost that war. It failed on every count of Clausewitz's trinity. It provided no security. It was corrupt. It was illegitimate. Too many Afghans lacked the will to support a government whose legitimacy was never properly established. I doubt the Afghan government could have ever won the war. It lacked a strategy to win that it was willing to forge or execute. Whether the Taliban succeeds in maintaining control over the country is an open question. Competitors challenged its authority immediately. My sense is that while Afghans want to live in peace and security, they're not going to buy into what the Taliban is selling.

As an executive, winning is mainly about profits and loss. I'm a consultant. Mark Penn, who served as Hillary Clinton's pollster and is one of the smartest in the business, once advised me that you're not a consultant unless you get paid. You're not in business unless you earn a profit, although the content of what constitutes a profit to you may or may not be pecuniary.

Success requires understanding your identity and that of your target audiences. That's about culture, values, language, history, geography, and politics. Not everyone shares the same values as Americans. Difficulty in grasping this hampered our efforts in Korea, where Douglas MacArthur misread Chinese

---

thinks about the need of leaders to arouse unity and support for their actions while sapping or destroying the will to resist an adversary.

intentions and culture, and Vietnam in the 1960s and 1970s, the 2003 Iraq War until 2005-2006, and the Afghanistan War. It impairs our policy in the Middle East. Those in the region value accountability and responsibility from government, but they judge that by their own culture and their interpretation of Islam, not democracy or Christian values.

The corporate world operates along parallel lines. In their open insistence on proving credibility, perhaps Japanese consumers rank among the most suspicious and demanding. But we all want to trust the people we deal with and their products. No surprise that online retailers who stream thousands of products are finally taking heat for giving visibility to no-name products and exploiting price point to win sales without providing value. I'm curious to see where that ends up. Congress is already debating whether to break up large Internet companies like Google, Amazon, and Facebook. A lot of factors integrate into that political calculation, but their large commercial impact is one of them.

You can – and should, for each strategic situation – write down your own list. Tough problems don't lend themselves to quick fixes or overnight solutions. You need to be *brave*. That can scare the hell out of any rational person. Starting up a new business these days can be harrowing. One key is to maintain a healthy concern, but never to let that spill over into worry.

Properly profiling audiences and targeting them carefully is essential. You can rarely change the fixed beliefs or convictions of audiences. That goes for the military, especially the ones who conduct operations in foreign nations in the hope of reshaping their politics to suit operational or strategic interests.

All of us want to be armchair strategists. *All of us.* I suspect that even the most deranged of us believe in their heart they could call better football plays and create better game plans than most coaches (no, not deities like Alabama's Nick Saban or the Patriots' Bill Belichick; the mortals!). Sadly, far more executives than you may imagine fall short when it comes to defining strategy or what it consists of, and even more lack the skills to devise and execute a working strategy.

Napoleon was the one who first used newspapers effectively to build political clout, in the tradition that Martin Luther had done with his broadsheets attacking hypocrisy in the Roman Catholic Church for selling indulgences. A combination of ego and power sent him astray. The battles of Austerlitz and Jena remain masterpieces of military strategy. Success went to his head. He misread the politics of Spain and Wellington and the Spanish handed him his head there.

That failure cast a shadow on his later invasion of Russia, a debacle from start to finish.

Julius Caesar and Scipio Africanus are remembered as extraordinary military leaders who defeated extraordinary opponents partly because they were great strategists. They commanded admiration and respect from their troops. When the hard fighting took place, they were in the thick of things. They led. They inspired. They persevered. The founders of Harry's Razors, Moment, Innocent, and Warby Parker brought the same elan and strategic sense in building their success.

Crises affect us all. The chapter on crisis management analyzes what we must deal with, how to do so, and looks at key case studies. I selected them as they stand out for actionable lessons. Put them to work.

Now it is *Your* Turn

Finally, what this book most aims to do is to provoke thought and discussion. I've included discussion questions at the end of every chapter. These flow from the content of the chapter. I encourage you to think carefully about them and decide how they apply to you or your situation.

Understanding the challenges you face, possessing the faith, optimism, enthusiasm, and confidence that you will persevere and overcome, and then making it all happen is what life is about. It's what makes it worth living.

James P. Farwell

New Orleans, Louisiana
February 2022

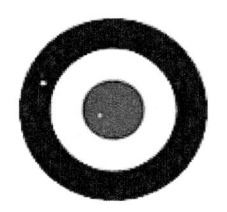

INDEX

Surnames starting with "al" are alphabetized by the subsequent part of the name.

A

Abrams, Creighton, 114, 146
Abu Ghraib prison, 179–85, 191, 200, 204, 213–14, 231, 236
Adidas, 15, 45, 48, 106–8, 151–52, 165
Advertisements. *See also* Marketing strategies; Target audiences
    backfiring of, 168
    cultural considerations, 99–100
    emotion in, 13–15, 49, 56, 69–71, 133–37
    messages in, 13–14, 153–55
    misleading or deceptive, 59, 166
    narratives in, 13–14, 36, 94, 97
    political, 59, 67, 69–70, 167
    production values, 68, 69, 95n256, 153, 166–67
    themes in, 13–14, 66
Afghanistan. *See also* Taliban
    command and control in, 162–63
    cultural engagement in, 55, 246
    failure to define end-state in, xii, 27–28, 246
    humor and entertainment in, 92
    lessons learned in, 27–28
    obstacles to success in, 147
    political dynamics in, 122
    Soviet intervention in, 130
    Special Inspector General for Afghanistan Reconstruction, 27, 147, 163
    U.S. withdrawal from, 5, 29, 62–63, 122, 246
AI. *See* Artificial intelligence
Aidid, Farrah, 43
Airbnb, 135
Air Force, rivalry with Marine Corps, 158
Algerian civil war, 207, 242
Allison, Graham, 29
Al Qaeda
    identification of members, 39
    Iraq War and, 11, 27, 52n129, 174, 208
    narratives promoted by, 55, 128, 172n452
    strategies for countering, 52–53, 131
    tactics utilized by, 52, 96
    theme of actions taken by, 129
Amazon, 15–16, 53, 112, 165–66, 205–6, 247
Ambrose, Stephen E., 147
American Airlines, 205
American Revolution, 109
Analytic empathy, 40–41
Anderson, Warren, 188–89, 191
Anheuser-Busch, 49, 167
Apple
    brand loyalty to, 88

center of gravity for, 31
global visibility of, 73
marketing strategies, 56, 59, 70, 85–86, 92
message discipline by, 213
narratives used by, 13–14, 85
1984 (Orwell) reference in advertisement, 13, 47, 95, 95n256
team management at, 165
Artificial intelligence (AI), 11, 53, 163–65, 217, 243
Ashland Oil storage tank collapse (1988), 186, 233
Attachment strategy, in crisis management, 182, 183
Attorney-client privilege, 229
Authenticity, defined, 112–13
Authoritarianism, 13, 31, 62, 91, 203
Automobile industry. *See also specific brands*
electric vehicles, 4, 90
failures within, 63, 90–91, 146
marketing strategies in, 57, 73–74
mirror-imaging by, 59
self-driving vehicles, 205
technological advances in, 4
Avoidance, in crisis management, 182

B

Bachchan, Amitabh, 212, 215
Baghdadi, Abu Bakr, 91–92
Baker, Farah, 61
Balon, Adam, 34
Barker, Matt, 107
Barnes, Stephen, 217
Bastian, Ed, 206
Beatles (music group), 86–87
Beckwith, Charles, 158, 159
Beebe, George, 40–41
Benghazi attack (2012), 208
Bergh, Chip, 98, 99
Berra, Yogi, 170
Berthier, Louis-Alexandre, 149
Bezos, Jeff, 15, 53, 112
Bhopal disaster (1984), 187–91

Biden, Joe
campaign themes and messages, 129
COVID-19 vaccination promoted by, 234
foreign policy under, 31, 78n194
Interim National Security Strategic Guidance, 12
on SolarWinds hack, 219
on U.S. withdrawal from Afghanistan, 5, 29, 122
Bin Laden, Usama, 3, 52, 104, 147
Bin Salman, Mohammed, 57
Bismarck, Otto von, 29
Blackhawk Down incident (1993), 43
Bloomberg, Michael, xiv, 87, 210
Blue ocean strategy, 45–46, 54, 62, 245
BMW, 56, 88
Boeing, 182, 191–94, 204, 210, 214
Bogost, Ian, 93
Bombfell (men's clothing subscription service), 40
Boucher, Richard, 183
Bowerman, Bill, 15, 15n36, 66
Boxing Day tsunami (2004), 12, 132, 184
Branch, Austin, 11–12, 25–26
Brand identity, 73, 98, 129
Brand loyalty
in COVID-19 pandemic, 49, 50
elements of, 157
long-term, 33, 47
reasons for switching, 22
status perceptions and, 113
strengthening of, 11, 88, 98
Brand strategy, 14–15
Branigan, Edward, 127–28
Branson, Richard, 50–51, 173
Bremer, Paul, 150, 162, 162n412, 172n451
Brown, Michael, 219, 228–29, 231–32
Bruns, Andreas, 97
Brzezinski, Zbigniew, 158
Budweiser, 49
Burke, James, 186, 192, 213
Bush, George H.W., 79, 190–91, 213
Bush, George W., 25–27, 96, 146, 150, 182, 208
Business gaming, 124

Business world. *See also specific companies and industries*
    competition in. *See* Competition
    corporate responsibility in, 18, 98–99, 205
    crisis management in, 185–96
    cybersecurity in. *See* Cybersecurity
    entrepreneurs in, 54, 113, 125, 164
    environmentally friendly companies, 47, 89, 99, 107, 132–33, 168, 206
    government relations with, 12, 59, 85
    leadership in. *See* Leadership
    startups in. *See* Startups
    strategy in. *See* Strategy
    success in. *See* Success
    technology in. *See* Technology
Bynum, Al, 108, 115

C

Cadbury, 212, 214–15
Calderon, Felipe, 29, 30
Campbell, Joseph, 14, 127
Carlson, Brian F., 66
Cars. *See* Automobile industry
Carter, Jimmy, 158, 159
Casper, 54, 164
Centers of gravity, 21, 28–29, 31–36, 82, 207
Challenger disaster (1986), 159–60, 173
Chandrasekaran, Rajiv, 162
Charisma, 14n31, 110, 147
Chief executive officers (CEOs). *See also specific names of CEOs*
    arrogance of, 242
    challenges for, 2
    crisis management by, 186–88, 192, 195, 198, 200, 209–10
    end-states utilized by, 21
    objectives of, 1, 80
    severance packages for, 193
    stakeholder engagement by, 118
    strategic planning by, 105
China
    cyber dangers posed by, 221
    grand strategy of, 42, 79–80
    intellectual property theft by, 42, 221
    Internet control in, 42, 62
    Muslim Uyghurs in, 207
    strategic communication in, 41–42, 244
Chivas Regal, 40
Christensen, Thomas, 78
Chrysler, 110
Cirque du Soleil, 46
Citibank, 71
Civil War, U.S., 110, 148
Clarke, Wesley, 114
Clausewitz, Carl von
    on centers of gravity, 21, 28–29, 207
    on frictions of war, 1, 2, 104, 173, 245
    on moral factors, 3
    on nature of war, 245, 245n628
    on strategy in war, 6
    on war as continuation of politics, 171
"Clear and hold" strategy, 146
Clinton, Bill, 43–44, 120, 213
Clinton, Henry, 109
Clinton, Hillary, 14n31, 122, 129, 208, 246
Coca-Cola
    failures by, 146, 156–57
    global visibility of, 73
    as investor in Innocent Drinks, 35
    marketing strategies, 13, 56–57, 93, 131, 153–56
    narratives used by, 133, 134
    Pepsi Challenge and, 60–61, 85
    on political issues, 207
    resource availability, 86
    response to Virgin Cola, 51, 173
Cognitive warfare, 164
Cold War. *See* Soviet Union
Collaboration
    leadership and, 113, 151, 162, 242
    in marketing strategies, 106, 107, 153
    with stakeholders, 115, 117, 120–21
Color revolutions, 62, 171
Combs, W. Timothy, 181–82
Commander's Briefs, 12, 21–22
Commiseration, in crisis management, 181, 182, 196

Communication. *See also* Media; Strategic communication
    channels of, 59–61, 66, 72–74, 165–67, 235
    in COVID-19 pandemic, 234–36
    email, 119, 198, 218, 220, 223–24, 236
    emotional intelligence and, 7, 129–31
    failures in, 158–61
    industry best practices for, 232
    strategies for effectiveness, 8–10
    in team management, 165
    unity of command and, 162
Communism, 41–42, 56, 58–59, 147, 181
Comparison marketing, 59, 85–86
Competition, 39–63. *See also* Global competitive marketplace
    admitting failure in, 63
    avoidance of hubris in, 62–63
    communication channels used in, 59–61
    credibility and persuasiveness of, 56–57
    as driver of marketplace shifts, 2, 106
    identification of, 39–40, 174
    information warfare and, 35
    language considerations, 55–56, 58–59
    mirror-imaging of, 57–59
    obstacles in, 61–62
    self-perception of, 51–54
    strength and weakness assessment, 40–51, 58
Computer Fraud and Abuse Act of 1986, 222
Confidential data, 223, 224, 227, 237
Consistent branding, 89, 90
Containment strategy, 79
Cornwallis, George, 109
Corona (beer), 49
Corporate culture, 36, 105, 112, 241
Corporate responsibility, 18, 98–99, 205
Costco, 165
Costello, Lisann, 151
Cost imposition strategy, 105–6
Counter information warfare, 222
Counterinsurgency guidance, 9, 58n146, 131
COVID-19 pandemic
    Chinese response to, 41, 42
    communication during, 234–36
    crisis management during, 207–8
    cybersecurity during, 234–38
    marketing strategies during, 36, 49–50
    motion picture industry during, 53–54, 54n136
    retail industry during, 17, 167
    vaccinations and, 129, 234
Creative briefs, 21, 106, 176
Credibility
    of Al Qaeda, 52n129
    character of companies and, 241
    of competition, 56–57
    in COVID-19 pandemic, 238
    crisis management and, 182, 192, 193, 202, 208, 214
    cybersecurity incidents and, 230–31, 233
    elements of, 113, 247
    of government, 28, 189
    as marketing strategy, 99
    of military, 11, 42–43, 109, 130, 180, 181
    of narratives, 137, 141, 235
Crisis, defined, 180
Crisis management, 179–215
    in business world, 185–96
    by CEOs, 186–88, 192, 195, 198, 200, 209–10
    credibility and, 182, 192, 193, 202, 208, 214
    cultural sensitivity in, 200–201
    empathy in, 195, 201–2, 205
    humor used for, 203
    influencer marketing and, 211–12
    media relations in, 213–14
    message discipline in, 183, 213
    by military, 179–85, 200
    narratives in, 192, 195–96, 204, 210–15
    political issues and, 205–7
    preparation for, 197–200, 210
    promotional giveaways and, 204
    for sexual harassment, 201, 202
    social media and, 204, 215, 233
    stakeholder engagement in, 207–8, 214–15

strategic communication in, 179, 181–83, 190, 196, 209
timing of responses, 208–9, 214
transparency in, 181–82, 188, 191, 193, 195–96, 231
victim management in, 201–2
Crocker, Ryan C., 27, 162
Cronkite, Walter, 56, 181
Crowd-sourcing, 61, 203
Crusades, 11, 128, 172n452
Custer, George, 173
Cybersecurity, 217–38. *See also* Hacking
in COVID-19 pandemic, 234–38
credibility and, 230–31, 233
crisis management and, 198n529, 208, 233
defending against attacks, 220–22, 226
preparation for, 228–29, 231–32
strategic communication and, xiv–xv, 217, 228–33
Cyber warfare, 219

D

Dailey, Dell, 104–5, 120
"Daisy" (political ad), 69–70
Darby, Joseph M., 179–80
Data breaches. *See* Hacking
Davis, Jacob, 97
Davis, Jefferson, 148
Davis, John, 4, 22, 111, 221–22, 229, 244
Davout, Louis-Nicolas, 149
Decision-making
contextual considerations for, 44
in crisis management, 200–201
in Fourth-Generation Warfare, 81–82
information resources for, 150, 159, 160
knock-on consequences of, 43
leadership effectiveness and, 6
stakeholder engagement in, 115
"team of teams" concept for, 175
value-based, 131
Deepwater Horizon oil spill (2010), 161, 196, 232–33
De Gaulle, Charles, 207, 242–43
Delta Airlines, 206

Democratic Alliance in South Africa, 71
DeSaix, Louis, 149
Desert Storm. *See* Gulf War
DiCaprio, Leonardo, 54
Direct-to-consumer (D2C) marketing, 54, 167, 172
Disassociation, in crisis management, 181, 182
Disney, 53–54, 53–54n135
Dixon, Patrick, xxi
Dodge, 133–34
Dole, Bob, 92
Dollar Shave Club, 32, 33, 54, 86, 124–25, 174
Douglas, Stephen, 148
Dove, 134, 137–42, 213
Downing, Carol, 180–81, 196
Drug wars, 29–31
D2C marketing. *See* Direct-to-consumer marketing
Dublin, Michael, 109, 124–25
Duncan, Karen, 236

E

EAGLE CLAW, 157–59, 173
Eastwood, Clint, 133, 134
Eikenberry, Karl, 162
Eisenhower, Dwight, 103, 104, 128, 145, 147, 148, 211
Electric vehicles, 4, 90
Elimination strategy, in crisis management, 181
Email communication, 119, 198, 218, 220, 223–24, 236
Emotions
in advertisements, 13–15, 49, 56, 69–71, 133–37
in information warfare, 88
in marketing strategies, 7, 88–91
in narratives, 88, 129–31, 133–37
in strategic communication, 129–31
Emotional intelligence, 7, 129–31, 133
Empathy
analytic, 40–41
in branding strategies, 142
commiseration and, 181

in crisis management, 195, 201–2, 205
cybersecurity incidents and, 231, 236
in leadership, 8
End-states, 21–36
    centers of gravity and, 21, 28–29, 31–36, 82
    characteristics of, xii–xiii, 16, 21
    failures to define, xii, 11, 26–28, 30, 246
    knowledge acquisition for, 23–26
    in strategic communication plans, 104, 105
    in strategic thinking, 21–23, 35
    wargaming against, 123
Enron scandal (2001), 161
Entrepreneurs, 54, 113, 125, 164
Environmentally friendly companies, 47, 89, 99, 107, 132–33, 168, 206
Equifax, 208, 208n555, 233, 236
Equinox, 206, 230–31
Espionage, 218, 218–19n578
Exxon Valdez oil spill (1989), 196, 210

F
Facebook
    Adidas' use of, 107
    commercial impact of, 247
    in COVID-19 pandemic, 237
    Dove Self-Esteem Project and, 141
    fraudulent postings on, 166
    ISIS posts on, 169
    in political campaigns, 87
    Taliban's use of, 170
    traditional media disrupted by, 181
    Ukrainian resistance and, 171
Federal Trade Commission Act of 1914, 59
Feelings. *See* Emotions
Ferling, John, 109
Films. *See* Motion picture industry
Fisher, Walter R., 127
5G Internet, 11, 42, 217
Flom, Joseph, 86
Forrest, Nathan Bedford, 110
Fortum & Mason, 72–73
Forward-thinking, 163–65
Fourth-Generation Warfare (4GW), 81–82

Fox, Vincente, 30
Franks, Tommy R., 26n58, 147
Fridman, Ofer, 5, 6, 80, 130
Fritz, Ben, 53, 54

G
Gaddafi, Muammar, 122
Garcia, Jerry, 93
Gates, Bill, 86, 87, 202
Geneva Conventions (1949), 180, 180n463
Genocide, 43–44, 52, 162
Gerges, Fawaz, 52n129
Germany
    Nazi Germany, 96, 128–29, 148, 211–12
    special operations conducted by, 3
    strategic thinking by, 23
Gerstner, Louis, 116
Giesler, Bob, 21, 44–45, 82–83
Gillette, 32, 33, 135
Gingrich, Newt, 119–20, 213
Gladwell, Malcolm, 60, 86–87, 167
Global competitive marketplace, 1–18
    marketing strategies in, 13–18
    operating environment of, 2, 243, 245
    social media connections in, 168
    Special Operations theory and, 2–10
    target audiences in, xii, 2, 10–13
    winning on competitive playing fields, 1
Glow, Lee, 13, 13n30
Godin, Seth, 88, 93, 95, 96, 130–31, 153
Goizueta, Robert, 156
Goldring, Bill, 113
Google, 134, 166, 175, 247
Gorbachev, Mikhail, 106
Government
    authoritarian, 13, 31, 62, 91, 203
    business world relations with, 12, 59, 85
    corruption in, 30, 55, 96, 246
    credibility of, 28, 189
    Internet controlled by, 42, 62
Grand strategy, xiii, xiiin2, 28–29, 42, 78–82, 84, 246
Grant, Ulysses, 110, 148
Greenstein, Fred L., 147
Grieshaber, Michele, 117

Grouchy, Emmanuel de, 149
Groupthink, 24
Grow, Lee, 95
Guderian, Heinz, 110
Gulf War (1991), xii–xiii, 79, 191, 235
Guy, Jack, 77
Guzman Loera, Joaquin (El Chapo), 30

H
Hacking
    case law related to, 227–28
    crisis management for, 208
    damage inflicted by, 224–25
    defending against attacks, 220–22
    examples of, 217–19, 221, 223–25
    financial costs of, 217–18, 223, 225–27
    regulatory costs of, 226–27, 233
    stakeholder notification of, 229–30, 233
Hall, John, 186
Hammes, Thomas X., 81–82
Harassment, 201, 202, 210
Harley Davidson, 96–97
Harris, Izzy Liyana, 141
Harrods, 72–73
Harry's Razors, 31–33, 32n76, 59, 125, 165, 174
Harvey, Paul, 133, 134
Hayward, Tony, 210, 232
Health Insurance Portability and Accountability Act (HIPAA), 237
Heine, Heinrich, 244
Higgins, Elliot, 61
Hitler, Adolph, 96, 148, 211–12
Holbrooke, Richard, 162
Holtz, Lou, 241–42
Hooker, R.D., Jr., 78, 78n194, 79
Howe, Jonathan, 43
Hubris, 33, 62–63, 152, 242
Huggies, 35
Humanitarian operations, 80, 132
Humor, 36, 91–93, 203
Hush Puppy, 37, 167
Huxhold, Paul, 123, 129

I
Iacocca, Lee, 110, 112
IBM
    global visibility of, 73
    history and evolution of, 63, 116
    intelligence gathering by, 173
    marketing strategies, 56
    message discipline by, 213
    narratives used by, 36, 134
    self-stated purpose of, 112
    stakeholder engagement by, 116–17
IKEA, 71–73, 164
Influencer marketing, 211–12
Information warfare
    competition and, 35
    emotional appeals in, 88
    in Iraq War, 84, 151
    narratives in, 127, 130, 171
    social media in, 5, 6, 170
    status perceptions in, 96
Inglis, Chris, 220–22, 227
Ingrassia, Lawrence, 86, 124–25, 164
Inman, Bobby, 7–8
Innocent Drinks, 33–35, 132, 206
Innovation. *See also* Technology
    adaptive, 61, 84
    by entrepreneurs, 54
    in leadership, 124
    in marketing strategies, 32, 45
    pace of, 245
    in retail industry, 72–73
    Special Operations theory on, 4
    in strategic communication plans, 31–32
    in strategic thinking, 4–5
    value innovation strategy, 46
Instagram, 50, 90, 181, 237
Intellectual property, 42, 219, 221
Intelligence
    artificial, 11, 53, 163–65, 217, 243
    classified briefings on, 24
    collection of, 39, 44, 173
    emotional, 7, 129–31, 133
    integrating information and, 172–73
    in Iran hostage crisis, 159

ongoing updates of, 173–75
perishable nature of, 4
International Military Tribunal Nuremberg Charter (1945), 180, 180n463
Internet
    color revolutions and, 62
    entrepreneurial uses of, 164
    5G, 11, 42, 217
    government control of, 42, 62
    inventory reductions due to, 125
    as marketing tool, 61
    unicorn startups and, 86, 171, 246
Iran hostage crisis, 157–59
Iraq War
    Al Qaeda and, 11, 27, 52n129, 174, 208
    command and control in, 162
    counterinsurgency efforts in, 9
    cultural knowledge and, 25, 246
    failure to define end-state in, xii, 11, 26–27
    information warfare during, 84, 151
    intelligence gathering during, 174
    lessons learned from, 26–28, 146
    narratives of, 11, 150, 172n452
    public affairs strategies in, 8–10, 61, 151
    surge in (2007–2008), 8, 10, 27, 162
    tactical strategy in, 79, 84
Isaacson, Walter, 148
ISIS. *See* Islamic State
Islam and Muslims
    Bosnian, 43
    Crusades against, 11, 128, 172n452
    interpretations of, 52
    narratives for appealing to, 55, 128
    Shiites, 25, 27, 52
    Sunnis, 25, 27, 52
    Uyghurs in China, 207
Islamic State (ISIS)
    as genocidal organization, 52, 162
    monetary reserves of, 29–30, 170
    narratives promoted by, 55
    social media use by, 168–69, 210
    strategies for countering, 42, 91–92, 131, 203
    tactics utilized by, 52, 96
    Taliban war against, 42, 170
Israeli-Palestinian conflict, 61

J

J. Press, 40, 73
Jack Daniels, 55–56, 73, 112–13
Jack in the Box, 201
Jackson, Thomas "Stonewall," 110
Jaguar, 73–74
Japan
    advertisements in, 99–100
    Pearl Harbor attacks by, 29, 173, 211
    suspiciousness of consumers in, 99, 247
Jiwa, Bernadette, 131
Jobs, Steve, 7, 14, 47, 66–67, 95, 109, 148
Johansson, Scarlett, 53, 53–54n135
Johnson, Kevin, 18, 195, 213
Johnson, Lyndon B., 56, 69–70, 145–46
Johnson & Johnson (J&J), 186–87, 192–93, 196, 207, 214, 231–35
Johnstone, Keith, 96
Jones, David, 158
Jordan, Michael, 87, 166
Julius Caesar, 10, 108, 248
Justification, in crisis management, 182

K

Kael, Pauline, 134
Kamprad, Ingvar, 72
Karpinski, Janis, 179
Katz-Mayfield, Andy, 32
Kearney, Frank, 27, 104–6, 114–15, 123, 138
Kehne, Seth, 152
Kellerman, Mary, 185–86
Kelly, F. John, 26
Kemp, Brian, 206
Kennedy, John (IBM), 116
Kennedy, John F., 119, 146, 146n372
Kenney, Jim, 194–95
Kersey, Jim, 99
Killeen, Buzzy, 88
Kim, W. Chan, 45–46
Kim Jong Un, 221, 224n594
Kimmitt, Mark, 182–85, 192, 200, 209, 214, 231, 236

Kissinger, Henry, 147
Knowledge acquisition, 23–26
Koha, Rebeka, 68
Korean War, 246
Kozlowski, Don, 117
Kurzman, Dan, 187–88, 187n480
Kyle, James H., 158

L

Lawn Butler, 152
Law of Armed Conflict (LAC), 218–19n578
Leadership. *See also* Chief executive officers
    charisma and, 14n31, 110, 147
    collaboration and, 113, 151, 162, 242
    in crisis management, 181, 197, 200
    entrepreneurial, 164
    innovative, 124
    management vs., 111
    moral, vi, 7
    motivation through, 115, 120
    political, 114, 181, 207
    Special Operations theory on, 4
    strengthening of, 1
    traits for, xi, 6–8, 10, 110, 114, 242–43
    values-based, 35–36, 111–12
Lean Cuisine, 136
Lee, James, 97
Lee, Robert E., 110
Leer, Genrikh Antonovich, 6
Leonardo da Vinci, 245
Leonhard, Gerd, 11
Levi Strauss & Co., 97–99, 132
Lexus, 88
Libya, U.S. intervention in, 12, 122
Liddell Hart, B.H., xiiin2, 77–78
Lin, Michael, 97
Lincoln, Abraham, 28–29, 110, 148
Listening, 25, 43, 115, 118, 199, 201, 242
Lodge, Henry Cabot, 145–46
Lombardi, Vince, 108
Lopez Obrador, Andres Manuel, 30–31
Loyalty. *See* Brand loyalty
Lukaszewski, James E., ix–x, 7, 186–87, 197–98, 201–2, 214
Luther, Martin, 247

Luttwak, Edward, 78–79
"Luxury disrupted" strategy, 17
Lysol, 135

M

MacArthur, Douglas, 211, 246
Machine learning, 165, 243
Mack, Mary Bono, 230
Mahinda, Keshab, 189
Malaysian Rebellion, 58–59
Mao Zedong, 40
Marcus Aurelius, 244
Margolies, Tracy, 16
Marine Corps
    in Afghanistan, 162–63
    Counterinsurgency Field Manual, 131
    cultural engagement by, 55, 65
    emotional intelligence of, 133
    in Iraq War, 151
    ISIS attack on, 169–70
    rivalry with Air Force, 158
Marketing strategies. *See also* Advertisements; Target audiences
    centers of gravity in, 21, 33, 34, 36
    collaboration in, 106, 107, 153
    communication channels for, 59–61, 66, 72–74
    comparative, 59, 85–86
    in COVID-19 pandemic, 36, 49–50
    cultural considerations, 28, 71–72, 99–100
    direct-to-consumer, 54, 167, 172
    emotion vs. reason in, 7, 88–91
    in global competitive marketplace, 13–18
    humor in, 92–93
    innovation in, 32, 45
    Internet-based, 61
    language considerations in, 56–57
    message discipline in, 15, 33, 90, 155
    narratives in, 17, 31, 34–36, 66, 85–86
    obstacles to, 62
    quirkiness in, 93–94
    social media in, 50, 73, 89–90, 107, 156

status and, 16, 96–99
Marks, James "Spider," 118
Marshall, George, 23, 148, 211
Mauborgne, Renee, 45–46
Mazzetti, Mark, 162
McChrystal, Stanley, 111, 114, 163, 174–75, 235
McClellan, George, 148
McDonald's, 196, 203, 204
McNamara, Robert, 145–46
McRaven, William H., 3, 3n6, 19, 159, 159n403
Media. *See also* Advertisements; Public relations; Social media
   beauty standards set by, 138–41
   in global environment, 181
   Iraq War reporting in, 27, 150
   responsibilities of, 9
   strategies for interacting with, 9–10, 213–14
   training for dealing with, 213
Mercedes, 57, 73, 88
Message discipline
   in crisis management, 183, 213
   importance of, 49, 89, 146, 238
   in marketing strategies, 15, 33, 90, 155
   strategies for instilling, 10
Messages. *See also* Message discipline
   in advertisements, 13–14, 153–55
   characteristics of, 129
   of competition, 45, 55–56
   in creative briefs, 106, 176
   in crisis management, 183, 190, 195–96, 203–4, 212–13
   cultural considerations, 175
   environmentally sensitive, 132
   in marketing strategies, 15, 17, 66
   in military operations, 113
   in strategic communication, 41, 127, 244
   for target audiences, 98
Method (cleaning products), 132, 168
Metrick, Mark, 17
Mexico, drug wars in, 29–31

Military. *See also* Special Operations; War and Warfare; *specific branches of military*
   Commander's Briefs in, 12, 21–22
   credibility of, 11, 42–43, 109, 130, 180, 181
   crisis management by, 179–85, 200
   emotional intelligence of, 133
   humanitarian operations, 80, 132
   leadership in. *See* Leadership
   narratives used by, 11, 109, 113, 130–32
   Operational Art in, 1, 22, 62, 108
   on public relations, 182
   SolarWinds hack and, 218–19
   strategy in. *See* Strategy
Millennials, 154, 164
Miller, Donald, 85–86
Miller, Geoffrey, 183
Mirror-imaging, 57–59, 87
Mission statements, 89, 138, 139
Mitchell, Mark, 22
Miteva, Anni, 156
Moliere, 91, 203
Moltke, Helmuth von, 103
Monaghan, Andrew, 78
Montgomery, Bernard, 110, 145
Moon, James, 97
Moral factors (Clausewitz), 3
Moral high ground, 131–32
Moral leadership, vi, 7
Morgan, Adam, 62
Morozov, Evgeny, 62
Motion picture industry, 53–54, 53–54nn135–136
Motor vehicles. *See* Automobile industry
Mueller, Robert S., III, 217
Muilenburg, Dennis, 192–93
Mulino Bianco, 94
Mulloy, Lawrence, 160
Murphy, Tim, 156
Musk, Elon, 209, 210
Muslims. *See* Islam and Muslims
Mussolini, Benito, 3

N

Napoleon Bonaparte, 6–7, 7n16, 10, 11n21, 149, 173–74, 247
Narratives, 127–42. *See also* Messages; Themes
    in advertisements, 13–14, 36, 94, 97
    assessment of, 124
    of competition, 45, 55–56
    components of, 127–28
    in creative briefs, 106, 176
    credibility of, 137, 141, 235
    in crisis management, 192, 195–96, 204, 210–15
    cultural considerations, 175
    Dove Self-Esteem Project, 137–42
    emotion in, 88, 129–31, 133–37
    environmentally sensitive, 132–33
    in information warfare, 127, 130, 171
    in Iraq War, 11, 150, 172n452
    of Israeli-Palestinian conflict, 61
    in marketing strategies, 17, 31, 34–36, 66, 85–86
    military use of, 109, 113, 130–32
    moral high ground and, 131–32
    in propaganda, 79
    status-related, 96
    in strategic communication, 41–42, 127, 244
    for target audiences, 55–56, 98, 234–36
National Defense Strategy, 12
Nationalism, 41–42, 55, 58–59, 99, 146
NATO. *See* North Atlantic Treaty Organization
Naveh, Shimon, 82
Navy, *Mercy* deployment by, 132, 184
Neate, Mark, 58, 83, 84
Netflix, 53, 54
Neurotechnology, 11, 163, 164, 243
Newell, Graham, 67
Ney, Michel, 149, 149n378
Nieto, Enrique Peña, 30
Nike
    center of gravity for, 31
    competition for, 45, 48, 106, 151
    global visibility of, 73
    key players in success of, 149
    marketing strategies, 13–15, 56, 66–69, 87, 166
    message discipline by, 213
    narratives used by, 31, 66, 134, 136, 175
    resource availability, 49
    team management at, 165
9/11 terrorist attacks (2001), 52, 173
Nokia, 160–61
Noriega, Manuel Antonio, xii–xiii
North Atlantic Treaty Organization (NATO), 1, 27, 44, 122, 151
North Korea, cyber dangers posed by, 221, 224
Nuclear weapons, 4, 69–70, 147
Nuovo, Frank, 160

O

Obama, Barack, 13–14, 14n31, 78n194, 87, 152, 167, 213
Obstacles to success
    in competition and conflicts, 61–62
    identification of, xiv, 39, 145–46
    language and cultural barriers, 175
    in marketing strategies, 62
    overcoming, 110, 119, 146–48
    for startup companies, 7
    strategic communication plans on, 115
Odierno, Raymond T., 10n19
O'Dwyer, Jack, 187
Oliver, Thomas, 156–57
Operational Art, 1, 22, 62, 108
Operational shock, 82
Operational strategy, xiii, 78, 138
Opium Wars, 41
O'Rourke, P.J., 242
Orwell's *1984*, reference in Apple advertisement, 13, 47, 95, 95n256
OUIGO, 94
Overy, Richard, 212
Oxford-AstraZeneca, 207–8

P

Padgett, Stephen, 31, 118–19, 123–24
Pampers, 35
Pandemic. *See* COVID-19 pandemic
Pascal, Amy, 223, 224
Patagonia, 132, 206–7
Patrikarakos, David, 171
Patterson, J. David, 10, 39–40, 117, 198, 200, 203–4, 233
Patton, George S., 108, 110
Peacekeeping missions, 13n27, 44
Pearl Harbor attacks (1941), 29, 173, 211
Penn, Mark, 246
Pepsi, 59–61, 85, 92–93
Petraeus, David, 8–10, 22–23, 27, 51, 115, 119, 162, 233
Picard, 94
Pinto, Maurice, 34
Pitman, Charles H., 158–59, 158n400
Pizza Hut, 112
Plank, Kevin, 45–48
Political advertisements, 59, 67, 69–70, 167
Political leadership, 114, 181, 207
Popeil, Ron, 167
Porsche, 57
Positioning strategy, 86–88, 106, 110
Preemption, in crisis management, 181
Press. *See* Media
Private data. *See* Confidential data
Procter & Gamble (P&G), 63, 106, 135–37, 139, 175
Promotional giveaways, 204
Propaganda, 41, 52, 56, 79, 184, 186
Psychological warfare, 147
Public relations, 50, 72, 140–41, 150, 182, 198–99, 210
Publishing industry, 89
Puma, 130
Putin, Vladimir, 61, 122, 130, 171

Q

Al Qasabi, Nasser, 203
Quantum computing, 11, 163, 217
Quincey, James, 207
Quirkiness, 93–94

R

Raider, Jeff, 32
Ramakrishnan, Keerthana, 68
Rapinoe, Megan, 68–69
Rather, Dan, 183, 213–14, 231
Rawl, Lawrence, 196
Reagan, Ronald, 69, 105–6, 114, 159
Rectification, in crisis management, 181, 182, 196
Red teaming, 58, 123, 124
Reebok, 15
Reed, Richard, 34, 35
Refutation, in crisis management, 181
Relative superiority, defined, 3
Reputation. *See also* Credibility
    building and rebuilding, 62, 202, 203, 212
    crisis management and, 180, 185–86, 196, 199, 202, 209
    damage to, 180, 217, 224–25
Responsibility to Protect doctrine, 12, 122
Retail industry
    in COVID-19 pandemic, 17, 167
    disruptions within, 15, 53
    innovation in, 72–73
    strategic communication in, 16
    technology in, 15–17, 16–17n41
Revolutionary War, 109
Rice, Susan, 208
Ricks, Thomas, 10, 10n19
Ries, Al, 86, 88
Roberts, Andrew, 149, 173–74
Robison, Peter, 193
Rohozinski, Rafal, 232
Rommel, Erwin, 110
Romney, Mitt, 152, 213
Rood, John, 24–25, 57, 120, 133
Roosevelt, Franklin D., 28–29, 96, 148–49, 211–12
Rorsted, Kasper, 107, 151–52
Ross, Stephen, 206
Rotfeld, Herbert Jack, 13

Rubio, Marco, 206
Rumors
    filling communication void, 215
    importance in intelligence gathering, 172
    speed in refuting, 238
Rumsfeld, Donald H., 26–27, 146, 183
Russia. *See also* Soviet Union
    cyber dangers posed by, 218–19, 221
    on grand strategy, xiii, 80
    intervention in Syrian civil war, 130
    Napoleon's invasion of, 174, 247
    strategic thinking by, 6
    Ukrainian resistance against, 171
Rwandan genocide, 43–44

S

Saddam Hussein, 11, 26, 52, 79, 95–96, 180, 191
Saks Fifth Avenue, 16–17, 164
Sanchez, Ricardo, 150, 162
Sandalova, Anna, 171
Schultz, Howard, 17–18
Schwartz, Tony, 69–70, 131
Schwarzkopf, Norman, Jr., 235
Scipio Africanus, 108–9, 248
Scott, Ridley, 13
Scowcroft, Brent, 190–91
Scudder, Ken, 197
Scudder, Virgil, 7, 25, 118, 185, 196, 198–200, 209, 233
Sculley, John D., 60, 84
Self-driving vehicles, 205
September 11 terrorist attacks (2001), 52, 173
Sexual harassment, 201, 202, 210
Sheridan, Philip, 110
Sherman, William, 110, 148
Shia Muslims, 25, 27, 52
Shirkey, Clay, 62
Shirreff, Richard, 1–2, 7, 24, 27–28, 35–36, 83, 124
Shock, in crisis management, 181
"Shock and awe" strategies, 95, 130
Shrivastava, Paul, 190

Shultz, George, 16
Sickler, Jonas, 195
SIGAR. *See* Special Inspector General for Afghanistan Reconstruction
Singh, Arjun, 189
Skorzeny, Otto, 3
Smith, Richard F., 230
Smith, Rupert, 164
Smith & Wesson, 146
Smoke-and-mirrors strategy, 130
Social media. *See also specific platforms*
    analytic research through, 65, 152
    in COVID-19 pandemic, 237
    crisis management and, 204, 215, 233
    for direct-to-consumer marketing, 167, 172
    in Dove Self-Esteem Project, 140, 141
    fraudulent postings on, 166
    in global competitive marketplace, 168
    in information warfare, 5, 6, 170
    in Israeli-Palestinian conflict, 61
    in marketing strategies, 50, 73, 89–90, 107, 156
    media space disrupted by, 62, 165–66, 181
    in retail industry, 17
    target audience analysis on, 65, 67
    weaponized, 166, 168–70
SolarWinds hack, 218–19
Somalia, Blackhawk Down incident in, 43
Sony Pictures hack, 221, 223–25, 224n594, 230
SoulCycle, 206
Soult, Jean-de-Dieu, 149
Soviet Union
    in Cold War, 79
    collapse of, 105–6
    intervention in Afghanistan, 130
Special Inspector General for Afghanistan Reconstruction (SIGAR), 27, 147, 163
Special Operations
    adaptability of, 84
    in Iraq War, 175
    operations arm of, 104

relative superiority and, 3
theory of, 2–10
in World War II, 3, 3n8
Standard Bank, 71
Starbucks
    crisis management by, 194–96, 204, 207, 214, 233
    environmental friendliness of, 89, 132
    marketing strategies, 17–18, 90
    mission statement of, 89
Startups. *See also specific companies*
    blue ocean strategy for, 45–46
    forward-thinking by, 164
    Special Operations theory and, 7
    strategic communication plans for, 124–25
    unicorns, 47, 86, 124–25, 171, 246
Starwax, 94
Status, 16, 96–99, 113
Stavridis, James George, v–vii, 3–4, 6–7, 28, 65–66, 80, 175
Stella Artois, 49–50, 50n119
Stengel, Jim, 7, 35–36, 63, 88, 94, 111–14, 132
Stephens, J. Christopher, 208
Stevenson, Jonathan, 43
Stories. *See* Narratives
Strategic communication. *See also* Marketing strategies; Narratives; Strategic communication plans
    in crisis management, 179, 181–83, 190, 196, 209
    cultural considerations, 72–73, 99–100
    cybersecurity and, xiv–xv, 217, 228–33
    economic elements of, 81
    emotional intelligence and, 129–31
    humor in, 91–92
    limitations of, 13
    narratives in, 41–42, 127, 244
    in retail industry, 16
    spokesperson/coordinators of, 235
    strengthening of, 1
    Taliban's use of, 5–6
Strategic communication plans, 103–25
    creative briefs as, 21, 106, 176
    for cybersecurity, 228, 231–32
    end-states in, 104, 105
    failure to think through consequences of, 44
    innovation in, 31–32
    orientation towards winning and inspiring, 108–14
    realistic nature of, 122–25
    stakeholder engagement with, 114–22
    for startups, 124–25
    written, 22, 103–8, 244–45
Strategic thinking
    in business gaming, 124
    on cybersecurity, 222
    end-states in, 21–23, 35
    factors in shaping of, 106
    innovation in, 4–5
    on nature of war, 6
Strategy, 77–100. *See also* End-states; Marketing strategies; Strategic communication; Strategic thinking
    blue ocean, 45–46, 54, 62, 245
    brand, 14–15
    "clear and hold" s, 146
    containment, 79
    cost imposition, 105–6
    cultural considerations, 99–100
    definitions of, 77–78
    grand, xiii, xiiin2, 28–29, 42, 78–82, 84, 246
    industry and, 82–86
    "luxury disrupted," 17
    National Defense, 12
    operational, xiii, 78, 138
    political, 27, 87
    positioning, 86–88, 106, 110
    "shock and awe," 95, 130
    smoke-and-mirrors, 130
    tactical, xiii, 78, 79, 84, 110, 138
    value innovation, 46
Subscription services, 32–33, 40
Success. *See also* End-states; Obstacles to success
    budgeting resources for, 176

delegation of responsibilities and, 150–52
forward-thinking for, 163–65
in global competitive marketplace, 13, 18
intelligence integration and updates for, 172–75
of Iraq War surge, 8
key players for, 148–50
leadership and, 7, 10
measures of, 105, 152–54, 246
sharing critical information with stakeholders and, 157
of Special Operations, 3
strategic view of, 46, 104
sustaining, 22, 85
team management for, 165
10,000-Hour Rule and, 86–87
unity of command and control for, 162–63

Suchet, Louis-Gabriel, 149
Sunni Muslims, 25, 27, 52
Sun Tzu, v, vi, 40, 80
Swann, Patricia, 180–81, 196
Syrian civil war, 130

T

Tactical strategy, xiii, 78, 79, 84, 110, 122, 138
Taguba, Antonio, 180
Taliban
    identification of members, 39
    ISIS war against, 42, 170
    narratives promoted by, 55
    social media use by, 5–6, 170
    strategies for countering, 28
    tactics utilized by, 96
    takeover of Afghanistan, 5, 170–71, 246
Talking points, 235–36
Tallerine, Leonard, 243
Tall poppy syndrome, 154
Target (retail store), 62, 165, 217–18, 226
Target audiences, 65–74. *See also* Advertisements; Marketing strategies
    analysis of, 39, 61, 65–67, 81, 89, 124, 164, 211, 247
    competition for, 40, 46, 56–57
    cultural considerations, 28, 71–72, 99–100
    engagement with, 73–74, 215
    in global competitive marketplace, xii, 2, 10–13
    narratives for appealing to, 55–56, 98, 234–36
    strategy formulation for, 83, 156, 246
Team management, 165
"Team of teams" concept, 114, 174–75
Technology. *See also* Cybersecurity; Innovation
    artificial intelligence, 11, 53, 163–65, 217, 243
    as driver of marketplace shifts, 2, 28
    Internet. *See* Internet
    machine learning, 165, 243
    nature of warfare and, 245
    neurotechnology, 11, 163, 164, 243
    operational impact of, 1, 163, 245
    psychology of warfare and, 4
    quantum computing, 11, 163, 217
    in retail industry, 15–17, 16–17n41
    social media. *See* Social media
    Special Operations theory on, 4
    video conferencing, 234, 238
Templar, Gerald, 59
10,000-Hour Rule, 86–87
Terrorism. *See also specific terrorist groups*
    cyber capabilities in fight against, 163
    global war on, 8
    9/11 attacks (2001), 52, 173
    recruitment for, 42
Themes
    in advertisements, 13–14, 66
    characteristics of, 129
    of competition, 45, 55–56
    in creative briefs, 106, 176
    in crisis management, 184, 204, 212
    cultural considerations, 175
    environmentally sensitive, 132

in marketing strategies, 15, 17, 47–48, 66, 93
in military operations, 113
in strategic communication, 41, 127, 244
for target audiences, 98
Thompson, Robert, 58, 58n146
Timothy's Coffee, 204
TJX-hack, 227
Toyota, 163, 165
Transcendence, in crisis management, 182
Transparency
    in crisis management, 181–82, 188, 191, 193, 195–96, 231
    as leadership trait, 8
    in stakeholder engagement, 121
Treverton, Greg, 172
Trout, Jack, 86, 88
Trump, Donald J., 31, 78n194, 87, 129, 192–93, 206, 210–11
Twin Metals Minnesota, 121–22
Twitter
    Adidas' use of, 107
    in COVID-19 pandemic, 237
    fraudulent postings on, 166
    ISIS posts on, 169
    power and consequences of, 210–11
    Starbucks' use of, 90
    Taliban's use of, 170
    traditional media disrupted by, 181
Tylenol poisoning incidents, 185–87, 191, 231–35

U
Uber, 205
Ukraine, social media use in, 171
Under Armour, 45–49
Unicorn startups, 47, 86, 124–25, 171, 246
Union Carbide Corporation (UCC), 187–91
United Airlines, 205
United Overseas Bank, 71
UNTUCKit, 40

V
Vaccinations
    Al-Qaeda rumors of poisoning from bovine vaccinations, 172n452
    COVID-19 pandemic and, 129, 234
Value innovation strategy, 46
Values-based leadership, 35–36, 111–12
Vance, Cyrus, 159
Vehicles. *See* Automobile industry
Video conferencing, 234, 238
Vietnam War
    cultural knowledge and, 246
    identification of enemies in, 39
    media reporting on, 56, 181
    obstacles to success in, 146
    "one war" strategy in, 114
    public opinion on, 207
    Tet Offensive, 56, 181
Virgin Cola, 50–51, 173
Vision statements, 138
Volkswagen, 90–92, 134
Votel, Joseph L., 2, 24, 43, 58, 83–84
Voting rights, 206, 207

W
Wade, Sandy, 44
Walmart, 98, 141, 165
War and warfare. *See also* Information warfare; *specific wars*
    centers of gravity for, 207
    cognitive, 164
    counter information, 222
    crimes of, 44, 156, 180n463, 212
    cyber, 219
    drug wars, 29–31
    Fourth-Generation, 81–82
    frictions of, 1, 2, 104, 173, 245
    global war on terror, 8
    humans as instruments of, 6
    nature of, 6, 245, 245n628
    psychological, 147
    tactical, 79
    unpredictability of, 103–4
Warby Parker, 54, 74, 165
Wargaming, 123
Warren, Elizabeth, 210

Warrillow, John, 33
Watts, Clint, 169
Weapons of mass destruction, 4, 11, 26. *See also* Nuclear weapons
Wedemeyer, Albert, 23
Westmoreland, William, 145–46, 181
Whitlock, Craig, 55, 163
Whole Foods, 131
Williams, Mike, 81, 91
Winning. *See* Success
Wintour, Ana, 121
Wirthlin, Dick, 88
Wolff, Josephine, 224
Wolfowitz, Paul, 10, 26n58
Wood, Graeme, 52
Work-product privilege, 229
World War II (1939–1945)
    actionable victory plan in, 23
    key players in U.S. successes during, 148–49
    military strategists during, 110
    Normandy invasion, 128, 129, 173
    Operation Market Garden, 145
    Pearl Harbor attacks, 29, 173, 211
    Special Operations during, 3, 3n8
Wright, Jon, 34
Wyndham Hotel Chain hack, 226–27

X
Xerox, 86
Xi Jinping, 41, 79

Y
Yellowtail, 46
Young, Miles, 134, 166

Z
al-Zarqawi, Abu Musab, 163

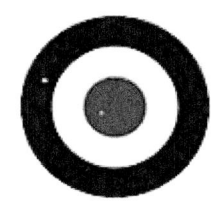

ACKNOWLEDGMENTS

Thanks are owed to many people in the course of writing this book. On and off the record, I interviewed several senior and flag officers in the United States and United Kingdom military, US Department of Defense officials, former US intelligence officers, as well as several of the most distinguished experts in corporate America on crisis and corporate communication.

A book like this is equally exciting and challenging. You can't produce a top book on your own. I had a lot of help from many generous, gracious, immensely talented individuals to whom I am deeply indebted.

Admiral (ret) Jim Stavridis was very gracious and generous to write the Foreword to this book. We met years ago at a dinner sponsored by the Center for Strategic and International Studies. At the time, he was the Supreme Allied Commander – Europe (SACEUR). His peers rightly view him as a star: a great leader, a superb strategist, a scholar, a wonderful friend. We struck up a friendship, and his advice and support have always meant a lot to me. His current book, 2034, is a cautionary tale about the dangers of human frailty and miscalculation in great power competition, and I recommend it highly.

Jim Lukaszewski was equally generous in writing about **The Corporate Warrior**. People become legends because they are blessed with supreme talent, understand human nature, have an intuitive grasp of strategy, and are effective. Jim's most recent book, The Decency Code, defines standards for integrity that every executive should respect and practice.

My publisher Phil Rothstein and his team, including marketing chief Glyn Davies, were terrific at every level. Some authors complain their publishers don't give them enough attention or get behind their books. Phil told me the day we talked that they try to identify the very best book on a topic and publish that book. He was flattering, offered within a day to publish the book, then proved that one reason Rothstein is so great to work with is that they are very tough on their writers, insisting on rewrites and edits until in their judgment the book would be worth any reader's time. They kept pushing, offering recommendations, and paying attention to details. I think this book has achieved its goals in conveying its key messages. If you agree, credit them in no small measure for the result.

Judy Katz is a close personal friend and longtime colleague. She is a top New York publicist and an exceptional editor and counselor. Judy has championed my work tirelessly and stood by me on this and other projects. She is remarkable, but even more impressive is the outstanding quality of her efforts on my behalf. She was one of five people, along with Phil Rothstein, Virgil Scudder, Ken Scudder, Jim Lukaszewski, and Kristen Noakes-Fry, whose edits vastly strengthened the clarity and structure of the book.

Lt. Gen. (Ret) Dell Dailey and Maj. Gen. (Ret) John Davis are great friends I met and had the honor of working with at the US SPECIAL OPERATIONS COMMAND, which I advised for many years. They led distinguished careers in the military before moving on to advise the corporate world. Their insights inform this book even as their friendship provided me with vital support to tackle the subject.

The same holds for other retired flag officers, Pentagon, and Intelligence Community officials who speak with me on the record. Brig. Gen. (Ret) Mark Kimmitt worked closely in Iraq with my close friend Rich Galen, whom the White House had sent to Baghdad on communication matters. His handling of the notorious Abu Ghraib incident – and himself – was a master class in strategic communication and a testament to what officers with ability and integrity can accomplish. He introduced me to Maj. Gen. (Ret) James "Spider" Marks, whose insights were acute and on-point. Dell Dailey introduced me to Lt. Gen. (Ret) Frank Kearney, who gave me a lot of time to walk me through his excellent, provocative views on leadership and decision-making. He illustrates what an outstanding flag officer should be as well as how to apply his ideas to the business world.

Leaders like Mark and Spider stand shoulder-to-shoulder with other distinguished, able US flag officers like General David Petraeus, General Joseph Votel, Admiral Bobby Inman, and Admiral Michael Brown. General Petraeus requires no introduction: he ranks among the most respected and recognized four-star Generals the military has produced. We first met at the Army War College in 2005. His observations are always acute. I met General Votel at a conference at the US SPECIAL OPERATIONS COMMAND. Extremely well-liked and respected, he went out of his way to answer my questions and added depth to the book.

People often ask me what I think of our flag officer corps; I've had the honor of meeting or knowing many flag officers. Those I interviewed are awe-inspiring, capable, tough leaders who combine patriotism, leadership, and dedication and compel admiration and respect.

Admiral Bobby Ray Inman was at first reluctant to grant an interview. No surprise, as he didn't know me. My friend and colleague Greg Treverton, who also gave me an interview and had headed up the National Intelligence Council (NIC) under President Barack Obama – the NIC is an elite CIA think tank – persuaded him to visit. Greg's views on the topic of this book were enlightening, as his opinions on every topic we work on together, which I've been lucky enough to do, always are.

Admiral Inman is a legend. Spending some time with him demonstrated why that is so. He is brilliant, concise, to-the-point, collegial, and a leader whose sound judgment manifests itself in every one of his sentences. I'm very grateful to him for taking the time and Greg for making that interview happen.

Most civilians think flag officers run the military. Some do, but operationally, and if I may generalize, the critical senior officers are Colonels. One of the joys of my career in advising the US Department of Defense for over two decades has been the honor of working with some extraordinary ones: USAF Col. (Ret) Al Bynum, U.S. Marine Col (Ret) Paul Huxhold, U.S. Marine Col. (ret) Stephen Nitzschke; United Kingdom Col. (Ret) Stephen Padgett, U.S. Army Col. (Ret) Jack Guy, and United Kingdom Col. (Ret) Sandy Wade.

I've worked closely with each of these guys for many years. They are close friends and respected colleagues. They are incredibly talented. They've been steadfast and generous in offering me their counsel and insight through the years, and words cannot express the depth of my gratitude to them. Col. Padgett and Col. Wade introduced me to UK Col. (Ret) Mark Neate and General (Ret) Sir Richard Shirreff. Distinguished in their own right and now running major businesses, their views provided important links between thought leadership in the military and civilian worlds. Thanks to them and their colleague Andy Welsh.

Chris Inglis is President Joe Biden's national cybersecurity chief and a former Deputy Director for the National Security Administration. His brilliance is well recognized, and his appointments are one of the President's best. Chris has been a friend, and his views on what it takes to erect defenses to cyber attacks inform this book. He was just nominated for his current position when we visited, and I'm grateful that he took the time to share his ideas with me.

John Rood served as the Undersecretary of Defense for Policy, the third most powerful position in the Pentagon. He worked closely with Dave Patterson, Peter Flory, and Greg Treverton, and were part of the team General James Mattis assembled as Secretary of Defense. US Special Operations Col. (Ret) and former Acting Assistant Secretary of Defense for Special Operations – Low-Intensity Conflict Mark Mitchell was part of that broader circle. They combine integrity, hard work, discipline, loyalty, as well as pragmatism and high intellect. They went out of their way to be helpful to me in writing this book.

The same is true for my good friend Bob Giesler, whose ability and achievements at the Pentagon made him legendary. He's held many important posts. I'll single out his tenure as the highest-ranking career official in the Office of Undersecretary of Defense (Intelligence). Bob's savvy, experience in business and national security, and generosity have made a difference in my work for the Pentagon and this book.

Darby Arakelian and Scott McDonald are great friends and colleagues from another part of the United States Government that deals with national security. Their talent stands out. They know how to cut to the heart of an issue and are unceasingly resourceful in identifying problems and executing solutions. They brought fresh perspectives to my thinking that informed this book. I'm grateful for their friendship and tremendous help.

George Beebe headed up the CIA's Russia Analysis and served as Vice President Dick Cheney's expert on Russia. He is a leading voice in discussions on how the US should deal with Russia today. His comprehension of strategy and great power competition puts him at the apex of experts in his field.

Dr. Neville Bolt, Dr. Ofer Fridman, and Dr. David Betts are friends and colleagues at King's College, University of London. I remain in constant dialogue with each of them on many topics. Each has always gone beyond the call of duty in discussing my ideas, offering critical insights, and has helped me to think through what needs to be said. Their help has always been invaluable, and I am incredibly grateful to them.

Austin Branch has made a notable mark for his expertise and leadership at the Pentagon in Information Operations/Influence Operations. He and his colleague Mike Williams helped to strengthen this book through their knowledge and experience.

I met and began working with John Matheny and Dr. Jeffrey Starr at the Pentagon right after 9/11. They played critical roles, along with my late friend Col. (ret) Dan Devlin, in recruiting me for work in national security. These guys epitomize what is best about those who serve our nation patriotically: integrity, high intellect, loyalty, warmth, regard for and support of colleagues, insistence on high performance, and significant contributions to the discourse and operations on matters in which they are or were involved. They also worked closely with Ambassador Brian Carlson, another great friend whose practical yet scholarly approach to public diplomacy epitomizes what every executive needs to know.

I'm by background an attorney and political consultant. Many friends and colleagues over many years have made a significant impact on my thinking in strategic communication and strategy, and I'm in their debt. Joe Gaylord, former Speaker Newt Gingrich's senior political advisor, has been a friend and partner in campaigns for many years. Rich Galen is well known in news media and political circles for his keen insights into politics, his online newsletter Mullings.com, and was also part of Newt's team. He understands the impact of news media in unique and compelling ways, and how to capitalize on news coverage. His insights were a big help.

Wally Clinton and I have been friends and colleagues since we met in 1969, during then state senator Billy Guste's campaign for Mayor of New Orleans. His expertise in telephone communications and influence is unparalleled. He has helped tremendously in shaping my thinking about that channel of communication. Steve Wegmann is my longtime collaborator in producing political media, and his help, support, ability, and friendship rank among the high points of my professional career.

Celinda Lake and Ed Goeas are top-shelf pollsters with international reputations whose advice, insights, and counsel uniquely helped make this book better. Celinda is President Joe Biden's pollster and ranks at the top of Democratic pollsters. Ed Goeas stands at the apex of Republican pollsters. Together, they conduct the respected "Battleground" opinion surveys on U.S politics. The Gallup Organization's Chris Stewart is also a top pollster, and no one should write a book like this without his insights. I met Mike Dabadie, another pollster, through the famous pollster Dick Wirthlin, another late friend who counseled President Ronald Reagan. Mike's fresh thinking and original approaches are, I hope, reflected here.

Dr. Marvin Weinbaum of the Middle East Institute is a longtime friend and colleague. He was my principal reader on my first book, The Pakistan Cauldron, and a source of endless wisdom that helped immensely with my views on strategic communication. Dr. Jim Giordano at Georgetown is also the Director of the Institute for BioDefense Research, where I am a Senior Fellow. The ethical and legal ramifications of weaponized neurotechnology are among my areas of subject matter expertise. He has played a central role in inspiring and developing my interest and knowledge in this area. A New Orleans native, my good friend King Mallory worked with Dick Allen to direct John Kasich's national security team during the 2020 election. Today he is at the Rand Corporation. King and I maintain an ongoing conversation, and I always feel better informed after our visits. His thinking influenced this book.

In the corporate world, several friends stand out. John Kotts and Boysie Bollinger are longtime close friends. They supported me when I wrote my first play that opened in London. They are astute and successful business executives who have always given me lots of their time and strong friendship. Their views on business were most helpful as I thought about applying leadership and imagination displayed by military leaders to the boardroom. Their friendship honors me. Billy Goldring is a megastar in business: the industry equivalent of Tom Brady in the manufacture of bourbon. His observations on that industry and what works or doesn't were invaluable. John Georges has distinguished himself nationally as an imaginative, persistent, effective executive. The opportunity to work with him over the years and be a friend has informed my work and views expressed here.

Virgil Scudder and I met in 1987. We worked on issue management for Fortune 500 companies. He has been a close friend, adviser, and colleague ever since. His expertise and insights, those of his talented son Ken – an ascending voice in crisis management – have helped to define my views on crisis management. Both provided attentive, savvy, and detailed edits to strengthen the manuscript.

Other close friends and colleagues are owed special thanks. James Babst has been a lifelong friend, law partner, and counselor, and his advice is pure gold. He is always there for his friends, and it's no surprise he's so well respected and loved. Vaughan Fitzpatrick and I have been close friends for decades. He served as a point man deployed forward for Chevron in working in Africa, the Middle East, and Russia. He is one of the most sophisticated, cultured, warm, and savvy people I know. His views on human nature and what works as companies strive to achieve goals are unique – and uniquely helpful.

Greg Hicks was the brave deputy chief of station in Tripoli during the tragic Benghazi incident. His integrity and fortitude illustrate what statesmanship and integrity mean. He called the events the way he saw them. This nation needs more diplomats like him. Richard Lavsky is an enormously gifted composer, the winner of 17 Cleos (the Academy Award for the ad industry) and 5 Golden Lions at Cannes. His guidance underscored the importance of music and tone in strategic communication.

Above all, my profound thanks to the most important and loving person in my life, my incredible wife, Gay LeBreton. She puts up with me, a Herculean challenge, and supports my work with cheers and enthusiasm that makes me think maybe I'm not such a bad writer.

Finally, a call-out to the individual to whom the book is dedicated: Ronald A. Faucheux. We met in 1969, courtesy of the legendary political consultant, Matt Reese, credited for winning the West Virginia primary for John F. Kennedy in 1960. Matt recognized the rapport we had, and we served as deputies to him and Billy Guste, a candidate for Mayor. Ron and I have been extremely close friends, colleagues, and often business partners our entire adult lives. He shines within the prestigious inner circle of top corporate and political pollsters. We developed our views on communication and politics together. A lot of what's in this book emanates from our daily conversations, stretching over five decades.

Finally, and most important, I thank my sweet wife, Gladys Fenner Gay LeBreton, for her unceasing love and support for my writing. Everything I do or achieve would be impossible without her.

Thank you, one and all, for helping me bring this book to fruition. I hope it will serve its mission and produce victorious outcomes in the C-suites of corporate America.

James P. Farwell

New Orleans, Louisiana

January 2022

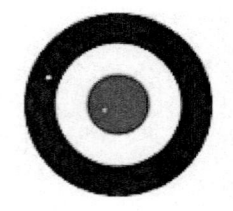

CREDITS

Philip Jan Rothstein, FBCI, is President of Rothstein Associates Inc., a management consultancy he founded in 1984 as a pioneer in the disciplines of Business Continuity and Disaster Recovery. He is also the Executive Publisher of Rothstein Publishing.

Glyn Davies is Chief Marketing Officer of Rothstein Associates Inc. He has held this position since 2013. Glyn has previously held executive level positions in Sales, Marketing and Editorial at several multinational publishing companies and currently resides in California.

Editorial Advisory Services

Kristen Noakes-Fry

Indexing

Enid Zafran, Indexing Partners LLC

Cover Design and Graphics

Sheila Kwiatek, Flower Grafix

eBook Design & Production

Donna Luther, Metadata Prime

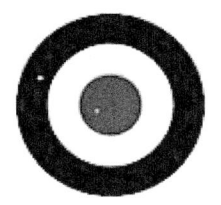

ABOUT THE AUTHOR

James P. Farwell is an author and national security expert in information warfare, corporate strategic communication, social media analytics, political media and strategy, cyber policy, cyber security, strategy, and authorities.

He has advised the U.S. Department of Defense, the U.S. SPECIAL OPERATIONS COMMAND, U.S. CENTRAL COMMAND and the U.S. STRATEGIC COMMAND.

Global Security

Mr. Farwell is a recognized expert internationally in the legal and policy issues for cyber war and cyber security, and strategic communication/information warfare. His geographic topical expertise includes political dynamics including for elections in North Africa, the Middle East, Pakistan, and the Mexican Drug War.

He has served as a consultant to the U.S. Department of Defense, including Office of the Under Secretary of Defense (Policy), Office of the Under Secretary of Defense (Intelligence), Special Operations – Low Intensity Conflict, U.S. Special Operations Command, and U.S. Strategic Command.

He has served as an advisor to the U.S. Special Operations Command (US SOCOM). He was a co-architect of SOVEREIGN CHALLENGE, a flagship program of SOCOM entailing outreach to the foreign military attaché and senior military officers in Washington. He advises on strategic initiatives and engagement. His work for SOCOM has included outreach to think tanks, foundations, and the academic community. For Combined Joint Task Force-Horn of Africa, he helped develop a new plan for Strategic Communication.

Legal

As an attorney, he was a partner at Chaffe McCall law firm, specializing in business law and litigation for major national and international clients, and later as Of Counsel to Elkins & Associates. He has served as Arbitrator for NYSE and American Arbitration Association.

Strategic Consulting

Mr. Farwell has worked with major multi-nationals including R.J.R. Nabisco, Philip Morris, Freeport-McMoran, Monsanto, Entergy Corporation, Microsoft, Boeing, and Monsanto. He has also worked for advocacy groups and business associations such as the Coalition for Affordable Power, Louisiana Lottery, Louisiana Council for Fiscal Reform, North Carolina Citizens for Business & Industry, and the American Insurance Association.

Education and Notable

He holds a B.A. from Tulane University, a J.D. in Law from Tulane University, and a D.C.L.S. in Comparative Law from the University of Cambridge (Trinity College).

He was cited by *Roll Call* as one of the top political consultants in the United States. He serves on the Business Council of New Orleans as Advisor.

Academic Appointments

Mr. Farwell is an Associate Fellow in the Kings Centre for Strategic Communications, Department of War Studies, King's College, University of London. He is a non-resident Senior Fellow at the Middle East Institute in Washington. He is a Senior Fellow in the Institute of Bioscience Research, Washington, D.C. He is a member of the Board of Advisors of the peer-reviewed publication, *Defence Strategic Communications*. He is a Visiting Scholar at the A.B. Freeman Tulane School of Business.

Special Certification

Certified Information Privacy Professional (CIPP/US) and Member, International Association of Privacy Professionals, in cybersecurity and data protection.

Contact Information:

James Farwell

The Farwell Group,

1214 Nashville Avenue

New Orleans, LA 70115

(202) 213.5815

james.farwell@gmail.com.

SKYPE: JamespFarwell

Twitter: @JamesFarwell

ABOUT ROTHSTEIN PUBLISHING

ROTHSTEIN PUBLISHING is the premier global content provider in the core disciplines of Business Continuity Management; Emergency Management; Disaster Recovery and Prevention; Information Security; Risk Management; Crisis Communications; Management; and Leadership, Since 1989, we've published an extensive, informational suite of books in these important subjects. More recently we've established ourselves as a serious publisher in the fields of Cybersecurity; Critical Infrastructure; Business Strategy; and Leadership.

Our founder **Philip Jan Rothstein, FBCI**, is an internationally known management consultant, entrepreneur, publisher, columnist, contributor to 90+ books, and an expert on the subject of Business Continuity and Disaster Recovery.

Our authors are globally recognized; several are uniquely distinguished international thought leaders as founders of their respective industries. Most have also been key participants in developing industry standards and best practices. Some are founding fellows of the Business Continuity Institute, as is our publisher Philip Rothstein, who was elected a Fellow in 1994 in recognition of his substantial contributions to the profession.

No matter the company size or your level of expertise, you'll find in Rothstein's publications the most current and practical advice, tools, & tips to protect your employees, facilities, and financial assets, manage your legal & reputational risks and grow your business.

Rothstein Publishing is a division of Rothstein Associates Inc., an international management consultancy founded in 1984.